OFF THE
Beaten Path

MADISON WRIGHT

Copyright © 2024 by Madison Wright

All rights reserved.

No portion of this book may be reproduced in any form without written permission from the publisher or author, except as permitted by U.S. copyright law.

Cover Design by Sam Palencia at Ink and Laurel

Developmental Editing by Made Me Blush Books

Copy Editing and Proofreading by V.B. Edits

Instagram: @authormadisonwright

To Noah Kahan and Gilmore Girls. I truly couldn't have done this one without you.

Prologue

- MASQUERADE -
THE ANONYMOUS DATING APP

SpeakingFromTheArt: **Hi! I love your bio!!!**

user6872: **My sister signed me up for this account without my permission because she's annoyingly meddlesome but I'm not looking for a relationship.**

BeautyAndBrainsss: **Hey cowboy**

user6872: My sister signed me up for this account without my permission because she's annoyingly meddlesome but I'm not looking for a relationship.

MustLoveDogs: Let's play two truths and a lie. You go first!

user6872: My sister signed me up for this account without my permission because she's annoyingly meddlesome but I'm not looking for a relationship.

AlwaysAndForever551: What do you like to do for fun?

> **user6872:** My sister signed me up for this account without my permission because she's annoyingly meddlesome but I'm not looking for a relationship.

> **LikeStrawberryWine:** Come here often?

> **user872:** My sister signed me up for this account without my permission because she's annoyingly meddlesome but I'm not looking for a relationship.

> **LikeStrawberryWine:** That's fine, I'm mostly looking for someone to rob a bank with me. You in?

> **user6872:** No.

LikeStrawberryWine: I have ski masks. You don't even have to provide your own.

user6872: I told you I'm not interested in a relationship.

LikeStrawberryWine: No, but you seem like you could use a friend.

user6872: I have friends.

LikeStrawberryWine: Are you this nice to them?

user6872: Worse, actually.

LikeStrawberryWine: I bet you're fun at parties.

user6872: I don't go to parties.

LikeStrawberryWine: That's not surprising in the least.

user6872: Well, this has been tolerable. I'm going to get off here.

LikeStrawberryWine: **Words every woman longs to hear.**

user6872: **Sorry, that was rude of me. My friends tell me I can be too blunt.**

LikeStrawberryWine: **I'm still not convinced these friends are real.**

One
- WREN -

"To the little cabin off the beaten path!" I yell, wincing as I pop the cork on the cheapest bottle of champagne I could find at the liquor store. The cork falls to the floor with a dull *thump*.

"Well," my lifelong best friend, Stevie, drawls. She sits propped against an exposed beam in the demolished kitchen of the cabin I'm renovating. "That was underwhelming."

I stare at the bottle in my hand, not hearing the telltale fizz of carbonation. "That's the last time I buy something from the liquor store in town."

Stevie snorts a laugh. "You said that last time."

The bottle thuds against the ground as I set it down. "I'm serious this time. The five-dollar strawberry wine from the market never fails me."

A smile lifts one corner of Stevie's mouth. "I thought you might say that." She reaches for the backpack she dropped to the floor when we came in. The zing of the zipper echoes through the empty cabin, and a second later, she pulls out a clear bottle filled with dark pink liquid. The metallic frog sipping from a large wine glass on the label winks in the sunlight slanting through the windows.

Stevie twists the cap and looks at me expectantly. "Did you bring glasses?"

My mouth falls open, and her lips curve in a wry grin before she kicks the bottle back and takes a swig. When she's done, she extends it to me. "Congrats, friend."

I close my fingers around its neck, take a long sip of the sweet strawberry wine, and look around the empty cabin I plan to renovate and rent out. We sat in this exact spot last month when I got the keys to this place. Because of the holidays, my contractor just got it stripped to the studs and ready to start the renovations on Monday, so I wanted to celebrate.

My little cabin in the middle of the woods, on the outskirts of my tiny speck-on-the-map town.

When I bought it a month ago, everything was outdated, all warm wood walls and peeling linoleum floors and countertops. Dust covered every square inch of the place, and the windows were dirty enough to mute the sun shining through them. It's certainly not the place I would have picked for myself, but it's got great potential as a rental. And since I live in a town that sees more tourists than residents year-round, it's exactly the kind of place I need.

"How are you going to manage renovating this?" Stevie asks, her gaze trailing my own, taking in the gutted expanse in front of us.

My shoulders lift in a shrug. "Jimmy said he could get it done in time, and he told me I could shadow him. This way I can learn the basics and DIY some things on the next flip. Plus, you know as well as I do how slow things are at the orchard in the winter." Her parents own Misty Grove, after all, and I've been working there in some capacity since high school. Now, I run all their events and marketing. And after the imported Christmas trees are hauled away at the end of December, not even the crickets come out to chirp until spring. I make the most of the downtime with small events, but the bleak beginning months of the year are usually spent twiddling my thumbs and praying for the flowers to bloom early so visitors return.

"Well, if you need my help with anything, let me know." She gestures around the room. "I have done some of this before."

Stevie lives in an Airstream deep in a patch of woods so far down the lake that you'd never stumble upon it if you weren't expressly looking for it. But when she bought the land, before she purchased the Airstream, she lived in the cheapest RV she could find for sale online. It was crumbling and deteriorating and only ran well enough to get up the hill the one time. When she finally upgraded, it had to be towed to the junkyard.

But somehow, despite all its shortcomings, Stevie managed to make the vintage RV homey, customizing it piece by piece.

When I started looking at properties in the fall, I planned to update a place on my own, with the help of Stevie and anyone willing to lend a hand, of course. But then this place came available, and while it wasn't the cabin I would have chosen, the location was hard to beat. Even with the windows covered in grime, you can't miss the view of the mountains sloping and climbing right outside or the trees older than the town itself springing up from the soil.

"You know we couldn't handle this amount of work on our own," I say, trailing my fingers along the now barren concrete floors. They used to be covered in a bubbling, peeling linoleum. "Or maybe we could handle it, but there's no way we could finish by April."

It's only January, with fat snowflakes falling to the ground outside, but tourist season takes a village of prep work, and although we're in a lull until March, things are going to get hectic fast.

Stevie takes the wine bottle from my hand, her throat working as she swallows a large gulp. "You're right. I'm just bored. No one is hiking for at least another month and a half."

Stevie works as a trail guide for her uncle's tour company, taking groups of tourists on hikes into the backcountry for anywhere from one afternoon to multiple days. During tourist season, she works constantly. And when she's *not* working, she's ripping apart at the seams, taking up different hobbies and somehow cooking enough food in her tiny Airstream kitchen to feed the town twice over.

She doesn't do well with sitting still or staying in one place, which is ironic since she's never lived anywhere but here in Fontana Ridge. I always thought she'd get out and see the world the first chance she could get.

"Do you need any help with the Galentine's Auction?" Stevie asks, perking up, a feverish gleam entering her dark eyes.

A laugh rumbles out of me. "You look deranged. Are you seriously *that* bored? I thought you were knitting for the family shelter in town."

Stevie's dark gaze darts away, a faint pink tingeing her cheeks. "They told me they have enough hats and mittens to last them through next winter."

I'm quiet for so long, stifling my laughter, that Stevie glances back at me. She presses her lips together, holding back a grin of her own. "It's not funny."

"It's a little funny," I say, holding my thumb and forefinger an inch apart. "Why don't you go on a vacation? You deserve it. You could take your Airstream and stay gone until April."

Stevie reclines against the counter, crossing her lean arms over her chest. Her eyes fix on an unidentifiable point on the floor. "I don't want to go on a vacation," she says finally, an odd tone entering her raspy voice. "Can I help you with the event or not?"

I'm shocked by the sharpness of her tone, but from the flickering muscle in her jaw, I get the sense she doesn't want to talk more about it. Instead, I say, "I'd love some help. You can be in charge of finding bachelors to sign up."

Flinty eyes meet mine. "That's the worst part of this event, and you know it."

A wry smile tugs at the corners of my mouth. "Also the most time-consuming."

She holds my gaze for a long moment before a reluctant grin splits her mouth. "Fine, I'll heckle bachelors, if you insist."

A laugh punches out of me, echoing across the barren walls of the empty cabin. "That didn't take much convincing."

Her shoulder lifts in a shrug. "Beats doing puzzles in my Airstream for the next two months."

"I'm having a planning session with the volunteers tomorrow. Why don't you come, and we can work on a list of bachelors to approach?"

Stevie's amber eyes narrow. "Will the biddies be there?"

By the biddies, she means two middle-age best friends, Myra and Melissa, who single-handedly keep the town gossip mill running. I find them charming. Stevie calls them intrusive.

At the smile I'm holding back, Stevie lets out a sigh, shoulders slumping. "Fine, but if they ask me about my love life even once, I'm leaving."

Better to just not come, then, but I don't tell her that.

"We're meeting at Smokey the Beans at nine," I say, screwing the cap back on the wine bottle and stuffing it into my bag. I'll finish it off tonight, snuggled in a nest of pillows and chunky knit blankets on my couch.

I follow Stevie out the front door, avoiding the porch step that snapped in half on our way in, and glance over my shoulder at the cabin. I've got my work cut out for me, for sure. Especially if I want to have this place finished by tourist season.

What I haven't mentioned to Stevie or my parents, who are always concerned for my perpetual tendency to jump into things without thinking them through, is that I *have* to have the place finished by April. I sank all my meager savings into purchasing and renovating the place. If I don't get visitors in by the start of tourist season, I won't be able to afford the mortgage.

In the hazy grayness of the falling snow, the cabin looks even more dilapidated. A storm cloud inches into my line of sight, and as icy snowflakes kiss my skin, I pray it's not an omen of things to come.

The cabin is on the very edge of Fontana Ridge, deep in the woods, but my home is a little cottage nestled between towering maples on a quiet street in the middle of town. It takes nine minutes to trek from one place to the other, even if I hit all four stoplights. The pale winter sunshine is already dipping below the horizon, blanketing the world in shades of gray, as I make my way through town.

Fontana Ridge, a pit stop on the Appalachian Trail and nestled in the heart of the Smoky Mountains, is vastly different during the winter months than it is in spring, summer, and fall. And despite only being a quarter of the year, those months can feel the longest. The town comes alive when the seasons change, when there are new blooms in the fields and hikers and tourists in the streets, when the inns are full and the restaurants stay open late. Everything in Fontana Ridge was made for those fleeting months when the air is warm and the sun shines longer.

But there's a special place in my heart for the slow months. It's quiet, peaceful. There's not the constant bustle of tourists or the pressure to make the town seem perfect. It's just us, the ones who are here even when the hikers and tourists return home.

Now, the shops are closed for the night, the shutters pulled tight and the lights flicked off until late tomorrow morning. The barest wisps of snow fall in lazy flakes, leaving drops of condensation on my windshield and glowing in the headlights shining from my car.

My street is all but shut down for the night, my neighbors already warming inside their old houses, golden light seeping through the gaps in the curtains. It's the kind of cozy quietness that comes with the post-holiday rush, when people haven't gone stir crazy yet from the cold and dark and all our town responsibilities are on hold for another two months.

As I steer my car down the street, my headlights beam across the lawns, dry and dead, until my house is illuminated, a speck of white with a bright yellow door among the bare trees of stick season.

I smile when I see the package on my neighbor's porch as I'm letting myself into my cottage. In the spring and summer, the window boxes are full of flowers, and there's always the faint sound of buzzing bees and chirping cicadas, but tonight, everything is quiet.

Mail crunches under my feet, dropped through the slot in my front door at some point today. I grab it, wincing when I see they're all bills. I'd kill for a catalog right now, even if I can't afford to buy anything. The constant reminder of my financial state is starting to wear me down.

Honestly, I probably shouldn't have spent my savings on the little cabin in the woods. I probably shouldn't have been investing in real estate at all, but I was looking for other avenues of income since my job at the orchard pays…enough, and that's it. If I were to ask Stevie's parents for a raise, they'd give it to me, but that means they'd lower their own salary to compensate, so I've never even considered it.

I'm toeing off my boots when my phone rings. My lips curve in a smile when I see the grainy, aged photo of a gap-toothed girl on the screen.

"Hi, Rae," I say, swiping to accept the video call.

My older sister is seated at her desk in her tiny Chicago apartment, a mound of copper curls piled atop her head. Dim lamplight bathes her skin in gold and reflects off the lenses of her huge, wire-rimmed glasses.

"I needed a writing break," Rae says without preamble.

I grin at her directness, moving through the darkness of my cottage to collapse on my couch. The room fills with soft light a moment later when I stretch to flip on the lamp on the end table.

"What are you working on?" I ask, tucking my chilled feet under a wadded-up blanket at the opposite end of my sofa.

"A piece on a nonprofit that's revamping a city park." She drags her hands over her face, pulling her skin taut. I don't miss the dark half moons under her eyes, a sure sign that she's been working more than sleeping lately.

Rae is a reporter for the *Chicago Daily*, and although she swears she takes breaks and has time off, I've yet to see it.

"Take a break and spend some time with your husband," I tell her.

She sinks a little further into her chair. "He had to work late, so I thought I'd get some extra work done until he gets home. Then we have a date."

That makes my chest ache, a spear of jealousy slicing through me. Tonight, she'll go out with her husband, and as soon as we get off the phone, I'll park myself on the sofa with my laptop and work on things for the Galentine's Auction until I inevitably pass out on my keyboard and type the letter *E* until my laptop dies.

Rae looks at me like she knows exactly what I'm thinking, her lips pursed and brows raised.

"You look just like Mom," I tell her. She stops so immediately that a bark of laughter escapes me.

"I'm barely thirty," she whines. "Before you know it, I'll be buying those stretchy colored pants she always gets from the thrift store."

I sink down into the sofa, avoiding her gaze, but she catches me and gasps. "Wren Isabella Daniels, tell me you didn't."

"They're not from Goodwill," I murmur, barely audible. When her eyebrows never return to their usual position, I sigh. "They're not from the thrift store, but I did buy a pair of sweatpants that, upon further inspection, look a lot like something Mom would wear."

Our mother found her style in the nineties and never updated it. She can usually be found in an assortment of brightly colored stretch pants and soft cotton tops with tiny prints on them. Last week, when we had lunch, she wore bright yellow pants, a white turtleneck, a knit sweater embroidered with bees, and clogs.

"You didn't," Rae breathes, clutching at her chest like she's desperate for air.

"They're just for around the house!" I yell.

A laugh rumbles out of her. I'm glad to see those shadows under her eyes disappearing into her laugh lines.

Reaching for the throw blanket to drape over my legs, I ask, "So when are you coming to visit?" She and her husband, Leland, spent Christmas with his family, and neither of them could get off work long enough to visit at Thanksgiving, so I haven't seen her since a long weekend trip they took in early fall, when apple season was in full swing and the farm was at its busiest. I barely even saw her on that trip.

She shrugs, picking at a stray thread on the knit blanket she has wrapped around her shoulders. It's cold here in Fontana Ridge, but being so close to Lake Michigan makes Chicago icy and frigid. I'm not sure how she and Leland manage it.

"It's hard to get away from work," she says, voice soft. My heart hurts for her. There's something to be said about living your dream, yet still feeling strapped by it. I love my job at Misty Grove and could never imagine doing anything else, but that doesn't mean I don't have days where I feel overwhelmed by it.

Her computer chirps in the background, and she sighs. "Speaking of, that's my editor asking for this piece, so I better go."

I nod, pulling the throw blanket up to my chin. "Night, Rae."

"Love you, Wren."

She clicks off before I have a chance to say it back, and I'm left in the quiet of my house. Not even the birds or cicadas chirp on a night as cold as this. I stare longingly at my fireplace, knowing I'm not going to bother lighting it.

It's nights like these when the house feels extra quiet and the loneliness settles over me like a familiar yet unwanted weight. I don't mind the quiet, but sometimes I wish I had someone to share it with. Sitting in silence wouldn't feel so bad with my feet tucked under someone's thigh, books settled in our laps, glasses of strawberry wine sitting on the coffee table.

A car door slams outside, followed by a peal of high-pitched giggles, and I smile to myself, knowing my night isn't going to be quiet for much longer.

Two

- HOLDEN -

"You've got sawdust in your hair," my mom says, standing on tiptoes to swipe at my mass of dark shoulder-length hair that's tied back in a messy bun at my nape. Bits of sawdust rain down around me like the snowflakes outside.

"That's a hazard of being a contractor," I grunt, pulling down a mug from her cabinet and filling it with the decaf brew she switched to at four o'clock. After taking a sip, I look around the kitchen for my daughter, who usually pummels me like an excitable puppy when I walk through the door. "Where's June?"

"I ordered her a friendship bracelet kit, and she's been making them all afternoon in her room," Mom says, holding up her wrist, which is decked out in multiple beaded bracelets in varying colors.

A grin twitches at the corners of my lips. "Think she made me one?"

"She made you five."

A piece of my heart grew cold and hard on a damp, dreary December day long ago, but June always has a way of thawing it. My lips tilt up in a tiny smile, and I take a sip of my coffee. The hot, strong brew burns my tongue as I try to hide the emotion clogging my throat. Mom watches me with perceptive eyes, seeing everything, as she always does.

She rests her folded hands on the countertop, pinning me with her gaze. "June told me that Mia mentioned her coming to visit in Paris for the summer."

Dread settles in my stomach, sitting like a rock the same way it did when my ex-wife brought it up on the video call yesterday. "She did."

My fingers clench on the mug until I'm afraid it might shatter as Mom's gaze narrows on me. Jodi Blankenship can't hide a single emotion from her face, and right now, she's angry.

"You need to tell her to stop promising things that are never going to happen, Holden. She gets June's hopes up every time, and June ends up crushed."

"You think I don't know that?" I rasp. "You don't think it rips me apart when June cries because her *mom* forgot she made plans to video call or promises to visit and then cancels at the last minute?"

"Then put your foot down," she says, jaw ticking, fury and hurt flashing in her eyes.

"I—"

"Daddy!" An excited, high-pitched yell comes from the end of the hallway, and despite the heaviness of the conversation with my mom clinging to me like dew to grass, a smile cracks across my face.

A head full of wild blond curls flings itself at me, and skinny arms wrap around my neck like tentacles, suffocating me in the best way. She's bony but strong, and I'm always surprised by her strength.

I band my arms around June's middle, breathing in her little girl scent—cheap watermelon shampoo and sweat, despite the frigid air and falling snow. "How was your day, June Bug?"

"Good!" she yells into my ear, fairly shattering my eardrum. "Olivia invited us over for a play date."

"Did she?" I murmur, setting her wriggling frame back down on the floor.

Mom presses her lips together to hold back a smile, no trace of the tension from our earlier conversation clouding her features. Her hazel eyes meet mine, twinkling like the first of the stars starting to appear in the twilight haze outside.

"Can we go?" June asks.

I reach for my mug so I can take a sip and avoid answering.

Olivia is a really sweet little girl in June's first grade class at school. *Her mom*, Charlotte, on the other hand...wants in my pants. She sent me nudes a few weeks ago. I didn't think people even did that anymore. After consistently turning her down since the girls became friends at the beginning of the school year, I made the mistake of agreeing to get coffee with her a month ago. Since then, she seems to believe she's finally snared me.

"Can we?" June asks again, undeterred by my avoidance.

"Yeah, Holden," Mom says, face lighting. "Are you going to go play with Olivia's mommy?"

I level her with a flat glare. She ignores me, humming as she bustles around the kitchen.

Turning to June, I say, "Maybe. We'll talk about it later. We should probably get home."

"We better hurry," June says, reaching for her backpack that's discarded on the kitchen floor. "Last night, Mommy said she would call me tomorrow, and now it's tomorrow."

Mom's gaze collides with my own, and that sick feeling settles low in my stomach again. We're lucky to get a call from Mia once a week with the time difference and her indifference toward the family she left behind. There's no way she's going to remember to call tonight, especially not when she's probably already in bed with whatever Parisian boyfriend she's currently entertaining.

The look Mom gives me is meaningful. She wants me to stand up to Mia. If I'm being honest, I'd love to give my ex-wife a piece of my mind about how she treats our daughter, but I fear it would only push her away further, until the weekly calls become monthly and then fizzle out entirely. I think Mia loves June, I really do. I just don't think she knows how to be anything but selfish. It isn't a trait I would have chosen for the mother of my child, but we hadn't even been together a year when the strip came back positive and our lives turned upside down. The only thing I can do now is make the best of the bad situation she put June and me in.

Sighing, I rest a hand on June's shoulder, leading her in the direction of her shoes that I noticed scattered by the front door when I walked in. It's best to keep her from finding something to distract her or we'll be here all night.

"Think about what I said," Mom yells after us as we walk through her front door and are met with an icy blast of wind.

I don't bother responding, just lifting a hand in a wave as I shut the front door behind us. Mom doesn't need to tell me to think about it. Mia's actions are always in the back of my head, looming over me like a storm cloud. There's always a voice in my ear telling me I can't raise our daughter on my own—even though I've spent more time as a single parent than I did with Mia here—reminding me that I don't know what I'm doing and I'm one mistake away from ruining June for life.

I didn't expect this when I met a girl with out-of-control curls on a sidewalk one long-ago August day, and I definitely didn't expect it three and a half years later when she left us on an especially cold day in December.

Out of those two days, it's December that I go back to most often, wondering where it all went wrong.

I finish buckling June in the back seat of the truck and climb into the front, cranking the heat. "How was school?"

"Olivia traded me a cupcake for my carrots at lunch, so it was a pretty good day," June says.

I meet her eyes in the rearview mirror. "I packed you carrots because I wanted you to eat carrots," I tell her, my tone stern.

June has the worst sweet tooth of anyone I've ever met. I even had her pediatrician run some tests last year to make sure I wasn't rotting her insides or putting her on track for diabetes. She said June was healthy, but I still want her to eat better. Which is great in theory, except she keeps conning her friends into trading her fruits and vegetables for sweets.

She's going to be a politician one day. I can feel it.

"Yes, Daddy," she says calmly, ignoring my stare by smoothing down the pleats in her skirt. "But cupcakes taste *so* much better."

I let out a puff of air that plumes white in the chill of the car. This girl will be the death of me.

"What else did you do today?"

June's chatter fills the truck as we drive the few minutes across town. Our little town is dead at this time of year, all the hikers and tourists gone until spring, just like I like it. It's cold and a little bleak, but it's quiet, and there's no traffic. Once spring arrives, the town will be bustling again until the leaves turn, and I won't be able to get groceries without waiting in a mile-long line.

My headlights slice across our front yard as I turn down the long gravel drive that leads to our detached garage. I let out a curse under my breath when I catch sight of the stack of boxes on the porch.

"You still have to put money in the swear jar even if you whisper it, Daddy," June says from her booster seat. I mumble another curse, exasperated by how good her hearing is.

I throw the truck into park, grumbling the whole time I help June from the back. Her high-pitched giggle rents the night air as she runs up to the porch. Her hair swings around her when she spins around after reading the labels on the packages.

"They're not ours," she yells, loud enough to alert the neighbors.

She didn't have to yell for me to know that I didn't order six boxes' worth of packages. No, that amount of destructive online shopping can only belong to one person.

"Go inside, June. I'll be back in a minute."

She giggles again, no doubt running inside to the window that faces our neighbor's front porch, eager to watch the action. If I had more cash, I'd let her watch from the porch, but her hearing is too good for my wallet.

Gathering the packages in my arms, I stomp across the yard separating our houses, dead grass and snow crunching beneath my boots. My hands are icy, but my blood is boiling as I pound on my neighbor's summer yellow front door. Even the color is making me angry.

It swings open a second later, and Wren stands across the threshold, smiling brightly. She looks like a ray of eye-searing sunshine, and it makes me glare even harder.

"Good evening, Holden," she says calmly, glancing down at the packages in my arms. "Oh, some of my packages must have been delivered to your house by mistake."

The sparkle in her blue eyes and the smirk on her face tell me this was no accident, not that I thought it was even for a second. At least once a week, I come home to her packages on my porch, and every time I storm over here to deliver them, she seems more and more delighted.

Wren Daniels likes to mess with me. Sending her packages to my house, parking her car in my driveway instead of her own, putting plastic forks in my yard on mowing day, leaving her Christmas lights up way too late.

It's the middle of January, and those fat, bright bulbs are still lighting up the whole neighborhood.

"Stop sending your packages to my house, Wren," I say through gritted teeth.

She props her tiny hands on her hips and tips her chin, giving me a hard stare. "You called the cops on me last week for not taking my Christmas lights down."

"It was the nonemergency line," I say, as if that makes it better. Honestly, if anyone else in the neighborhood had left them up, I wouldn't have given it a second thought, but Wren has a way of getting under my skin. That, and I'm pretty sure she's the one who told my mom that there was a woman at my house two weeks ago, which my mom didn't shut up about for three days. I'm never hiring a housekeeper again.

"Next time, I'm taking these to a dumpster," I say, dropping the packages at her feet. Something rattles in one of the boxes, sounding almost like breaking glass.

Her eyes flare wide, and she drops to her knees, setting the packages to rights. "Holden, there's breakable stuff in there."

Despite everything, I feel a little bad, but I don't show it. Instead, I cross my arms over my chest and stare down at where she's crouched on the ground. "Don't send breakable stuff to my house, then."

She tears open the biggest package, and guilt pools low in my stomach when I see the shattered remains of a broken light fixture. Hard blue eyes meet my own.

"Look what you did," she says.

The words snap me out of my guilt and back into anger. "What *I* did?" I practically yell, shoulders stiffening. "Stop sending your damn packages to my house." I enunciate every word, and her jaw ticks with each one of them.

"Fine," she says, voice rising. And then she slams the door in my face.

I stare at that stupid yellow door for way too long before spinning on my heel and going back to my house. June is standing at the threshold, a jam jar stuffed to the brim with bills in her hand.

"I heard that," she says, grinning up at me with her gap-toothed smile.

I love June more than anything or anyone else in this world, but my favorite part of my day is after she's gone to bed. I get to set the house to rights, putting everything back in its intended place. Then I turn the lights down low, make myself a cocktail, and settle into the deep leather chair by the fireplace to read.

Tonight, the sweet, spicy scent of bourbon perfumes the air. Logs crackle in the fireplace and cast warm, golden shadows on the forest green walls. A brand-new copy of my favorite author's latest mystery novel sits in my lap. I take a sip of my old-fashioned, savoring the layers of citrus and sweetness before cracking open the spine of my book.

Just as I start the first page, my phone vibrates on the dark wooden side table next to me. The screen lights up with an incoming message on a now familiar app. Laying my book face down on my outstretched legs, I reach for my phone and swipe it open.

> *LikeStrawberryWine:* **Hello, my love. How was your day?**

> *user6872:* **I told you to stop calling me that.**

> *LikeStrawberryWine:* **Yes, but I like to imagine a vein popping in your forehead every time I do.**

> *user6872:* **Stop imagining me.**

> *LikeStrawberryWine:* **But in my imaginings you're so dreamy. Like Frodo Baggins. Or Phil from Hercules.**

user6872: That's what does it for you?

LikeStrawberryWine: I have very specific tastes.

user6872: I have bad news. Unfortunately, I am exactly your type.

LikeStrawberryWine: Do you have a hunchback??

user6872: And disfigured toes.

LikeStrawberryWine: Oh gosh. I'm a goner.

LikeStrawberryWine: Did you do anything fun today?

user6872: No.

LikeStrawberryWine: Ah, so just like every day. Well, I did something fun, thank you for asking.

user6872: I didn't ask.

> **_LikeStrawberryWine:_ I see we're still getting the hang of this friend thing.**

Despite my best efforts, a faint smile curves my lips, like it often does during my conversations with the perky stranger. I'm still not sure how we started talking every night in these quiet moments I used to reserve for myself, but I can't deny that I've come to look forward to it. A couple of weeks ago, she got sick and didn't message for three days, and I felt just as fevered and foggy.

It's probably a sign that I should nip this in the bud, but it feels nice to have something of my own for the first time in God knows how long. I've been splitting myself into pieces for ages, giving so much to June and my family and my job that I've felt like a shell of who I used to be.

But here, with this anonymous stranger, I almost feel like I'm putting myself back together.

I glance at my whiskey glass, assessing how much I've drunk to end up in such a sappy mental state.

> **_user6872:_ Right, sorry. How was your day?**

> **LikeStrawberryWine:** You're going soft on me.

> **user6872:** I don't usually have that issue.

I send it before I can think better of it, smiling down at my phone as I wait for her response. She doesn't disappoint.

> **LikeStrawberryWine:** Did YOU just make a sex joke? I'm so proud. I knew this day would come.

> **user6872:** You can write it down in my baby book.

> **LikeStrawberryWine:** If you think I haven't already, you don't even know me.

> **LikeStrawberryWine:** To answer your question, I had a pretty great day. Well, the beginning was good. The ending has been okay.

I stare at her message for a long moment before I respond, and even though I've never actually heard her voice, it's like she's urging me in my ear to try out this friend thing.

> **user6872:** Why was the ending bad?

I must have shocked her into silence by asking a question, because her reply is a long time coming. We've been talking nightly for months now, since Finley signed me up for the stupid app back in the fall, and while she's always trying to pry my secrets out of me, I don't usually ask for hers.

> **LikeStrawberryWine:** I know you don't ever wish for a partner in life. You've made that abundantly clear. But sometimes I want someone to help carry the burden, you know? Sometimes my house feels too quiet and my bills are too much and making dinner for myself or lighting a fire in the fireplace is too hard. And I just want someone to be there, doing all of it with me.

That's the moment I know she's never been in a serious relationship, because if she has, she'd know they're not like that. There's always one person carrying the majority of the weight, shouldering more than their fair share. Maybe there are a select few people out there who find what she's talking about, but most of us don't get that lucky. I know I didn't.

I don't know how to tell her that what she's looking for is a fairy tale, so I stare at the screen until it goes blank, then open it and respond as truthfully as possible.

> **user6872:** I hope you find it.

Three

- WREN -

I FELL ASLEEP ON the couch last night, still dressed in my corduroy pants and sweater from the day before, waiting on the response from **user6872**. My mascara-crusted eyes drift around the room, landing on the empty wine bottle sitting on the coffee table, and the memory hits. I sent a brutally honest wine-fueled message to my anonymous friend last night.

My phone somehow has maintained 1 percent battery, so I swipe the screen and see the message that must have come in after I dozed off.

> **user6872:** I hope you find it.

I stare at the message until my phone goes black, finally surrendering that last 1 percent, a sleepy smile curving up the corners of my mouth. It's taken months, but he's finally started to come around to this whole friend thing. If I'm being honest, I don't know what drove me to keep messaging him in those early days when it was clear he didn't want to talk to me. Maybe I sensed that despite the surliness, he needed connection as much as I did.

Regardless, I'm glad to have him—even if I have no idea who he is. Sometimes living in a small town can be incredibly lonely, but it's nice to know I have someone just a tap away.

Glancing up at the clock on the wall in the kitchen, I groan. I forgot to set an alarm last night, and I have to meet with the volunteers for the Galentine's Auction in less than an hour. I push up off the couch and bump into every piece of eclectic vintage furniture in my cottage on the way to the bathroom. Icy water splatters across my skin when I turn on the shower, and I hiss, stepping back to be closer to the radiator. Through the tiny window, I can see the lights on at Holden's place, the silhouette of his frame and June's much tinier one moving around behind the sheer curtains.

The sight of him reminds me of the packages from last night, and that sick feeling returns to my stomach. I spent weeks scouring the internet for an affordable yet stylish light fixture for the cabin and finally found one online. It was a little outside my budget, and I probably spent too much on it, but I also want to invest in quality pieces to make the space feel luxurious. Except *Holden* dropped it on the ground, shattering the glass inside into fractured pieces. I left the box on my kitchen table next to the stack of cabin bills that I've yet to look at. Between the bills, the construction materials, the furniture and decor I've budgeted for, and what I'm paying the contractor, I'm starting to feel like I'm drowning.

Turning away from the window, I hop into the now warm shower, desperate to get my mind focused on something else—like the thousands of little details I still have to organize for this auction.

It doesn't take me long to shower and get ready, and I manage to make it to the town square on time, though the ends of my wet curls grow stiff and crunchy in the chilly air. I probably should have driven, but I love surveying the town in winter, with snow crunching under my feet and flurries landing on my eyelashes.

When I let myself into Smokey the Beans, the only coffee shop in town, it's already bustling, which isn't unusual for a Saturday morning. My mail carrier is sorting through mail at a table in the corner. My high school Spanish teacher, Mrs. Garcia, is reading a bodice ripper on one of the couches, her hand pressed to her throat. The teens behind the counter are making a video of themselves dancing.

My volunteers are at a table near the window, bickering about something, and I can't help but smile as I make my way over to them.

"Wren!" Melissa, a sixty-three-year-old woman with dyed auburn hair and bright green eyes that always sparkle, calls out when she sees me approaching. "You can settle our argument."

Myra, her best friend, places her folded wrinkled hands on the table and leans forward. "How long do you think it will take Carl Sanders to realize that his new wife is older than she says?"

Carl Sanders owns a urinal cake manufacturing plant on the edge of town, and he's probably the richest resident in the county. About every five years, he trades out his wife for a newer model. What he hasn't realized is that his newest wife is probably three years older than his last. She just drives three hours to Charlotte every couple of months to get Botox.

"I'm going to need coffee before I start in on something like that," I respond to the group of women eagerly awaiting my reply.

Stevie launches out of her seat. "I'll go with you." Tagging me toward the counter, she hisses, "You're late. You left me alone with Myra and Melissa for too long and they cornered me about matrimony."

I snort a laugh. "What did you tell them?"

"That I gave up men cold turkey."

"And that worked?" I ask, cocking a brow.

She shakes her head. "Not even close. They said it's now their mission to show me the value in men."

"If you were going to lie, you should have just told them you're seeing someone," I say as we approach the counter. One of the teens, still filming her dance, holds up a finger at me, signaling they need another moment.

Stevie leans a hip on the counter. "Like that would have worked. Plus, my mom is there, so that would have opened another can of worms."

I hum in the back of my throat just as one of the teens comes to the register, out of breath and smiling. "What can I get for you?"

After I order my usual chai latte, Stevie and I make our way back to the table. I pause to ask Mrs. Garcia what she's reading so I can pick it up at the bookstore later today. If she's blushing that hard, I want it.

"We're back," I singsong, sitting in the chair next to the one Stevie collapsed in. I have to hold back a smile at the way she's got her arms crossed over her chest, as if physically warding off any of the meddling women around the table.

Looking around the table at my volunteers, I say, "Let's get started. We've got four weeks until the auction. Mom, where are our donations going this year?"

My mom hasn't worked since Rae was born, but she's on every board in town, and she's more connected than anyone I've ever met. She pushes a lock of red hair that's going white at the temples behind her ear as she consults the tiny notebook she always keeps in those colored sweatpants. Rae and I both inherited her hair color, but we got our curls from Dad.

"The main bridge in town needs repairs, so the Bicycle, Pedestrian, and Traffic Safety Committee would love for donations to be put toward that."

"The bridge it is," I say, making a note in my own journal. Turning to Stevie's mom, my boss, I ask, "Is the budget for this year the same?"

Jamie nods. "Yes, ma'am."

"Stevie," I say, and I can practically feel her wince when all eyes land on her. "Did you come up with a list of bachelors to approach?"

"If not, Melissa and I can help," Myra says, winking one of her brown eyes.

I have to press my lips together to hold back my smile.

"I have a list," Stevie says, pulling a paper from her bag and sliding it over to me.

After scanning the bleak options, I glance up at her. "Stevie, there are only four guys on here."

She shrugs. "Jess Peters signed up three years in a row, but now he's dating the woman who bid on him last year."

"I didn't realize they were still together," I say.

Melissa pipes up. "Oh, yes. He just bought a ring." She's loud enough to draw the attention of everyone in the shop, meaning the whole town should know about poor Jess's proposal by noon.

"And Dean Barker is dating someone from that anonymous dating app everyone in town started using last summer," Ava, Stevie's aunt, says from across the table. She runs a store on the farm's property, selling handmade candles, soaps, and perfumes. She's also the mother of one of my childhood best friends, Hazel, which makes her one of my favorite people in the world.

The mention of that particular dating app has me itching to change the subject. If any of the women found out that I've been talking to a man on that dating app for months, they would never stop hounding me.

"Well," I say. "How about we each make a list of potential bachelors, and Stevie can be in charge of tracking them down?"

"I'll try to get Holden to sign up," Jodi, Holden's mom, says, grinning mischievously. I have no doubt Holden would bring in a good chunk of change, because despite his surly demeanor, he's kind of...hot. Tattoos cover his tan skin, and his hair is probably as long as mine, although it's always tied back in a bun, so I've never been able to confirm it. His hazel eyes change colors with his outfits, and his jawline, hidden under a thick, neatly trimmed beard, is sharp enough to cut glass.

But there's no way in hell he would ever agree to sign up for something like this. When he pisses me off, I like to tell Jodi I saw a woman at his house late at night, but the truth is, in the four years I've lived next door to him, I've never seen any woman but his mom, sister, or the occasional housekeeper step inside his home.

"Good luck with that," I say under my breath, and flip to the next page in my notebook. "Moving on. I met with the caterer last week."

There's a place in town that no one else knows about where I like to go when I need to think. Or at least I assume everyone has forgotten about it since I haven't encountered another soul here since I found it in my junior year of high school.

It's easy to assume that the best views around could be found just beyond the entrance to the Great Smoky Mountains National Park, but I personally like the view from an outlook on the very edge of town. Just off the beaten path, nestled in a copse of trees, is a dirt overlook barely large enough to park my car in. When the weather is nice, I'll climb out on the hood and watch the sunset or stare up into the sky as the stars blink to life. In the winter, I usually order a hot drink from Smokey the Beans, drive up to my little hideaway, and look out my windshield at the vast expanse beyond.

That's my plan today, but when I arrive, for the first time in over ten years, there's another car parked in my spot. And I know who it belongs to.

Holden is standing against the hood of his truck, hands wrapped around a thermos. When he notices me, his shoulders go rigid.

"What are you doing here?" he asks the moment I shut off my car and climb out into the bitter cold, chai latte in hand. He's dressed in a thick olive jacket with a sherpa collar. Although it looks warm enough, I don't know how he's standing outside, snow landing softly in his hair and melting on his red-tinted nose and cheeks.

"What am *I* doing here?" I ask, my voice pitching with incredulity. "This is my spot."

He scoffs. "I've been coming here since I was in high school."

"So have I."

A muscle in his jaw ticks as he stares down at me, and I realize I've moved into his personal space. It's a little intoxicating, being this close to him. I'm not sure what to make of that.

"I'm older than you," he says, lips twisting in a faint smile I've never seen on his face before. For the first time, I think I understand why all the single women in town lost their minds when he moved back here from Charlotte after his divorce four years ago.

"Thank you for that astute observation."

His hazel eyes narrow, more green than brown today, thanks to his jacket. "That means I've been coming here longer. It was my place first."

This is true, and probably also why the place felt like it hadn't seen another human visitor in years, since Holden had moved to Charlotte for college by the time I started high school. I just don't know how I haven't run into him here in the last four years.

"You forfeited your right to it when you moved away," I shoot back.

He gives me a flat stare before returning his gaze to the view ahead, effectively ignoring me. *I* can't focus with him here, taking up space in my field of vision, but he doesn't seem to have that issue.

Huffing out an annoyed breath, I move to lean on the hood of my own car, determined to be as unaffected by his presence as he is by mine. Then I see his jaw tick, notice the way his hand flexes on his thermos, and I realize maybe he *is* annoyed after all. And there's almost nothing that brings me more joy than annoying Holden Blankenship.

"We could share the spot," I say, my breath fogging in the air.

Holden slants a look in my direction. "Pass."

I take a sip of my latte to hide my smile. "You get it on weekends; I get it on weekdays. Or maybe Monday, Wednesday, Friday, and alternating weekends."

The noise he makes is so aggrieved that I feel a burst of pleasure shoot through me. "I'm not having joint custody of an overlook, Wren."

"Well, you're not getting full custody of it, Holden."

He turns toward me fully this time, flames licking in his eyes, a fire that lets me know I've pushed him right to my favorite spot—where all that reserved composure turns into unrestrained emotion. "Why are you always so difficult?"

I grin at him across the space between us. "I prefer vexing. It sounds sexier."

"Why are you always so vexing?" He practically growls it, his voice rough as sandpaper.

I press a hand to my throat just like Mrs. Garcia did in Smokey the Beans. "Wow, that worked for me. Can you try saying it in a British accent?"

His jaw tightens enough to break a tooth. "Get out of my spot."

"I'm not leaving." I pair my statement with a smile that I know makes him see red.

"Well, neither am I."

"Then be quiet so I can have some peace."

He shifts his body so he's facing the view ahead, shoulders stiff. "Fine."

"Fine."

A heavy quiet falls between us, the only sound the wind rustling the bare branches of trees. I try and fail to focus on the view, to ignore the cold biting at my nose and seeping into my hands despite the latte. I'm practically shivering, and I risk a glance over at Holden, who is standing stock still, like the chill isn't even bothering him. He doesn't even seem to notice the snowflakes gathering on his lashes, the hollows of his cheeks, the bridge of his strong nose, the tips of his hair escaping his messy bun. In fact, something about it makes him look stronger, more solid, in the face of the harsh elements.

I can't help but let my gaze linger on him out of the corner of my eye. As much as he drives me to madness, he really is nice to look at. All hard, lean lines. The unyielding slash of his brow and the ever-changing color of his eyes.

One of his sleeves is hiked up, exposing the ink on his wrist. I know it trails up his arms, disappearing beneath the rolled-up sleeves of his flannel, but I don't know where those tattoos end, and I've always wondered. Maybe it's the cold that loosens my tongue, or maybe it's the need to speak to remind my body that I'm still alive despite the way I'm freezing straight through, but I ask, "Holden?"

He sighs, eyes angling in my direction. "What, Wren?"

"How far up does that tattoo on your arm go?"

Holden looks at me directly this time, shifting his body to face me. "What?"

"It's a simple question," I say, not bothering to look in his direction, even though I can feel the weight of his stare lingering on me.

"Why do you want to know?" I can hear the wary tone in his voice, and I have to hold back my grin.

"Curiosity."

"I hear it kills," he says, and then he's silent for so long that I think he's not going to answer. "Which tattoo are you talking about? I have lots."

I finally allow myself to look at him, noticing the way his cheeks and nose are tinged pink in the cold, how it looks so delicate on him, a juxtaposition that sends a bolt of awareness through me. "All of them. Do they go all the way up your arm? You're always wearing flannels."

"They go up and onto my chest."

My tongue darts out to wet my dry, chapped lips, and I think his gaze tracks the movement. "Interesting."

"Why?" he asks, the suspicious tone returning to his voice.

"You should show them off more. Women like tattoos."

He rolls his eyes. "I'm not trying to get a woman."

"You had a woman at your house two weeks ago." I told his mom about it after he yelled at me for being too loud after neighborhood quiet hours on New Year's Eve.

"She was a housekeeper," he says, throwing his free hand up in the air like he's already had this discussion more times than his patience allows. His gaze narrows on me, like he's finally putting together how his mom found out about his visitor. "How do you even know that?"

I shrug easily. "I saw her through the windows. I can see straight into your living room from my bathroom."

He holds my stare for a long minute, and then his lips curl in a slow smile I've never seen before. Frankly, it's disorienting. "I know."

My breath feels halted in my lungs under the weight of that smirk, so when I speak, my voice comes out thin and raspy. "How do you know that?"

"Because I can see straight into your bathroom from my living room." He pauses, letting the words sink in. "You should really start closing the blinds when you shower."

Whatever trance that grin had me in snaps like a broken rubber band. I stare at him, jaw open. "You're kidding."

He grins wider. "Do you not understand how windows work, Wren?"

I push up off the hood of my car, rounding toward the door. "I'm leaving."

"It's too bad my bathroom faces Mrs. Sputniski's house, or you'd know just where those tattoos stop," he hollers as I slide into the driver's seat.

"Goodbye, Holden," I say, slamming my door closed and backing out of my little haven that now feels tainted. He's still smirking when I turn onto the main road, and I can feel it lingering in the back of my mind like an earworm.

That night, I make sure to shut the blinds in my bathroom.

Four

- HOLDEN -

Saturday nights are reserved for family dinners. For as long as I can remember, we've gathered around my mom's scarred wooden dining table. Mom worked a lot when we were kids, raising Finley and me on her own, but she always took Saturday nights off. That was our time, carved in stone.

Music is playing when I let myself in the front door. Frank Sinatra, which means Mom is making some kind of pasta. She likes to listen to music reflecting whatever she's cooking—says it puts her in the mood.

It's something my best friend, Grey, has found charming since he started coming around in high school, and by that time, it was so ingrained in me that I no longer noticed. At first, I thought he was making fun of me, but then I went to his house and saw that my happy-go-lucky best friend lived in a silent, beige cookie-cutter home and spent most nights eating a microwave dinner in his bedroom. It gave me a new appreciation for my loud, sometimes obnoxious upbringing, even if I do need a couple of hours to decompress after the noise and stimulation of a family gathering.

From the foyer, I can hear Grey and Finley arguing. My mom's laughter at their antics rings out, and June's high-pitched giggle follows a moment later. I've missed my daughter today. Saturdays are typically reserved for the two of us, since she stays the night with my mom after family dinner, but Finley begged for a girls' day with her, which is how I ended up at the overlook. With Wren.

I'm still not entirely sure what happened there. One moment she was driving me crazy, and the next, I was admitting that I have, on occasion, seen into her bathroom. Never on purpose, and I've never lingered, but she really needs to close the blinds.

Shaking myself from the way my thoughts are headed, I make my way into the kitchen.

"Daddy!" June yells, launching herself at me. "Aunt Finley put pink in my hair."

It's then that I notice the strip of pink hidden in June's wild, knotted curls. My head snaps up to look at Finley.

She waves me off from where she's sitting at the counter, seltzer in hand. "It's not permanent."

I level her with a flat glare. "From here on out, consult me before making changes to my daughter's appearance."

Finley ignores me, holding her hand up in front of her mouth to cover it as she whispers loudly to June. "Don't tell him about the belly button ring."

June giggles, and I let out a long sigh, massaging the spot between my eyebrows. The women in this family have made it their personal mission to make life as difficult as possible for me.

Grey smirks in my direction and nods at the fridge. "I brought beer."

"You shouldn't need alcohol to get through a family dinner," Mom chides from where she's stirring her pasta dish on the stove.

"You're right," I say, pulling a beer from the fridge and popping the cap off on the edge of the counter before taking a long sip.

Mom rolls her eyes, turning back to the stove. "Dinner is almost ready."

I move past her, pausing to drop a kiss on the top of her head. As much as this family teases and taunts one another, we'd all do anything for each other, especially for Mom. I've never known my father, and Finley's dad passed away before she was old enough to remember him, leaving Mom to raise a one-year-old and a five-year-old all alone.

Most days, I'm barely making it trying to keep June alive and healthy. I can't imagine how she did it with two of us.

"What can I help with?"

Mom smiles at me over her shoulder. "Nothing. Everything is ready."

The five of us move through the kitchen easily, a choreographed dance perfected over the years. It's chaotic and loud and sometimes makes me want to pull my hair out, but it's also simple and easy in a way most things aren't anymore.

"I met the nicest woman in the shop today," Finley says as soon as we're all sitting down, plates and silverware clattering.

I ignore her, using tongs to scoop salad onto my plate, knowing exactly where she's planning to take this conversation.

"She's single too," Finley continues, her voice taking on that singsong quality I hate.

"I'm sure Grey knows her," I deadpan.

Grey smirks at Finley, propping his chin on his fist. "Yeah, Fin, can you describe her for me?"

"She's off-limits to you," Finley says, glaring at him before turning back to me. "I gave her your number."

I lob a crouton in her direction, and she squeals, the sound echoing through the house.

"Children," Mom scolds, and we all get quiet enough to hear the clock ticking on the wall.

"Sorry, Mom," I murmur under my breath before fixing Finley with a withering stare. Somehow, when I walk into this house for family dinner, I revert to my childhood self. Childhood Holden had a lot less restraint when it came to dealing with the nuisances in his life,

"So tell us about this woman," Mom says, a mischievous lilt to her voice.

I let out a long breath, the dull throb returning right between my eyes.

"Her name is Emily, and she's twenty-nine," Finley says, pushing a lock of her long, golden blond hair behind her ear.

I cut her off. "Sounds like a perfect next wife for Carl Sanders. Did you hear his new wife is almost ten years older than she told him she is?"

Grey gasps, rearing back. He's wearing his glasses tonight, and the frames tilt with the movement. "How long do you think it will be before he figures it out?"

"Probably when he gets that bill from her plastic surgeon."

"*Emily* is a vet tech at Fontana Ridge Animal Hospital."

Grey waves a finger in Finley's direction, a grin lighting up his face. "Ah, I do know Emily." He turns the smile on me. "Great girl."

"See? I can't go out with her," I tell Finley and Mom.

"If you couldn't go out with anyone Grey has dated, you wouldn't be able to find a woman in the entire county," Finley retorts.

"Careful, Fin. You might sound jealous."

Her hazel eyes go flat. "There's not enough money in the world."

"For what?" June asks, looking between all of us. Marinara sauce has already dripped from her spoon, staining the mustard yellow dress she's wearing. It just adds to her wild child look, pink cheeks and freckled nose, bare, dirty feet and untamable curls.

"To pay me to date your Uncle Grey," Finley tells her sweetly. "Now, back to Emily."

I let out a long breath and run my palm down my face. My head throbs, and I would give almost anything to be sitting in my chair next to my fireplace with something stronger than a beer in hand. "Finley, I'm not going out with Emily."

Her jaw clenches, that determined look entering her eyes. I know what she's about to say is going to burrow right under my skin, an itch I'm not supposed to scratch. "Do I need to set you up on another dating app?"

"You set him up on a dating app?" Mom asks.

I want to strangle Finley for bringing this up. It takes all of my restraint not to fling an entire handful of croutons in her direction this time.

"Yes," she says with a roll of her eyes. She takes a sip of her seltzer, pinning me with a look. "And he threw such a big fit about it."

"Women wouldn't stop messaging me for days!" I'm practically yelling across the table, but all the aggravation I've felt about my mom and sister constantly butting into my love life, or lack thereof, has finally come to a head. It doesn't matter that I've told them I don't want to date, or that I've got too much going on in my life, or that I don't want to bring someone else into June's life who could ultimately leave her again. They don't listen.

"Holden," Mom says, her voice soft and soothing, like she's talking to a cornered wild animal. I *feel* like a cornered wild animal. "We just want you—"

"I want both of you to stay out of it." Setting firm boundaries is the only way to get through to them, or Mom, at least.

Her face pinches in displeasure, but she finally nods, tongue pressed to the front of her teeth.

Finley clears her throat. "I guess now isn't the best time to tell you that I also signed you up for single parent speed dating at the Baptist church next week."

"Speed dating," I grumble into my beer an hour later, perched atop a high stool at my favorite bar in town, Matty's.

A laugh rumbles out of Grey's chest, and he shakes his head. "She's good."

I glare at him over the rim of my glass. "I'm not going."

"You made that abundantly clear." This is true, but obviously, my firm tone wasn't going to work on Finley. I had to revert to throwing more croutons at her head and threatening to post her embarrassing middle school photos on the town Facebook page if she didn't let up on the matchmaking. She relented, but I'm not holding my breath that it will last long.

Finley ditched us the moment we left Mom's, headed to meet her boyfriend, Gus. Grey and I have never been his biggest fans, mostly because he doesn't treat Finley very well, but also because I've never had a conversation with him that doesn't involve cryptocurrency. So Finley doesn't invite him out with us much.

"She drives me crazy," I say.

He slants a look in my direction. "You love her."

I grunt low in my throat. "She still drives me crazy."

Grey shrugs, his eyes leaving mine to flit around the bar. He's probably looking for someone he *hasn't* approached before, but Finley wasn't kidding when she said he would need to leave the county for that.

"I wish I had siblings," he finally says. "You're lucky."

Guilt pricks in my chest. Grey's home life has never been *bad*, but I get the sense it's never been good either. In all these years we've been friends, he's hardly talked about it, but it's like the minute he came to my house in high school, it became his as well.

His parents have never really been happy with one another, but they've stayed together anyway. I always mourned that Finley and I never had two parents, but I never considered what it would have been like to have two parents who were only partly there.

"I am lucky," I say. My voice sounds rough, even to my own ears. "But you are too."

He smirks in my direction before turning back to focus on the woman across the room that he has been making eyes at for the last few minutes. "I hope to be. I'll be back."

Without another glance back, he slides off the barstool and weaves his way through the tables. The woman is standing by the vintage jukebox, coins jangling in her shaking hands, and he presses his palm to the wall next to her, smiling down.

I don't know how he does it. Even before June, I was never that smooth. I was all nerves and bumbling hands, saying the wrong thing and hoping women found it charming instead of standoffish.

It had been that way with Mia at first. I ran smack into her in a crowded bar in the city, my mind a mess with all the sounds and smells and voices clambering over one another. My drink spilled across her shirt, and before I could think about what I was doing, I was reaching for her to try and dry it up. It only took a moment to realize where my hands had landed, and by then, I was stumbling over my apology and bumping into other people as I tried to back away. But when I looked at her face, she was smiling. And I knew right then that I was a goner.

I knew even then that my life was taking a sharp turn in another direction. I just never expected this is where I'd end up.

The front door to the bar opens, and snow blows in on a gust of wind a moment before I see curly strawberry blond hair and smiling pink cheeks. This time there's no one to laugh at me as I groan into my beer.

Stevie Lynch walks in behind Wren, her dark hair piled atop her head, little wisps falling out to frame her face. They're laughing at something, and I can't help but notice how *happy* Wren looks. She's always wearing an expression of mischievous glee or barely contained hostility around me, or, for the first time, earlier today at the overlook, flustered embarrassment. I shouldn't have been so pleased to see her like that, but she's always getting under my skin, and I feel like I've never been able to turn the tables on her.

Who knew all I had to do was admit I've seen her ass because she can't figure out blinds?

Wren's eyes land on me, and the smile slides right off her cold-kissed face. An annoyed look enters her eyes and she pins me with it. Surprisingly, this makes *me* smile, just a faint twitch of my lips, but I know she catches it when her gaze gets even stonier.

I watch out of the corner of my eye as she and Stevie settle into one of the ripped red leather booths on the other side of the bar, the warm golden lights sending shadows over their skin. Wren looks even paler next to Stevie's tan, her freckles standing out in stark contrast like constellations over every exposed inch.

I'm not sure why I keep watching as they duck their heads and talk among themselves, but for some reason, my eyes keep drifting in that direction, focusing on red-gold ringlets catching in the overhead light. It's why I notice when Wren stands up, gaze fixed on me, and walks in my direction.

My heart ratchets up in my chest, beating loud enough that I can hear it in my ears, feel it in the tips of my fingers where they rest on the sweating glass. I probably shouldn't have admitted I've seen her naked. I can only imagine what she's going to do to get me back for that accident. I'll probably come home to hundreds of packages on my front porch and those giant Christmas lights hanging from my rafters.

"Holden," Wren says, sidling up next to me, her elbows landing on the bar top.

"Wrennifer."

Her nose wrinkles as she considers me, and my lips twitch again, straining to smile. Warmth gathers somewhere low in my stomach when her eyes track the movement. I push the feeling away, downing the rest of my beer.

Setting the glass on the counter, I ask, "Are you following me? This is the second time I've run into you today."

Her sigh is so exasperated that I want to laugh. She places her folded hands on the bar, swiveling to face me. "Yes, Holden. I'm following you because it's my deepest desire to make you fall madly in love with me and bear your children."

I stare at her, unblinking, and she rolls her eyes.

"No, Holden, I'm not following you. I'm only into men with hunchbacks and disfigured toes. You're much too proportional for my tastes."

My world narrows down to just Wren as she waves at Matty, who has been talking to someone on the other side of the bar. I barely hear his voice as he shuffles over, mouth stretched in his signature friendly smile.

No, I'm focused entirely on what Wren just said. On what *Wren* said. Wren and not **LikeStrawberryWine**.

"What did you just say?" I ask. My voice sounds strangled even to my own ears, because surely, *surely* this is a coincidence.

Wren flashes me a puzzled look, brows pinched together, full lips pursed. "What?"

"What did you say?" I ask again, enunciating more clearly this time.

Matty is now giving me the same look as Wren. I want to assure him that I'm not going crazy or suffering some kind of medical event. It's just that my world has been flipped upside down, and I'm walking on the ceiling, wondering why everyone else is still down on the ground.

Wren's gaze swings between Matty and me, her face painted in confusion. If you looked the word up in the dictionary, her current expression would be right beside it. "I told Matty I wanted strawberry wine."

And that's the moment I know I wasn't confused, but I have made a mistake.

Five
- WREN -

"Strawberry wine," Holden says from beside me, sounding strangled.

My gaze drifts over him—long nearly black hair pulled into a messy bun, flannel sleeves rolled up to reveal the tattoos I've secretly always wanted to examine up close, hazel eyes blown wide in shock.

I nod, not sure why he looks so spooked. "Strawberry wine. It's wine, but strawberry." I say this slowly, emphasizing the words like I'm talking to a toddler.

He just stares at me with that blank stare. Then, so low I almost don't hear him, he murmurs, "Like strawberry wine."

Realization clicks into place, and I blink at him, no doubt sporting the same confused look he is. Holden can't be…

Although now that I think about it, it makes so much sense. The grumpiness. The interfering sister. The absolute abhorrence for dating.

User6872 is Holden. My Holden—my *neighbor* Holden. The one who drives me crazy and calls the cops when I prank him and who has apparently *seen me naked* and has never once actually smiled at me for a reason other than mischief. *He* is my friend, the one I look forward to talking to each night, who I have to force myself not to message throughout the day so he doesn't think I'm trying to come onto him.

The surprise starts to dissolve into something warmer. A pleasure that feels like sunshine after days of rain. "I *knew* you weren't as grumpy as you pretend to be," I say, shoving his shoulder with the palm of my hand. It's more firm than I expected, and he doesn't even budge, his giant body completely unmoved by me.

He's quiet, something I've grown familiar with, but this silence feels different because his gaze is traveling the length of my body as if he's never seen me before. Everywhere his eyes rove over feels like I spent too much time out in the sun, my skin going pink.

Hazel eyes, that I'm just now discovering are flecked with varying shades of greens and golds, catch my gaze and hold. For some reason, the breath stalls in my lungs.

"No," he says simply, definitively. With a flick of his wrist, he motions at Matty that he wants another drink, no longer focused on me at all.

I blink slowly, only realizing after a lengthy pause that my mouth is hanging open. "What do you mean *no*?"

Matty returns with my wine and Holden's beer, glancing between us as if he can feel the tension radiating off us in waves. He doesn't say anything, just leaves with a dip of his chin. I'd be worried Myra and Melissa would be spreading this tale through town in the morning, but if there's anyone in Fontana Ridge who can keep a secret, it's the local bartender.

"Sorry, that was rude of me," Holden says, glancing at me out of the corner of his eye as he takes a sip of his drink, the long column throat working as he swallows. After he sets his glass back on the counter, he swivels to face me, his knees bumping into mine. "No, *thank you*."

He says this with a sticky-sweet tone and follows it with a closed-lip smile that has me seeing red. I plunk down onto the stool next to him. "You don't just get to say no, thank you. You can't just decide that I'm not the person you've been talking to for the last four months, Holden."

His broad shoulders lift in a shrug, straining at the fabric of his flannel. And that dismissive gesture is what sends me over the edge.

I'm not sure what's going through my mind as I grab him by the collar of his shirt and tug him forward. I do know that he has to allow it, giving into my pull, or else I'd never be able to make him budge.

Tugging until we're nose to nose, I say through gritted teeth, "We're friends, whether you like it or not. You can drop the act now." My voice lowers, going smooth as silk. "I know you're really just a big softie inside."

And then I pat him on the chest, right where my fist was a moment before. His gaze tracks the movement before returning to mine. This close, I can see every color in his irises, every freckle dotting the strong line of his nose, but everything beyond him is a blur, like adjusting the focus on a camera until the subject is in view.

It's only because my hand is still on his chest that I can feel him swallow, only because he's so close that I can see the way his gaze dips for just a second before returning to my eyes. I wonder if we're close enough that he can feel my skin heat. If he can feel my shudder as a zip of electricity runs up the length of my spine.

"Hi, Holden." A woman's voice pierces through the fog surrounding us, and Holden and I spring away from each other. I swear I can still feel the soft cotton of his flannel on my palm like it's been imprinted there.

Charlotte Danbury is standing directly behind Holden, a pinched smile on her face, and when he swivels in her direction, his knees tangle with mine. Charlotte tracks the movement, her eyes narrowing into slits.

"Charlotte," Holden fairly croaks, and I look between the two of them, trying to figure out the cause of the thick tension in the air. "Nice to see you."

"Nice to see you too," Charlotte says, but she's not looking at Holden. Her dark brown eyes are fixed squarely on me, and I get the feeling she's trying to read the situation she walked into the same way I am.

Turning back to Holden, she asks, "So what are you two up to tonight?"

Holden opens his mouth to respond, but the opportunity to get him back for the shower incident dangles in front of me, and I decide to snatch it.

"Holden asked for my help picking up women."

The look Holden gives me is sharp enough to cut glass. Or my throat. Which I can perfectly imagine him doing when Charlotte leaves us alone.

Charlotte looks to Holden, a more genuine, almost hungry smile lighting up her face. "I'm sure he wouldn't have any trouble in that department."

"You wouldn't think," I say and pat his thigh. It stiffens under my touch. He's tense enough to explode with one wrong movement. "But he's surprisingly bad with women. No charisma."

"Oh, I don't know." Charlotte's voice drops to something lower and huskier, and a thrill of excitement shoots through me. I decide to press my advantage.

"You know," I say. "Holden was just telling me that there was one woman in town he's been wanting to ask out, but he didn't know how. Holden, who was—"

"Excuse us," Holden says through clenched teeth, fairly launching out of his barstool. His hand binds around my upper arm, tugging me with him in the direction of the bathrooms.

I glance at Charlotte over my shoulder and toss her a wink. "Men, right?"

She giggles, something high pitched that I know has to grate on Holden's nerves, and I make a mental note to double down on my efforts to make him take her on a date, just so I can go to the same place and watch.

Holden pulls me into the dim hallway leading to the bathroom and spins me so my back is to the wall. This close, he towers over me. His eyes are lit with an angry flame that burns so hot I can practically feel it singeing my skin.

"What are you doing?" He enunciates each word, his jaw tight. Every line of his body is tense, and I can't help but notice the muscles flexing in his neck, the unyielding expanse of his shoulders, the flicker in his jaw.

I've never seen him this close to coming undone, and part of me wants to push another button, just to see what he would look like when he lost all control. I think it would be a little like watching a flame catch in the fireplace, all-consuming and impossible to look away from.

I smile sweetly at him. "Getting back at you for watching me in the shower."

His teeth clench hard enough to break, and he blows out a long breath through his nostrils. "I don't *watch* you in the shower, Wren."

"So you were lying?" I say, cocking an eyebrow.

He sighs, focusing on a spot down the hall, a flush creeping up his neck. "No, I have seen...just not on purpose."

I'm not sure what I was hoping to accomplish with this line of questioning, but suddenly, the space between us feels too small, the air in here a hundred degrees hotter than the rest of the bar. I know if he ever looks away from that riveting spot on the wall, he'd see the evidence of my embarrassment on my cheeks too.

His anger feels a million miles away, buried under the thick awkwardness hanging between us. Irrationally, I hope I was wearing cute underwear on whatever days he happened to be walking by his living room window.

"Sorry about Charlotte," I say, desperate for a change in subject.

His eyes snare mine, a muscle jumping in his jaw once more. This time, I think the red on his sharp cheekbones is from exasperation. That, at least, feels familiar.

Holden leans into my space, his hand landing on the wall beside my head. His lips part to deliver what I expect to be a lashing blow, but he's cut off by a noise at the end of the hall. Our gazes snap in that direction to see Charlotte, who's staring at us with wide eyes.

"Oh," she blurts, looking between us.

Holden jumps away from me, dropping his hand from the wall. It's surprising how much colder it feels without him close.

He palms at the back of his neck, avoiding Charlotte's glance, and I clear my throat. "Well, I better get going."

"No," Charlotte says, holding up a hand. "I was just coming to find Holden to tell him I was ducking out. I didn't mean to interrupt."

"You didn't—" I say, but she cuts me off.

"Good night, Holden." Charlotte spins on her heel, not sparing me another glance, and I turn to Holden, feeling like I'm missing something.

"Are you two dating?"

His eyes blow wide. "No."

I look back at the spot she vacated, analyzing the situation over and over again. "Does she know that?"

Honestly, I didn't think through the comments I made earlier. I would have said it to any single woman of a certain age in town in order to get back at him. My hope was that he'd have to sit through a terrible date or fend off the hordes of women who thought it was finally time to shoot their shot.

"We went out on one date. Kind of," Holden finally concedes, pinching the bridge of his nose. "I didn't think it was a date, but I'm pretty sure she did. Now she won't leave me alone."

I make a humming noise in the back of my throat, shifting my weight from foot to foot. "Oh."

He glares at me. "Yes, *oh*."

Irritation flares inside me. "Well, she left, didn't she? She thinks we're back here necking in the hallway."

"Don't say *necking*," he says with a wrinkle of his nose.

I cross my arms over my chest. "She's been gone for a while now. She's probably thinking we're doing a lot more than necking. I'm wearing my overalls dress too, so it's really easy to—"

"Wren," Holden snaps, and a grin touches my lips. He rolls his eyes when he sees it.

"I know, I know," I say. "I'm so—"

"Vexing."

My smile widens, and under the warm, dim lights, I think I see his lips twitch. I feel that bare hint of a smile all the way down to my toes.

"There you are," another voice comes from down the hall behind me, and I spin around to see Stevie walking toward us. "I thought you left."

"No, I was back here necking with Holden."

He sighs so heavily that I can feel it on the back of my neck, even with the two feet of space between us.

"Any good?" Stevie asks, not missing a beat.

I shrug. "Kind of out of practice, if you ask me."

"We were not necking," Holden says, his tone laced with exasperation.

I nod at Stevie. "Sorry, he's not a fan of that word."

"I'm leaving," Holden says flatly, his shoulder brushing against mine as he moves down the tight hallway, not looking back at me.

"Use some ChapStick," I yell after him. "It'll make it better next time."

He disappears around the corner, but I catch his hand holding up a middle finger in my direction, and my laughter echoes down the hall.

Stevie looks between me and where Holden just departed. "What just happened here?"

I can still feel the memory of his warmth, imagine the sharp line of his jaw and the intensity of his stare. My skin tingles in all the places his eyes touched, and there's a lingering electricity in the air that has never been there before.

"I honestly don't know."

"I only have four guys signed up for the bachelor auction," I whine to Myra and Melissa on Monday morning. They meet up at the local coffee shop, Smokey the Beans, every weekday morning and order black coffees that they get refilled for free while they sit here and gossip. If anyone needs to know anything in town, they know to come to Smokey's before lunch.

Outside, chilly rain is pattering on the windows. The sky is gray and hazy, making the mountains barely visible. Inside, the coffee shop has been buzzing with customers seeking warmth in the form of hot beverages. The air smells of strong coffee and rich caramel, cinnamon, and peppermint.

I've been here all morning, hoping to rope single men into joining the auction but having very little luck. The auction has gotten a bit of a reputation for attracting...older women, and after the winning bid for every bachelor under thirty was made by women old enough to be the guys' mothers—or grandmothers—last year, finding willing participants is tricky.

"Should I put an age limit on the bidders this year?"

Myra's dark eyes blow wide. "Absolutely not. How else am I supposed to rope a dashing younger man into taking me out to dinner?"

I press a hand to my mouth to cover my smile. *This* is the reason I'm considering the age limit. It's not fair that the rich old women of this town are monopolizing all the available men.

Switching tactics, I say, "Some of us would like to actually find someone."

Melissa waves a hand. "Then go to a bar. Or church. You all have 364 other days a year to snatch up these men."

But Myra is looking convicted. "Missy, maybe she's right."

"She's absolutely *not* right. I like having a younger man cut up my steak for me."

It takes everything inside me not to lose it at that comment. If I do, I'll lose all the traction I've gained.

"We had our time, Missy," Myra says, patting Melissa's hand. "These girls deserve a chance to see what this town has to offer. We can go to Asheville to find you a young man."

Melissa looks between us, resignation in her green eyes. "Fine, we'll tell the rest of the *old women* to quit bidding."

The bell above the front door chimes, alerting us to a new customer. Myra's and Melissa's heads swivel in the direction of the door, catching Grey Sutton, Melissa's nephew, walking in.

His eyes crinkle with his smile when he sees his aunt, and he turns to head toward the table instead of the front counter. "Hey, Aunt Missy," he says, stooping to press a kiss to the top of her bottle red hair. "What kind of trouble are you getting into?"

She pats his hand, smiling up at him, but I don't miss the mischievous glint that has entered her eyes. I only hope it's focused on him and that she doesn't have anything concerning me in mind.

"Wren here was just telling us she hasn't had much luck getting bachelors to sign up for the auction."

Grey meets my eyes, desperation coloring his features. I feel for him, I really do. But just not enough to try to get him out of this. I really do need bachelors. It's for charity. Kind of. If nothing else, it's for the town. And if the rumor mill is correct, Grey makes his way through town plenty without any financial encouragement.

"Unfortunately, I'm busy that night, Aunt Missy," he says, trying and failing to extract his hand from her iron grip. He might be a firefighter, but even he isn't strong enough to fight her off.

"Ah," Melissa says, undeterred. "What night is that?"

He glances at me once more, and I roll my lips inward to keep from laughing at the distraught look in his green eyes, the same color as his aunt's.

"The night of the auction," he chokes out.

"When is the auction, honey?" Myra asks, her voice loud enough to wake the dead. She may be sixty-four years old, but she still hasn't learned volume control.

Grey looks between the two of them, and I know the moment he gives up. His shoulders slump, and all the fight leaves his body. "Fine, I'll do it."

I grin at him, pleased with the turn my morning just took. "Think you can convince some of the other guys at the station?"

He lets out a long-suffering sigh and drags his palms down his face. "I'll see what I can do."

My smile widens. "Thanks, Grey."

"Thanks, *Grey*?" Melissa exclaims, pressing a hand to her ample chest. "I'm the one who made this happen."

"I've got to go," Grey interrupts, diffusing their rant.

I feel a pinprick of guilt for not helping him out. Not enough to let him back out of the auction, though. Having someone like Grey signed up will make other men in town reconsider.

When he heads toward the counter, I push up from the table. "I do too, ladies. I've got some errands to run."

Myra pats my back, the three taps she's been doing to everyone for as long as I can remember. "Let us know if we can do anything to help, hon."

"Keep heckling bachelors." I stuff my notebooks and event binders into my bag. "I've got Stevie on the case too, but it seems like you two have more sway." I tell them with a wink.

Moving around behind their chairs, I wrap my arms around their necks, hugging them close. Sun-spotted hands pat my arms, and I breathe in their scents—Myra, smelling of jasmine and citrus, and Melissa, who always smells like fresh laundry that's been hanging out on the line. They're so different in so many ways, but like opposite sides of the same coin in others.

I let them go, blowing a kiss in their direction, and brace myself to head out into the cold.

During the year, the square is always decorated. Banners hanging from streetlights and shop windows painted and dressed up to match the season. After the holidays is no exception, although I can't help but think it looks a little dreary. Maybe it's the generic winter theme or that half the town still has their Christmas trees out while the other half is pulling out pastels and florals for spring. Either way, when paired with the gray skies and icy rain, everything feels a little disjointed.

Or maybe that's me, still shaken by my discovery that *Holden* is **user6872**. We haven't talked since Matty's, not that I haven't picked up my phone to message him at least five times.

Every time I do, though, I remember it's *him* on the other end, and I can't bring myself to send it.

Everything feels jumbled up and weird with him. I don't know whether we're friends or neighbors who mostly annoy each other. I've even considered opening my blinds in my bathroom to peer into his living room, but I don't know what I'd do if I saw him looking back.

I still can't reconcile the two halves of him, and I'm starting to wonder if this is some elaborate prank Holden is playing to get back at me for all the packages I've sent to his house. And one time, last year, I bought a bunch of men's underwear, wrote his name in the waistband, and donated them to the town-wide charity auction.

He really has a lot of reasons to mess with me, and if **user6872** hadn't started ghosting me immediately after my run-in with Holden, I wouldn't be convinced they're the same person.

My phone buzzes in my pocket, and I hate myself for getting my hopes up that it's *him*. My contractor's name flashes across the screen, and a little thrill of excitement zips through me.

"Hey, Jimmy," I say as soon as I swipe open the call. Jimmy Chin is a longtime family friend, and he helped my dad when my parents renovated their farmhouse a few years back. As much as this cabin remodel has stressed me out, Jimmy, at least, has always been steady.

"Wren, hi." He sounds a little frazzled, and I hear shuffling in the background. "Are you available to talk for a moment?"

I stop in the middle of the sidewalk and duck under the awning of an antique shop, unintentionally landing in a puddle that soaks through my boots. "What's up?"

Dread pricks at my stomach, sending waves of anxiety curling through me.

"Listen, Wren, I'm so sorry to have to do this, but I'm going to have to back out of the remodel." His words hit me like shrapnel, and my mind starts whirring. "It's my mom. She fell and broke her hip last night. She's having surgery on Monday. They said that with her age, it will likely be a lengthy recovery. I'm going to have to take time off work to care for her."

I nod, even though he can't see me. It makes sense, and I agree that he's making the right choice, but my eyes still drift to the mountains surrounding the town, knowing there's a dilapidated, gutted cabin up in those trees that has to be renovated in less than three months.

"Wren?" Jimmy asks, pulling me from my downward spiral.

I clear my throat, hoping he won't hear the frantic tears clogging it or sense the anxiety clawing at my insides. "Don't give it another thought, Jimmy," I say. "I'm so sorry to hear about Miss B. I'm glad she has you to take care of her."

Jimmy lets out a relieved sigh, and I can imagine him pinching the bridge of his nose between his graying eyebrows, his forehead lined with concern. "Thanks for being so understanding. I'm happy to get you the contact information of some of my contractor friends. Maybe one of them can help you out, although I'm not sure how quickly."

"That would be great, thanks," I respond, and my voice cracks on the last word. "Listen, I've got to get off here, but keep me posted on how Miss B is."

"Will do, Wren. Thanks again."

I press *end* on the phone call and lean against the cool glass of the antique store window, only now realizing that the wetness on my face is tears and not rain. My phone beeps again. I glance down at it, hoping it's Jimmy saying this was all a mistake, but it's a notification from my credit card company that my payment is due soon.

The bell above the antique shop door chimes, and Mrs. Heeter, the owner, steps out, pulling her cardigan tighter around her shoulders. "Wren, what are you doing out here in the cold?"

My lips stretch in what I hope is a convincing smile. "Just had to take a phone call, Mrs. Heeter. I'm heading out now."

Her eyes soften with worry as she no doubt notices my red eyes. "Are you sure, honey?"

I nod, holding my stiff smile in place. "I'm fine. See you later. I'll probably be in to look for some furniture for the cabin soon."

This brings some levity to her expression, her eyes lighting up. "I'll hold back some pieces for you."

"Thanks, Mrs. Heeter. See you soon."

That is, if I can find someone to renovate this cabin. As I stare up at the mountains again, I feel as gutted and hopeless as my cabin.

Six
- HOLDEN -

There's a package on my porch when I return home for lunch on Monday, and unfortunately, I'm not even angry about it. My gaze darts over to Wren's cottage. The bright yellow of her front door looks especially cheery on this gray day. The rain falls in heavy sheets, almost obscuring my view, but when I make out the warm glow of the lights on in her living room, my heart picks up speed.

We haven't talked since Matty's, not in person or through messages, and I'm shocked at how much I miss it. To be honest, I haven't been sure what to say. A small piece of me worries that now that she's gotten close enough to know me, she didn't like what she saw and bolted. That's undoubtedly related to Mia, or if I go back further, to my father, who left the minute the strip turned pink. It's probably something I should talk about with a therapist, but just thinking about that gives me hives.

Needless to say, the whole Wren situation has taken up more mental space over the last few days than I care to admit.

Now, though, I have a reason to go over there and see what's going on in her head, once and for all.

Icy rain beats down on my skin, soaking through the material of my jacket. It weighs down the thick mass of my hair, landing with heavy drops on my eyelashes, as I make my way across the yard separating our houses.

The closer I get, the brighter the lights in her living room glow, assuring me she's home. Her vintage yellow Volkswagen Beetle is parked in her gravel drive, but Wren likes to walk through town, even in the worst of weather. Sometimes I'll look out the window and see her standing in the rain with her face lifted up to the sky. If June notices, she begs to run outside too, and I'll hear her peals of laughter from across the yard as the two of them jump in puddles or dance to upbeat music Wren cues up on her outdoor speakers.

My hand shakes as I pound on her door. I hate myself for the bolt of nerves that spreads through me as I wait. The seconds tick by, painfully slow, and with each passing one, my jaw clenches tighter, my shoulders lifting until my collar is covering my ears against the damp cold.

I'm not sure what I'm expecting when she opens the door, but it isn't Wren's tear-filled eyes. She looks *wrecked*, and my chest pinches at the sight, my instincts screaming at me to fix whatever made her look like that.

"What's wrong?" I don't mean for it to come out like a bark, but when Wren flinches, I instinctively take a step closer and clench my fists at my sides. I scan her body, looking for an injury. "Are you hurt?"

She stares up at me with wide, surprised eyes before finally shaking her head.

I bend at the knees so I can get in her line of sight. "What is it? What's wrong?"

And then Wren collapses into me, her arms banding around my middle, her face finding the soft spot between my neck and shoulder. Warm tears soak through the collar of my shirt, and for a moment, I stand, unmoving, not sure how to respond. But when her body shudders on a sob, it's instinct to pull her a little closer, rest my chin on the top of her head.

"Jimmy quit," she says into my chest, so muffled by my flannel that I can hardly make out the words.

My free hand, the one not holding onto the bubble mailer, runs up and down her back in soothing circles. "Who's Jimmy?"

"Jimmy Chin."

"The contractor?" Jimmy is a staple in town, doing this since before I was even alive. I was afraid to step on his toes when I started my business after moving back from Charlotte, but he said there was enough work to go around, and I've always been grateful for that.

I'm just not entirely sure what Jimmy has to do with this particular situation.

Wren nods, not really answering my question.

"Jimmy Chin quit what?" I ask, keeping my voice gentle like when I'm trying to figure out what's bothering June. I never would have guessed I'd have a reason to use this tone with Wren, of all people.

But she just holds on tighter, fitting against me better than my favorite pair of jeans, the ones I've worn until there are holes in the pockets and at the knees.

"The cabin," she says, and my pulse jumps when her nose brushes against my chest through the worn fabric of my T-shirt.

Suddenly, this moment feels less comforting and more intimate, less like consoling June when she's sad and more like staring at my ceiling in the middle of the night, remembering what it felt like when it wasn't so empty. When there was a person I could reach for, someone who would reach back. When it was skin and hands and lips and teeth and feeling desired and wanted and needed.

I release my grip on Wren, putting some much-needed space between us. Her cornflower blue eyes are red rimmed, and there's a dent in her bottom lip from her teeth. Her hair is a mess and her freckles stand out against the ruby red of her cheeks. She looks wild and disheveled, and it's not at all helping the turn my thoughts are taking.

"What about Jimmy Chin?" I ask, desperate to get this conversation back on track. I can still feel the imprint of her sweater's fabric on the palms of my hands.

Wren blinks up at me, looking as dazed as I feel, although I'm assuming for very different reasons. Whatever this is, I need to snap out of it.

"He had to quit the cabin remodel because Miss B fell and broke her hip."

I'm not really sure which question to tackle first. "Is she okay?" I finally ask.

Wren nods, gripping her elbows and shivering. There's a chill in the air, and I only now realize it's because I left the front door open. Kicking it shut with my foot, I stride into her living room, just a few short steps from the foyer. Wren stares after me, her feet rooted to the spot.

"I think so," she says, watching with creases lining her forehead as I stack logs in her fireplace. "He said she's having surgery and it's going to be a difficult recovery, so he has to put his projects on hold." She trails off for a moment. "Holden, what are you doing?"

I glance at her over my shoulder, confused. "I'm starting a fire."

"Why?" She sounds wary, defeated, unlike I've ever heard her before. I can't say I like it. Quiet and introspective is my thing. She's supposed to be shitting rainbows.

"Because you're cold."

"Oh," she says, eyes fixed on the flame at the end of the lighter as I press it to the kindling. It catches, and I push the logs around with a poker until it begins to burn evenly. Then I make my way across the tiny living room into the kitchen.

"So Miss B is okay?" I ask, pulling open cabinets that are frighteningly bare. The fridge, too, is mostly empty, only a few slices of off-brand American cheese and bagged lettuce between half-full condiment bottles.

"Yeah, she will be," Wren says, still fixed to the spot by the door.

I turn around to face her, cold air escaping from the fridge. "Where's all your food?"

"I need to buy groceries," she answers with a shrug, some of her defensiveness returning. "There's bread in the cabinet by the stove."

I pull it open and find bread, along with a large assortment of crackers and cookies. She eats like I imagine June will when she moves out, no real food in sight, only snacks and desserts to survive on.

"You need to eat healthier. This is pathetic."

Her blue eyes harden. "You need to mind your own business."

I place my hand on the freezer handle. "How much ice cream is in here?"

"You can't even find it under the bags of pizza rolls and frozen french fries."

I let out a breath, rolling my eyes, but the tight ball that formed in my chest when I saw her tear-stained cheeks starts to loosen a little. *This*, at least, feels more normal. Or maybe what our new normal is.

"What does Miss B getting hurt have to do with you?" I ask, reaching into the fridge for the slices of American cheese and a tub of butter.

Wren's feet finally unglue from the floor, and she takes the few steps into the kitchen, leaning on the arched doorway. "Jimmy Chin was remodeling my cabin."

She says this as I'm crouched over, retrieving the bread from the cupboard beside the stove, and I smack my head on the upper cabinets when I shoot up.

"Oh my gosh." Wren is at my side in an instant, standing on her toes to reach the top of my head. Her fingers press into the tender spot, feeling for a lump. "Are you okay?"

"You're moving?"

She blinks at me, her face painted in confusion. "No, I bought the cabin to rent out."

I don't know why this makes me feel relieved. Wren is easily the most annoying neighbor I've had, and that includes the weed-smoking couple who lived above the first apartment Mia and I shared. They fought loudly and made up even more loudly.

But at least they didn't torture me on purpose.

It's my turn to say "oh." And then I nod, causing her hand to move with the motion. We're close again, and I find myself getting distracted by the plump curve of her bottom lip, the shades of blue in her eyes, the perfect ringlets that frame her face. I don't know how I've never noticed these tiny details before when they seem so intricately important now.

"Right," Wren says, and takes a step back. "Do you need ice?"

I shake my head, trying to hide my wince at the sharp pain the movement causes. Spinning around, I twist the knob to the gas stove until it clicks and the flame lights under the cast-iron skillet.

Wren moves until her back is against the island, hands pressed to the counter on either side of her. "Holden?"

"Hmm?" I'm pulling open her drawers, looking for a butter knife and spatula. Just the spatula will do in a pinch. I should have expected her drawers would be stuffed with utensils, no organizational efforts attempted.

Wren watches me searching through her drawers, not stopping me or moving in to help. "What are you doing?"

"Making you lunch," I say simply, because it's obvious she wouldn't have done it herself if she's this upset. I've spent my entire life surrounded by women, and if I know one thing, it's that being hungry and being upset never go well together. "Have a problem with that?"

She shakes her head, and her curls bounce with the movement. "No complaints here."

"Your kitchen is a mess," I say when I finally find the spatula buried under a mound of other utensils in the drawer. It likely means she's never used it. I guess you can just peel the pizza rolls off the baking sheet without one. I did find an incredible number of potholders and multicolored dish towels in one drawer, however, so I wouldn't be surprised to discover she eats straight from the baking sheet.

A small smile touches her lips. "Thank you."

I give her a flat look, and she lets out a laugh so quiet it's barely audible over the sound of butter hissing in the pan.

"So you bought a cabin?" I ask, returning to our earlier topic.

The smile melts off her face, and I don't miss the way her fingers tighten on the countertop. "I bought a cabin."

"Where?" There are cabins all over town, and even more in the mountains surrounding us, overlooking the lake or river or facing miles and miles of national park.

"Edge of town. You can see the river in the distance, but it's not quite on the river."

I make a noise in the back of my throat. Personally, those are my favorite locations. They have the best views without the hassle of being right on the water. Plus, the waterfront properties are stacked a lot closer together, with docks facing one another, but the cabins up in the mountains are spread farther apart, quieter and more remote.

After assembling the sandwich, I place it in the pan and turn to face Wren. "Why didn't you hire me to renovate it?"

She snorts, looking at me like I'm crazy. Only when she realizes my question is genuine does her face line with confusion. "Holden, you wouldn't have said yes. You reported me to the HOA last year for installing a picket fence without getting their approval first."

I have to bite back a smile. "That was only because you started it at six a.m. on a Sunday morning. It's my only chance to sleep in, since June is at my mom's."

Wren throws her hands in the air. "That's the only day my dad and uncle could do it!"

We've had this argument before, and I can't explain the rightness that settles over me at the familiarity of it. Things have felt so tenuous since Matty's, since I realized Wren was my friend, whether I meant for it to happen or not. Arguing with her still feels right, even if now I know what she looks like when she's falling apart or how she texts when she's tipsy on strawberry wine.

"Wren," I say, and she pauses mid-rant. "Do you want me to work on the cabin?"

She blinks at me, taken off guard, and I have to wonder if I've really treated her so badly over the years that this simple act of kindness is throwing her so thoroughly. I never meant for it to be like this.

"Jimmy was giving me a deal," she says, and it looks like it pains her to admit this to me.

I shrug, turning to flip the grilled cheese in the pan. "I can make it work. How much needs to be done?"

"It's gutted."

My eyebrows lift. "Completely?"

"Just the main living areas and the bathroom." Her fingers flex on the counter until her knuckles turn white. "The bedroom just needs a paint job, and the outside needs landscaping. I have the plans Jimmy and I came up with."

I nod, thinking through the details. Winter is always slower. I'm only overseeing a couple of minor projects between now and spring. This sounds more intensive, but I like being busy.

"I can come look at it tomorrow," I say.

Wren watches me, her bottom lip caught between her teeth, twin half moons formed in the space between her brows. I have an unwise urge to smooth it out with the pad of my thumb, but I shake the thought away.

"You'd really do that?"

Her blue eyes look brighter, standing out in stark contrast against the puffy redness. Her skin is paler than it is in the summer, not tinged with that barely there golden glow that makes her look like sunshine. Even her hair has frizzed in the rain and her lips are chapped from the cold. I've always thought she looks unbreakable, unfazed, like Mia. But their differences have never been so plain.

Wren looks like she's barely keeping her head above water, and something inside me snaps because of it. "Yeah, Wren, I'd do it." I'm beginning to wonder if there's anything I wouldn't do if she looks at me like that.

She holds my gaze for a long moment, looking like she's assessing me, trying to find her footing on this new, uneven ground between us.

Then her nose wrinkles and she sniffs the air. "The grilled cheese is burning."

Seven
- HOLDEN -

Elementary students shouldn't be allowed to put on theater productions. This year, Fontana Ridge Elementary is performing *Seussical the Musical*, and I got roped into building the sets. The plus side of the musical is that since June is a background performer and it just so happens to be the night of the Galentine's Auction, I have an iron-clad excuse for getting out of being a bachelor. The downside is that Charlotte is in charge of costume design, meaning we have to spend a lot of mornings working in close proximity.

"Morning, Holden," Charlotte says from behind where I'm crouched over the frame of an arch I've been working on. The gym is empty this period, and I've spent the last thirty minutes enjoying working in silence. Once the first gym class of the day starts, I won't be able to even hear myself think.

I stand, wiping my dusty palms on my jeans. "Hey, Charlotte. How was your weekend?"

A smile touches her lips. "Not sure if it was as eventful as yours."

After the run-in with Wren at Matty's and then what happened with her in her house yesterday, I sort of forgot about seeing Charlotte Saturday night.

I grip the back of my neck, flexing my hand in an attempt to loosen some of the tension there. "About that—"

"We should get dinner sometime," she cuts me off, green eyes wide with expectation, and guilt pricks at me. Charlotte is forward, for sure, but I recognize the loneliness in her eyes, know exactly how cold the other side of the bed feels every night.

I sigh, stuffing my hands in the pockets of my jeans. The left pocket is worn so thin that I can stick my pinky finger through the hole in the fabric. "Charlotte, Wren and I—"

"Oh," she says, and I peel my gaze from the speck of dirt on the floor and meet hers. Her eyes blow wide. "Oh." This one she says slower, drawing it out. "You and Wren?"

"Wren and I, what?" I ask, not following her line of questioning.

"You're together." She says this almost to herself, nodding as if she's figuring out a complex equation. "I knew you two were necking in the hallway at Matty's."

"What is with the *necking*?" I grumble under my breath.

Charlotte looks at me, blond brows raised so high on her forehead they disappear beneath her bangs. "You are together, right?"

I don't know what makes me say it except that if Charlotte thinking I'm with Wren means that she will stop pursuing me, then I think it's worth it. "Yes," I say slowly, almost like a question. "We're together."

Despite asking the question, Charlotte looks completely taken aback by the answer. "I can't believe it. How long have you been together?"

"Uh," I say, running a hand over my beard. "Four months." Seems best to stick as close to the truth as possible.

Pink creeps into Charlotte's cheeks, and she catches her bottom lip between her teeth. "So when I sent you those...photos a few weeks ago."

I blow out a heavy breath, wishing I could be literally *anywhere* but here. Clearing my throat, I say, "I deleted them, and—"

She waves her hands wildly, cutting me off. "Let's pretend this never happened."

Gladly. "Can do."

The door to the gym squeals open, and twenty six-year-olds barrel through the gap, followed by one harried looking gym teacher. Every time I leave after working on sets, I pass him sitting on an upturned garbage can behind the school, smoking a cigarette on his break. Maybe I should say something to the administration, but I'd need a smoke break after dealing with that many elementary-aged kids too.

"Daddy!" June yells, and I'm grateful for the intrusion to break up the heavy awkwardness in the air between Charlotte and me.

June runs up to the edge of the stage, looking up at me with wide blue eyes. Her hair is a mess today, even more so than usual. I spent thirty minutes last night trying to coax her into letting me brush out the tangles, but she cried every time we attempted it.

Smiling up at me with that gap-toothed smile, June says, "Hi, Daddy."

I feel my own smile spread across my face like a flower opening its first petals in spring. People say dogs are always happy to see you, and I don't doubt it, but there's nothing like watching the happiness on my daughter's face and knowing it's because she gets to see me. I don't deserve it, and there's a sharp pang in my chest every time she flashes me those two missing front teeth.

Moving to the edge of the stage, I squat down to be closer to her. "Whatcha doing today, June Bug?"

"Olivia traded her cookies for my blueberries at snack today." She says this proudly, her pert little nose tipped up in cheeky defiance, and I sigh.

I glance at the clock hanging on the wall above the door, trying to ignore the chaos that has become the gym. "It's ten o'clock, June."

She grins broadly. "Good job, Daddy. Those clocks are hard."

Charlotte smothers a laugh behind me, and I decide to let this one go. "I'm going to be able to pick you up from school today. I don't have a project this afternoon."

"Really?" June asks, bouncing on the balls of her feet, a happy pink flushing her cheeks.

I nod. "I've got to go check out a project, but it shouldn't take too long, so I'll be back to pick you up, 'kay?"

She blows me a kiss, and I pretend to catch it. "See you after school." Without another look back, she spins on her heel and bounds off in the direction of the group of kids climbing the rock wall without supervision.

"You see the gym teacher anywhere?" I ask Charlotte, scanning the gym for the skinny man with the smoker's cough.

Charlotte moves beside me, looking around, and blows out a heavy breath through her nose when neither of us can locate him. "I'll go tell someone in the office."

I look at her with wide eyes. "And leave me here alone with them?"

She grins at me, walking backward toward the steps that lead down from the stage. "You've got it."

Maybe she's not as cool with Wren and me as I hoped.

"So this is it?" I ask Wren a couple of hours later. We're standing outside a well-built but dated cabin high up in the mountains. She wasn't kidding about the location. It's perfect. The cabin, not so much, but it's worth it for the views. I'd love to get my hands on a new build on this lot, with a wide back porch facing the mountains where you could sit outside in the mornings and drink coffee as the haze begins to dissipate on the peaks in the distance. It would be a dream.

Wren nods, shivering next to me in her light jacket. "This is it."

Even from here, I can hear her teeth chattering. "Why didn't you wear a warmer coat?" I ask.

She glares up at me, a fire beginning behind her eyes. "I wasn't planning on standing out in the snow staring at the cabin. I figured we'd be inside."

"We *just* got here. How much faster do you think we can go?"

Another shiver racks her frame, and she bounces in place. "Faster than this."

I sigh and square my shoulders, motioning to the stairs leading up to the porch. "Go on."

Wren shoots me an annoyed look before bounding up the stairs, her left foot slipping on the ice coating the stairs and making her almost wipe out. I catch her arm and haul her upright without looking in her direction, although I can feel her gaze on the side of my face, her breath on my neck.

The door opens beneath her palm, and I frown at it. "You don't keep it locked?"

She looks at me over her shoulder, brows pinch together. There are snowflakes melting in her hair, and her cheeks are ruddy red from the cold. "No, this is Fontana Ridge. And barely, at that."

"Wren, you need to keep your door locked, especially out here in the middle of nowhere."

"The only people who would bother coming in here are teenagers," she says with a wave of her hand.

I cock a brow. "And you really want teenagers having sex in here?"

"Well, it's too cold for them to go to the fire tower, Holden." The fire lookout tower at the top of The Mountain is infamously...carnal. There's not a surface in the whole thing where I'd feel comfortable putting my hands.

"You have building materials in here, Wren. Lock the doors."

She rolls her eyes. "Fine, I'll lock the doors. Happy?"

"Not now," I grumble.

Her eyes narrow into slits. "It's good to see that our friendship hasn't ruined our rivalry," she says with a patronizing smile.

I ignore her comment, allowing my gaze to travel around the interior of the cabin. Wren wasn't kidding when she said it was gutted, although it looks like Jimmy made some progress, replacing some of the drywall and installing new trim on the walls that weren't knocked out.

"Where are the plans Jimmy drew up?" I ask her. She motions to the kitchen, where a worktable has been set up in the corner.

She moves ahead of me, pulling a stack of papers from underneath some tools on the worktable.

I look over the plans Jimmy made up, glancing back and forth between the papers and the spaces he designed them for. What I imagine was probably a dated galley kitchen will be replaced with modern cabinets and a farmhouse sink. The living room used to be closed off from the kitchen, but Jimmy tore down the wall separating them, making it much more open concept. It looks like he sketched out an idea for a library on the wall in the living room and an electric fireplace in front of where the couch would go.

It's a lot of work, but nothing I can't handle.

"What do you think?" Wren asks from beside me.

I shrug. "Looks doable."

Her eyes brighten, the exact color as the lake in summer, when the morning sun glints on the surface, sending fragments of light across the trees. Right now, she looks like all the seasons, pale skin tinged red from the cold like crisp winter berries, red-orange hair like leaves changing when the weather gets cold in autumn, summer eyes and blooming pink petal spring lips. I don't know how anyone manages to look so alive.

"You really think you can do it?" she asks, pulling me from the turn my thoughts had taken.

I glance back at Jimmy's plans again, tilting my head back and forth as I assess them. "Yeah, I can do it."

"By April?"

My head tips up from the plans to meet her gaze. She looks so hopeful, and for once, I don't feel the urge to press her buttons or make that wrinkle form between her brows. I want to keep her looking at me just like that. "I'll get it done in time."

A smile splits across her face, startling in its brightness. I swear I can feel it in my chest like a sharp prick. "Thank you,

Holden. I feel the overwhelming urge to drag you back to the hallway at Matty's and show my gratitude the proper way."

I roll my eyes. "With some—"

"Necking," she says, her grin spreading wider. "You're catching on."

Heat creeps up my neck as I remember what I told Charlotte. I'm going to have to confess to Wren about it, and she's never going to let me live it down.

Shoving my hands in my pockets, I say, "Listen, Wren, I have to tell you something."

"Is this about you telling Charlotte we're dating?" She leans her hip against the worktable, and when I just stare at her, blinking, she asks, "What? You didn't think it would already be all over town? We should probably get our stories straight."

"You're kidding."

"No, I'm not kidding," she says with a roll of her eyes. "When the most eligible bachelor in town suddenly announces he's dating someone, that news spreads fast."

I sputter, sure this is just another one of her ploys to mess with me. "But I only told Charlotte."

Wren shrugs. "And she told everyone."

"Who did she tell?" This comes out louder than I intended, but Wren doesn't seem fazed.

"Beats me," she says, shrugging. "Myra called me on my way over here to ask about it. Smokey the Beans was absolutely silent, so I bet she had me on speaker."

"She wouldn't."

Wren pats my shoulder soothingly, her thumb tracing up the line of my tricep so softly I'm not sure she knows she's doing it. "She would, babe."

I give her a flat look. "Don't call me babe."

"But I told your mom that's what we call each other," she says, her voice sticky-sweet, like adding sugar in cereal.

My jaw hinges open. "You didn't talk to my mom."

Wren nods, her eyes widening. "She was the third person to call me."

I step back, running my hands down the length of my face, a headache forming at the base of my neck. "Please tell me you're lying," I say.

The grin she gives me is evil. "Afraid not, babe."

Eight
- WREN -

"Thank you all for agreeing to participate in the bachelor event," I say to the group of men assembled before me. Between Myra, Melissa, and Stevie, they managed to bully ten bachelors into signing up for the auction. There are a couple of guys, like Grey, who had no intention of signing up, a widower who is ready to get back out there, Sam Jenkins, who is hoping to lure some single men to the auction, and a couple of repeats from last year. All in all, I think it's going to be a really good group, and if they don't manage to raise enough money to fix the bridge, I plan to take photos of them working on it shirtless to sell as a bachelor calendar to raise the rest of what we need.

"The auction is in three weeks," I continue. "I need all of you to send me a photo you'd like me to use for promo, and I'll get those listed on the website later today."

Sam raises his hand, and I have to stifle my smile. We're in the meeting room at Smokey the Beans. All the bachelors are seated at the long table while I stand at the front, addressing them.

"Yes, Sam?"

"Is it fine for me to promote the event on my podcast?"

He lives on a homestead on the opposite side of town and hosts a very successful podcast, where he talks about sustainable farming and interviews a wide range of people in related fields. Promoting the auction on his podcast would garner a lot of publicity.

"Please," I tell him. "That would be amazing."

Sam flashes me a grin, and it buoys my spirits. Since getting the phone call from Jimmy a few days ago, I've experienced a wide range of emotions. First was panic, followed quickly by guilt for panicking about my situation when Jimmy and Miss B were struggling. When I got home and saw the growing stack of bills on my counter, guilt turned to dread. And dread turned into panic once more.

And then Holden showed up. I'm still not sure what to make of that entire encounter. I can't believe I cried on him. I can't believe he *let me*. I'm not sure whether it was subconscious or whether he remembered that time I spilled my guts to him about being too tired to cook for myself or build a fire in my fireplace, but then he started doing those things for me, and all I could do was watch, transfixed.

Holden moved with such an effortless grace, especially for someone who is way too big for my tiny, cramped cottage with sloped ceilings and compact appliances. I can still picture the way his flannel pulled tight over his shoulders as he built a fire in my grate, one that burned for longer than mine ever do. How his brow wrinkled when he found my cupboard of junk food and not a single vegetable. I thought that discovering Holden is **user6872** was going to be the only revelation I had about his character, but he was even different then than he was in his messages.

Then there's the deal with Charlotte. I still don't know what to think about that.

One of the reluctant sign-ups raises his hand with a question, and I spend the next twenty minutes going over the ins and outs of the event. Despite tourism being slow in the winter, the bachelor auction is one of our biggest town events, a last hurrah before the tourists arrive in the spring, and there's a lot of work left to be done.

When the meeting is over and I've secured headshots from each of the bachelors, I have just enough time to grab lunch with Stevie before I have to meet Holden at the hardware store to pick out samples.

There's a little café in an old, renovated cottage just a few blocks from Smokey the Beans, on the main street that leads in and out of the square. In the spring and summer, hydrangeas spill out from around the perimeter, and you have to let yourself through the white picket fence and walk up the cracked sidewalk to reach the cherry red front door. The whole place constantly smells like berries and sugar and feels like stepping into the pages of your favorite fairy tale. It's my favorite business in town. Stevie says she feels like she's going to break something and that she can't speak at a normal volume, but she always agrees to meet me here for brunch or lunch anyway.

I find her at a table in the back, her mass of dark hair sticking out from under a dark teal beanie and her hands folded primly on the table. Her foot is tapping quietly against the floor, though, and I can practically see the energy vibrating off her. I was made for dainty teacups and barefoot picnics in the sunshine. Stevie was made for dirty hiking boots and wide-open spaces and never staying in one place for too long.

"How long have you been here?" I ask, settling into the chair across from her and reaching for the glass of sparkling water on the table. Miss Janet, the owner, doesn't serve flat water, and it's one of my favorite things about the place.

"Got here right before you did. How was the bachelor meeting? Did Oliver give you any trouble?" Oliver is the owner of the hardware store in the square, and he used to date Stevie's cousin and the third member of our trio growing up, Hazel. When Stevie told me he approached her about being a bachelor for the event, I was a little surprised, since we were never his biggest fans in high school, but she said he seemed sincere enough.

"No, he seemed really interested. Asked lots of questions."

She nods and takes a sip of her coffee. "Good."

Her nose and cheeks are pink and her lips are chapped from the cold, and I can see mud caking her booted foot sticking out from under the table. "Did you go hiking this morning?"

"Yeah, just a quick hike up The Mountain." The Mountain is the tallest peak in Fontana Ridge city limits, and although it has an actual name, the residents have called it The Mountain for so long that I don't even know what the real name is. Stevie makes it sound easy, but in reality, it's fairly strenuous—a narrow, steep trail leading to an old fire lookout tower. In high school, we used to sneak up there after dark, risking the trek with flashlights and contraband bottles of liquor packed in our backpacks, but there's very little that could convince me to make the hike now, especially in the dead of winter.

I shake my head. "You and I have very different ideas of fun."

"I'm going stir crazy," she says with a shrug. Her dark brown eyes meet mine, lighting up. "So what's this about Holden taking over the cabin renovation?"

After the night at Matty's, I caved and told Stevie about the dating app and **user6872**. I'm not really sure why I kept it to myself before, but I think what I had with him felt so unexpectedly precious to me that I didn't want to ruin it with comments about how he could be a murderer or an old man. And surprisingly, I'm actually happy with who it turned out to be, although I'll never tell Holden that.

I shrug and tug on the sleeves of my sweater until they're covering my hands. "I was kind of falling apart after Jimmy had to back out, and Holden offered."

Stevie's eyes narrow. "And you don't find that odd?"

"I find it very odd," I say, but a small part of me is questioning the validity of the statement. Yes, it felt out of character for *Holden* to offer to help *me*, but it's not something I would have doubted **user6872** would do for **LikeStrawberryWine**. Thinking about the two of us now, so intricately intertwined, makes my head spin and an odd sensation stir deep in my chest.

"So did him agreeing to work on the cabin come before or after he told the whole town you're dating?"

"Before," I tell her with a roll of my eyes. "Enough about me. What's new with you? I feel like I've hardly seen you."

Winter is usually when we have the most time to spend together, but with the cabin renovation and everything that has entailed, we've barely been able to make time to spend together. I miss our cozy movie nights on my old corduroy sofa in the cottage or making some kind of decadent treat in her tiny Airstream kitchen at one in the morning.

She shrugs. "Nothing really. I joined a book club."

This takes me by surprise. "You don't even like reading." I have books stacked on every available surface in my cottage, and the most Stevie has interacted with them is when she moves them out of the way so she can find somewhere to sit.

"Seemed fun," she says, and takes a sip of her coffee, the steam curling in front of her face. "Alicia Bennington started it because she said she heard about some women in Illinois who used romance books to show them what men should be acting like so they could stop settling for douchebags."

A smile touches my lips. "So that's what you're trying to do, then?"

"No," she says over the rim of her mug. "But I did think it might be a fun distraction in the offseason." Leaning forward, she scans the café before focusing on me again. Her voice lowers to a whisper. "You would not believe some of the things in these books, Wren."

A laugh barks out of me, drawing the attention of the three other patrons in the café. "Ah, Stevie, you're just getting started."

"Neutral colors would be more marketable," Holden says, his brows wrinkled as he stares at the paint chips in my hands. Every color of the rainbow is represented, plus some. Shades of sunshine yellow, sea-foam green, pale lilac, cornflower blue, and cherry red.

I glare up at him. He's wearing another one of his many flannels today, his hair tugged back in a loose bun at the base of his skull. There's a piece of glitter on his eyebrow, and I've decided not to tell him about it.

"I bet your entire house is shades of neutral."

He crosses his arms over his chest, jaw ticking beneath his beard. "And if it is?"

"That's so like you," I say.

His eyes sharpen, turning a glittering topaz. "What's that supposed to mean?"

I let out an exasperated sigh. "You're boring."

Holden opens his mouth to reply, but then Oliver, the hardware store owner, walks by our aisle and winks in our direction. "The lovebirds."

My free hand falls on Holden's bicep, and when I lean into him, I can feel the muscle twitch beneath my palm. "It's a good thing you didn't come back here two minutes ago, Oliver," I say cheekily, and I can hear Holden's faint groan in the back of his throat. He's going to take a bat to my Christmas lights tonight for that one.

Oliver's chuckle follows him down the aisles, leaving us alone once more. Holden shrugs off my hand, and I step back, putting space between us. The glare he gives me sends a jolt of pleasure up my spine. There's a certain thrill in making him a little crazy like this.

"What was that?" There's a sharpness in his tone that hasn't been directed at me in weeks.

"We're supposed to be dating, remember?"

His eyes flash, jaw tightening. "You made me look unprofessional. I have to come here for work, Wren."

I give him a flat look. "Jimmy put up fliers on the board by the register promoting his bachelorette party dancing services when I was a kid. I don't think Oliver is going to be offended about us necking in the paint aisle."

"Enough with the necking, Wren." He practically yells this, and for the first time, I realize he's serious. That me touching him and making comments about us without checking with him first made him uncomfortable.

Guilt pricks at me. "I'm sorry, Holden."

He stares at me for a long moment, looking a little surprised, his full lips parted and a sigh escaping between them. "It's fine. Let's look at flooring samples."

He moves down the aisle in quick strides, purpose written in every line of his body. I follow him to another part of the store and stop beside him, leaving plenty of space between us.

Holden is quiet as he examines the flooring samples, his bottom lip caught between his teeth, fingers flexing on his bicep where his arms are crossed. He has the kind of quiet, settled energy I've always envied, if not a gruffness that makes me see red. My mind never seems to stop, even when I wish it would, but Holden's mind always seems to be calm and quiet, at least when he's not barking at me.

"These look good," Holden says, pointing to a sample. "They're good quality. I've installed them before."

I don't bother looking at the sample after seeing the price sticker. "No, thanks."

Holden's eyes slant in my direction, his jaw flexing again. He has to hurt his teeth with how often he does that. "Why not?"

I match his stance, arms crossed over my chest. "I don't like it."

"You didn't even look at it," he counters.

He's got me there, but I don't feel like explaining to him that I dug in my couch cushions for spare change to buy a drink at the gas station last night since it wasn't in my newly revamped monthly budget.

When I don't respond, he blows out a breath through his nose, nostrils flaring. "Is this about what I said?"

I blink, not tracking. "What?"

Warmth creeps up his neck, coloring his cheeks as he looks anywhere but at me. I marvel at uncovering a new layer to

Holden Blankenship, here in the hardware store of all places. Sheepish embarrassment looks good on him.

A low sigh escapes him. "Listen, I shouldn't have snapped."

"What?"

The bell above the front door chimes, and a second later, a female voice follows. "Hey, Oliver."

Holden's eyes snap to mine, and it takes me only a moment to recognize the voice. Charlotte is here after all.

This time, I don't have to reach for Holden, because he's already moving toward me, his palm landing on the shelf above my head. Suddenly, he's everywhere, so close that everything around him blurs.

His voice is soft, a rasp I can feel more than see when he says, "Is this okay?"

I realize that the scene a moment ago could have been avoided if I'd asked that simple little question. The thing is, I'm not sure how to answer. I should be annoyed with him this close, in my personal space, but instead, I feel it like a tug deep in my stomach, the shiver of a fingertip against skin.

"Yeah, it's fine," I finally answer, hoping he doesn't notice the breathlessness of my voice.

My body jolts when his free hand settles on my hip, heavy and warm, even through the thick layers of my sweater. "And this?"

If I'm not mistaken, his voice sounds huskier too, his eyes slipping into a deeper shade of hazel. I don't trust my voice, so I settle for a nod.

He mirrors the movement, his eyes lingering in the oddest places—the line of my jaw, the tip of my nose, the exposed curve of my ear where my hair is tucked behind it, the swell of my bottom lip.

"Is this unprofessional?" I ask him.

His gaze trips back up to meet mine. "Not yet." My heart stutters when one corner of his mouth kicks up. "There's been no necking." As quickly as it arrived, the smile disappears, his eyes going serious. "I'm sorry for snapping earlier."

My shoulder lifts in a shrug, brushing against his chest. "It's fine. I should have asked first."

He holds my gaze for so long that everything else goes hazy, only his eyes staying in focus. "You don't have to ask to touch me, Wren."

"Oh." A female voice startles us apart, and we look to the end of the aisle to see Charlotte. "Sorry, I didn't mean to interrupt."

Holden's hand flexes on my hip before he releases me. "You didn't interrupt anything."

I'm not so sure that's true.

Nine
- HOLDEN -

"June, get your hands off that brownie."

June freezes, her little fingers still resting on the plate of brownies on the counter. She's got chocolate smeared on her face and a line of it streaking across her cheekbone and covering the smattering of freckles there.

"You already had a brownie," I say again, spinning fully to face her, crossing my arms over my chest. I may be well over six feet and stocky enough to break down a door, but June can melt me in an instant if I let her get any traction.

Right now, she's doing the puppy eyes, her bottom lip, also covered in chocolate, sticking out to form a pout. "Just one more," she begs, drawing the word out in a plea.

I shake my head, narrowing my eyes. "No, you'll make yourself sick."

She drops her hand from the plate. "Fine," she says before disappearing down the hall. The front door opens a minute later, and I hear Grey's voice before June's high-pitched giggle, her anger gone as quickly as it arrived.

Grey walks into the kitchen a moment later, boots thudding on the hardwood. "Honey, I'm home," he singsongs, dropping a six-pack onto the counter. "Ooh, brownies."

I'm starting to understand where this sweet tooth came from, because it definitely wasn't from me. If I want to indulge in something, I spend a half hour crafting a cocktail and sip on it all evening.

By the time I turn around, Grey has already disappeared with the plate of brownies, and the NFL theme song starts playing through the speakers in the living room. I shake my head, putting the last of the leftover dinner in the fridge, and make my way into the living room.

Grey and June are sitting on the couch, the plate of brownies between them, Grey's socked feet propped on my coffee table. June is dropping brownie crumbs all over the couch.

"June Elizabeth Blankenship," I say, and June whirls around, a piece of brownie falling out of her mouth and landing in her lap. "I told you no more brownies."

She points at Grey, eyes wide. "Uncle Grey told me I could have one."

I turn my glare on my best friend, but to my annoyance, he doesn't look fazed. "Chocolate is good for the soul, Holden."

"Yeah, Holden, chocolate is good for the soul," June mimics.

Grey looks at her, absolute delight lighting up his face.

I don't even know where to begin with that conversation, so I start by taking the plate of brownies back to the kitchen before returning to the couch. June squeals as I pick her up, depositing her in my lap.

"No more brownies, understand?"

There's laughter in her eyes, like she knows she has me in the palm of her hand as surely as the rest of the brownie, but she nods. "Sure thing, Daddy."

And then she takes another bite.

"June," I groan.

"I can't finish this one?"

Snatching the brownie from her hand, I pop it into my mouth. It's so sweet I can feel it in my teeth, and I cringe knowing she's already had two of these. Her dentist is going to kill me.

"Nope," I say around the bite. She glares at me, spinning around to face the TV, but I know she's not really mad because instead of wiggling to get down, she nestles back into the crook of my arm, her head resting on my chest. She smells like watermelon shampoo and sugar, and it makes me want to hold her tightly. She may drive me absolutely crazy with how smart and sassy she is sometimes, but it doesn't stop me from waking up in the middle of the night and panicking about how quickly she's growing up, knowing one day she's going to leave me all alone in this house.

Rolling my head around the back of the sofa to face Grey, I ask, "Put out any fires today?"

He doesn't look away from the game on the TV. "Literally or figuratively?"

"Both, I guess," I say with a shrug, and June huffs out a breath at being jostled. Her knotted blond curls end up splayed across my chest and chin with the movement, and I try in vain to smooth them down. It would be much easier if she would ever let me brush them out.

"No actual fires, although I did save a cat from a tree."

I lift an eyebrow in question. "Seriously?"

He nods and takes a sip of his beer before responding. "One of Mrs. Heeter's tabbies got up a tree, and she couldn't get him down."

"What would our town do without your valiant acts of courage?"

Grey's blue eyes narrow into slits. "If your house ever catches on fire, you're going to be very thankful for my valiant acts of courage. But anyway, the figurative fires were much more dangerous today."

I turn back to watch the game right as our safety intercepts the ball. "What's that supposed to mean?"

"Melissa, who I am no longer referring to as my aunt, told all the single women in town that I joined the auction to look for someone to settle down with."

A laugh rockets out of me, the kind I don't do very often, where June looks at me and giggles just because she wants to be in on the joke too.

Grey glares in my direction. "It's not funny."

Between wheezing breaths, I say, "You've dated every woman in town. Of course you don't want to settle down."

Grey isn't laughing. In fact, my words seem to sober him even more. His bottom lip catches between his teeth, a wrinkle forms between his brows, and his fingers tap against his bottle.

"I mean, you don't want to settle down, right?" I ask, watching him carefully.

He doesn't look in my direction, but I get the idea he's not really watching the game either. "I don't date around because I like dating around, Holden."

I stare at him, trying to process his words. For the longest time, I've assumed that Grey doesn't go out with anyone more than a handful of times because he's not looking for a serious relationship. I never considered that he was searching for someone and coming up empty every time. It makes me unbearably sad for him.

After Mia, I can't imagine easily giving my heart over to someone else. She would have to be really special, as well as stable and safe. I'm not counting on finding a person who makes me feel that way, so I haven't even bothered looking.

To think that Grey has been doing just that for years, potentially, is a little heartbreaking.

"Hey, I'm sorry," I say, but Grey waves me off.

"I know my reputation," he says, staring into his beer. I can't help but notice that he doesn't sound happy about being seen as the town playboy.

Swallowing against the lump forming in my throat, I say, "Hey, maybe you will find someone at the auction."

This time, he's the one to laugh. "I can't imagine anyone new will be in the crowd, and I haven't found anyone here I want to go on another date with."

I make a humming noise in the back of my throat, considering his words. Frankly, I'm still processing this new information and looking back at all of Grey's actions in a new light. The women in town. The tourists. The hikers. Him hoping to find a soulmate in all of them.

"You'll find her," I assure him. "She's probably just right out there." I gesture with a hand toward the back door and the trees beyond.

"Out in the woods?" Grey asks skeptically.

I roll my eyes at him. "No, not out in the woods. I just meant that somewhere in this town or the next or across the country, she's waiting for you too."

My front door opens, and I hear Finley call out, "Hey, anyone home?"

"In here," I yell back, and a minute later, she comes around the corner.

Looking between the three of us on the couch, she frowns. "You're having a party without me?"

"Aunt Finley!" June's voice fairly pierces my eardrums, but Finley's frown transforms into a smile at the sound of it.

Climbing over my legs where they're propped on the coffee table, Finley motions to Grey. "Move over so I can sit next to my girl."

Grey makes a face at her but scoots over, and she wedges in the space between us, June climbing off my lap and into hers. Scrunching her nose, Finley turns to Grey. "Why do you smell like cat?"

When I wake up on Saturday morning, the world is bathed in snow. Sharp icicles hang from the roof and glisten in the sun, sending fragments of light across the blanket of white.

The mountains in the distance are capped with snow too, and from this vantage point, Fontana Ridge looks like the inside of a snow globe.

The wood floors are cool under my feet as I tiptoe into the kitchen, trying not to wake June, who stayed up way too late last night. When she finally passed out on the couch, Finley, Grey, and I stayed up until the early hours of the morning playing cards at my kitchen table. Now, my eyes are crusted mostly shut, and I think there's a crick in my back from sitting in the hard wooden chairs for a few hours.

But surprisingly, I feel lighter than I have in a while. Maybe it was Wren texting me on the app last night, tipsy after an evening out in Asheville with Stevie and making terrible dad jokes. Maybe it was spending easy, carefree time with my best friend and my sister, like Wren has been nagging at me to do on that app for months.

Regardless, as I open the fridge and pull out the pancake batter that I prepared last night, I feel like some of the weight has been lifted off my shoulders.

June wakes up midway through making breakfast, no doubt lured by the smell of pancakes and frying bacon. She shuffles into the kitchen, her plush pink blanket wrapped around her shoulders and dragging on the floor.

"Morning, June Bug," I say, holding back a smile at the grumpy frown on her face. While she may be a bundle of energy the majority of the day, she's not a morning person.

"Something smells good," she mumbles, climbing up onto one of the barstools and reaching for a piece of bacon.

I flip one of the pancakes onto a plate. "Pancakes."

Her ratty curls shake with the movement of her head. "Uh-uh," she says, more of a sleepy grunt than actual words. "Smells minty."

That would be the pine-scented candle Finley pulled out of her bag last night. She said she got it to "liven the place up." Although, looking behind June at the pastel yellow wall in my living room, I'm not really sure how much more lively it can get.

The sunshine accent wall was *not* my idea. I've decorated the whole house in shades of navy and hunter green, dark wood tones and leather furniture. But then June saw into Wren's house one day and couldn't stop talking about the yellow wall in her living room. So we spent a Saturday afternoon in the summer painting the accent wall, June dripping yellow paint all over my dark wood floors. I got most of it up, but there's still little dried droplets of sunshine scattered all over the living room.

"Aunt Finley brought us a candle," I say, pointing to the lit candle on the other side of the kitchen island. I drop the last of the pancakes onto the plate and push it in June's direction. "What should we top them with today?"

She taps her pointer finger on her chin, looking more awake now that she's debating sugary toppings. "Hmm, whipped cream."

I nod and pull open the fridge door, repressing a shiver at the blast of cold air. Today is one of those days that even the heater is struggling to warm up the house.

"And syrup," June says.

I glance at her over my shoulder and find her grinning, her front two teeth missing.

"And chocolate chips."

"One topping," I tell her, attempting my firmest voice.

"Two."

"One."

"How about a little bit of two?"

I stare her down for a long moment, waiting for her to cave, but I should have known better. "Fine. Which ones do you want?"

"Chocolate chips and whipped cream."

A few minutes later, I have her plate made, the tiniest dollop of whipped cream and four chocolate chips on each pancake, stacked next to a heaping pile of eggs, fruit, and one piece of bacon. I slide the silicone plate toward her and make my own, adding only one pancake, which I added a scoop of protein powder to, two pieces of bacon, and the rest of the eggs.

"What do you want to do today, June Bug?" I ask, climbing onto the stool next to her. Her little knee bumps against mine under the counter.

"Let's build a snowman."

Thirty minutes later, we're bundled up in heavy jackets, and June's hair is sticking out from under a beanie, the pom-pom bouncing atop her head. Her cheeks are already ruddy from the cold, but she seems impervious to it, giggling as she catches snowflakes on her tongue.

The snow fell in a heavy blanket last night, coating the ground and piling up to my lower calf and June's knees, but she trudges through it with a smile on her face. I feel that overwhelming ache in my chest again just looking at my little girl, who's growing up without my permission, growing sassier and wiser and more independent by the day.

The older she gets, the more I feel like I don't know what I'm doing, that I'm not prepared to raise a *girl* on my own. Most days, I can't even manage to get her hair brushed and put matching socks on her feet. But for the first time, instead of blaming Mia and mourning what she stole from us, I wonder if maybe there might be someone out there for me, like I was telling Grey last night. If there might be someone who would look past all my emotional baggage and my surliness and look *at* my perfect daughter and not see a burden but a blessing.

I haven't allowed myself to think like that because it feels too much like hope, and the last time I allowed myself to hope—when I stared at a little bundle wrapped in my wife's arms—I got burned, and badly.

Maybe hope wouldn't be so bad.

Without meaning to, my eyes drift across the snowy yard to Wren's cottage. The lights are off, and her car isn't in the driveway. There are no tracks to indicate she's been home since the snow fell. Something sour stirs in my gut as I remember her tipsy texts last night and wonder where she ended up, whose bed she slept in if not her own.

I turn away from her lawn, knowing I have no business feeling whatever *that* was.

"This looks like a good spot," I tell June as we stop a few feet from the road, right where everyone will be able to see our snowman as they pass and just far enough to be out of the glow of Wren's Christmas lights, which she still hasn't taken down, even though January is almost over.

"I think so too," June huffs, her breath fogging the cold air. She's got her hands on her hips, staring at the spot like a suburban dad surveying his lawn, and I have to hold back a smile.

June looks up at me, her blue eyes squinted against the bright sun. I probably should have put sunglasses on her. "What now?"

"We start with a snowball."

June chatters as we work on the snowman. Our hands grow wet and cold despite our gloves, but she looks like she's having too much fun for me to contemplate going inside. She decides she wants our snowman to look like a particular one from a princess movie, so we set to work making it lopsided and smiling with one very prominent front tooth.

When our snowman is almost finished, Wren's yellow VW Beetle comes sloshing down the freshly plowed street, and as she turns into her driveway, I get an idea. Turning to June, I say, "Let's get Wren with some snowballs."

Her eyes light up, bright as the winter sunshine in the sky. "Let's do it."

We trudge across the yard as quickly as possible, trying to get to Wren before she climbs out of her car. We make it just in time to form one snowball each. Wren's door cranks open, loud in the stillness, and when she sticks her leg out, it's covered in sheer black tights that end in black Chelsea boots. When she stands, her black dress falls to mid-thigh, and for a moment, I just stare at her, forgetting what I'm supposed to be doing.

That is, until June's snowball hits Wren right in the chest.

Ten
- WREN -

A ball of fluffy white snow explodes against my chest before I have a chance to react. The sound of the snowball smacking against me is quickly followed by a girlish giggle. I look up to see June with her little gloved hand pressed to her cold-kissed face, barely hiding the line of freckles that stand out prominently against her red cheeks.

My eyes land on Holden behind her, snowball in his hand, although his arm isn't raised. It's hanging by his side. His gaze is fastened on me, and there's a look I can't quite read on his face, which looks cold under the thick beard, but not nearly as chapped as June's.

"Don't you dare," I say, pointing at Holden, already feeling the chill from June's snowball seeping through the layers of my black velvet dress not covered by my unbuttoned trench coat.

Holden looks down at the snowball, seeming to remember it in his hand, then lobs it in my direction. I squeal, barely making it out of the way before June hurls another one right at me. This one lands, splattering across my neck and seeping down into my neckline.

I tug the dress away from my skin, hoping the snow will fall back out to the ground, but no such luck. It bleeds into my bra, chilling me to the core.

June is still laughing, trying to form another snowball, but Holden lifts her up, throwing her over his shoulder. "Okay, okay, that's enough, June Bug. Let's get some hot chocolate."

Amber eyes meet mine once more, and despite the snow and cold, something warms inside me, spreading into the tips of my fingers and the space behind my belly button.

"Want to join us?"

I'm momentarily stunned by the offer, caught up in the way the light refracts in his hair, illuminating the faintest hint of gray at the temples, the lines at his eyes that suggest that although he saves his smiles now, he used to give them freely. Holden Blankenship is an enigma, and I really want to figure him out.

"Hot chocolate sounds good."

We trudge through the snow to Holden and June's house. It's different from mine. It's larger, for starters, and while my siding is painted a bright white, theirs is dark gray with white trim and shutters.

Holden sets June down on the top step of the porch, and she spins around, scurrying inside. When he doesn't follow her, I stay back too, as fat snowflakes drift lazily from the sky and land on my exposed skin.

Despite the snow, the morning sunshine is bright, bathing Holden in rich golden hues that make his tan skin look tanner, while the cold only makes my pale, freckled skin look redder. His hair is tousled and damp, like he and June were playing out here for a while, crafting the snowman next to his mailbox. He looks...good, I don't fail to notice. I mean, he always looks good, but especially now, windblown and mussed, looking like he hasn't even had a chance to brush his hair since he woke up, which I'm only now noticing is down, growing slightly wavy in the chilly dampness, although nothing like June's untamable curls.

"You look nice," Holden says, startling me out of my thoughts, and my whole body feels like it's been pulsed by an electric shock at the comment, at knowing he was examining me and thinking the same thoughts I was having about him.

I'm wearing the same dress as last night, wrinkled from passing out on Stevie's tiny couch after one too many glasses of strawberry wine, *Gilmore Girls* playing on her TV mounted to the wall. I looked at myself in the mirror this morning, red curls frizzy and falling out of the messy bun I managed to tie them in last night, my eyes still sporting smudged brown mascara. I decidedly did *not* look good, but that doesn't stop me from feeling his compliment down to my toes and in the tips of my ears and every place in between.

"Thanks," I breathe, my breath fogging in the air between us.

Holden palms the back of his neck, his boot tapping lightly on the top step. "So," he says, the word dragging out.

I can feel my brows furrowing with the statement.

"Out all night, huh?" he finally asks, and I notice the streak of red across his cheekbones that, despite the cold, wasn't there before.

I want to see if I can make it spread. If it will disappear into the layers of his jacket and the flannel I expect is beneath.

"Mm-hmm," I say, and let the sound hang. "Same clothes too. Guess you caught me doing a walk of shame. It's a good thing June doesn't know what that means."

I was right. The redness does spread. I have the sudden urge to peel back the collar of his jacket and find where it stops. My fingers itch with it, and a startling beat of want courses through me at the thought.

"Right," Holden says, and I shake the thought away, feeling unsteady by it. I don't know where *that* came from, but it's dangerous. And unwanted. And unwarranted. Sure, Holden is nice to look at, but he's a jerk to me most of the time.

My brain unhelpfully decides to remind me of all the late-night messages and times that I felt less alone in my cramped, cluttered cottage simply because I knew he was just a tap away.

Swallowing hard, I say, "I was at Stevie's. I had too much strawberry wine to drive home."

I must be mistaken, because the expression on his face looks a lot like relief. Even his shoulders seem to loosen, like they're no longer holding a tension that was there just moments before.

"So you're a little hungover today?" he asks, holding his thumb and pointer finger an inch apart. I think I catch a faint twitch of his lips, the barest hint of a smile. I don't know why those half smiles always make me feel more victorious than someone else's laugh or grin.

Reaching out, I pinch his fingers a little closer together. His skin is warm against mine, his gloves pulled off and hanging haphazardly out of his jacket pockets, unlike mine, which has been exposed since I climbed out of the car in a jacket not made for this kind of weather.

"Just a teeny bit," I say.

Shock ripples through me when his hand closes over mine, the fingers he was just holding apart now coming to rest in the web between my thumb and forefinger.

"There's a pressure point right here," he says, his voice low and rough, whispering across my skin. "It helps with headaches."

"Oh," I respond, feeling his touch everywhere as he applies pressure to the spot firmly but not painfully. I expect him to let go, but he continues the pressure for several seconds, his lips moving as he counts silently.

When he reaches ten, he moves to my other hand, repeating the same process. My breath is heavy in the air between us, and it feels as if there's an electric current zipping up and down my spine.

Holden's eyes meet mine, his fingers still pressed to the pressure point on my hand. "Any better?"

"Mmm," I say, my mind not really able to form words. For some reason, I'm still zeroed in on the feeling of his skin against mine, rough and calloused from working in construction, so much bigger and warmer, smelling of that faint scent that I can never fully detect. Something exclusively Holden.

"Wren?" he asks.

I can feel his warm breath on the chilled, exposed column of my neck. I'm telling myself the goose bumps that spring up there are from the cold.

"Right," I say, focusing on his question. The pain is still there, a dull throb at the base of my skull from too much wine and not enough water. I never remember to drink enough water, which is why the wine always hits me harder than it should. "Headache is still there." Although slightly relieved.

Holden's hand drops mine, and I feel momentarily disappointed at the loss of contact, before he slips it beneath my hair, his fingers pressing into the exact spot the headache has gathered. My head lolls against his hand, my eyes meeting his. I think his might be as heavy lidded as mine feel.

He applies firm pressure to the base of my skull, although I notice his lips aren't forming the numbers as he counts. I'm counting, though, which is how I know he's gone past ten, how I recognize that the pressure in his fingers softens until his hand seems to just be supporting my head, threading through the fine curls at my nape. I can feel each tug of those tiny hairs *everywhere*, not just on the back of my neck but traveling down the length of my spine, settling warm and heavy in my belly, seeping into my cold fingertips, in the sensitive skin behind my knees and the hollow of my throat.

"Daddy!" June yells, bounding down the hall to the front door.

We spring apart, and I feel dizzy, my head swimming, although I'm not sure if it's from the hangover or his touch. I'm not even sure *what* exactly that was.

"Mommy's on the phone," June says, holding up what I'm assuming is Holden's cell phone. "Guess what? She said she's going to come to my musical."

The change in Holden is instantaneous, his jaw locking, his shoulders tightening, the furrow returning to his brow. He looks like every iteration of himself that has ever turned up on my doorstep, angry with me about some neighborly code I've broken. Nothing of the soft touches and heavy eyes and faint smiles remains.

"Do you want to talk to her?" June asks, looking at Holden with wide, innocent eyes.

Holden shakes his head. "No thanks, June Bug. I'll be inside in just a minute."

"Okay," she says, spinning on her heel to bound back into the house, chattering a mile a minute into the phone.

A muscle flickers in Holden's jaw as he watches her, and I grasp at something to say to soothe him, to bring back the soft version of him that fled at the mere mention of his ex-wife.

"Hey, you okay?" I ask, my hand landing on Holden's shoulder. But he moves, letting it fall back to my side. Cold sweeps in the place where he was just standing, and I feel it right down into my bones.

He doesn't look at me as he speaks, his eyes still focused on the spot June vacated. "I'll see you later, Wren."

"Oh," I say, unable to look away from him, though his eyes don't even flit in my direction. "No hot chocolate."

"Not today."

He doesn't give me any more than that, and although it's not much different from the Holden I've come to know over the last four years, it feels vastly different from my friend of the last few months and from the man who just had his hands tangled in my hair, his fingers moving gently against my skin.

I almost want to cry, can feel the tears pricking at the backs of my eyes, but I tell myself they're from the cold. Any other reason would be ridiculous. Hangovers always make me emotional, and I'm running on very little sleep. It's certainly not *Holden Blankenship* or his coldness that finally makes me feel the chill in the air, the dampness seeping into my bones, freezing the tears in my eyes.

It's not Holden Blankenship, because I know my place with him, and it's certainly not on his porch with his hands in my hair. It's across the yard, a neighbor who drives him crazy and a friend who sends him GIFs of cats on bad days.

That's where I belong, so I turn on my heel and head to my house without another look back.

Even if Unlikely Places weren't the only florist in town, it would still be my favorite. While I'm a fan of bright pops of color, there's something to be said about a flower shop decorated in muted earthy tones—forest greens, dusty blues, and warm pinks, natural wood and original scarred floors, creamy off-white walls and sunlight pouring in through the large windows. It's the perfect tribute to our little town nestled in the mountains and trees, and it makes the flowers lining every available square inch of the shop look like they're growing straight up from the wildflower fields at Misty Grove.

A little golden bell chimes as I let myself in the front door. It's covered in peeling white paint, an ivy trellis climbing up and over the door frame. Finley Blankenship looks up from where she's reading a book behind the counter, a smile brightening her face.

"Is it ten already?" she asks, consulting her watch. "Must have lost track of time."

Soft, quiet folk music plays through the shop, making it feel that much more cozy.

"What are you reading?" I ask, moving closer to the counter.

She closes the worn mass market paperback and slides it across the counter to me. There's a classic stepback cover depicting what I suspect is a Regency romance couple.

"I've read some of her books."

Hazel eyes, so much like Holden's, light up, crinkling at the edges. "I didn't know you were a reader," she says. "You should join the book club."

"The one Stevie is in?"

If possible, Finley's expression brightens even more, and she tucks a shoulder-length strand of golden blond hair behind her ear. "Same one. You should come."

I nod, warmth spreading through my chest. This is *exactly* what I need. I've been trying to fix my loneliness with Holden, of all people, but I realized yesterday that it might be fairly one-sided. Just because I think he's as lonely and in need of closeness as much as I am doesn't mean he's willing or wanting to do anything about it.

The problem with small towns is that you know everyone, but you never really know people the way you want to be known. I could go to Smokey the Beans and name every town resident who walked through the doors, but it's easy to feel lonely in a crowd of people who know you without understanding you.

"I'd love to," I tell Finley, pulling myself from my depressing thoughts. "Maybe after the Galentine's Auction and my cabin's finished. I still have so much to do."

"Right, flowers," she says, standing from her chair, a determined look entering her eyes. She disappears into the back room, coming back out with a worn leather notebook. "I've got a list here of all the centerpiece designs I thought would look good. If you want to pick a couple, we can test them out and see what you think."

Taking the soft leather-bound notebook in hand, I glance through her pages of meticulous notes, written in straight, neat lettering. Her attention to detail is unmatched, and although I don't know what every single one of these flowers is, I know whatever she makes will be beautiful and original.

When I look back up, I'm startled to find her watching me, an intense look on her face. Pink tinges her cheeks at being caught, and her eyes dart away from mine. "Sorry, I was staring. I've been told I can stare too much."

My shoulders lift in a shrug. "No big deal. I don't mind."

Her eyes meet mine for one quick second before moving away again to focus on my curls. "I just love your hair," she says.

A pleased warmth suffuses my cheeks, moving its way up to the tips of my ears. It's a lovely compliment, especially considering how long it took me to learn how to properly take care of my rambunctious curls. Always dampening my hair before brushing. Making sure it's dripping wet, making a puddle on my bathroom floor, as I apply my products. Sleeping with my hair tied up in a silk bandanna.

"Thank you," I say, tugging on one of my curls. It immediately bounces back up into place.

Finley watches the movement, assessing. "I think June's hair could look like this if she ever let anyone take care of it."

A smile touches my lips as I imagine June running through the backyard in the fall, rust and amber and currant leaves catching in the tangled locks as she jumps into the pile Holden spent all afternoon raking up. I remember wondering how he could look so carefree and happy watching her ruin all his hard work, but so surly at me for attracting raccoons by failing to toss out my jack-o'-lantern. I ordered a raccoon fridge magnet and sent it to his house later that week, but I don't know if he kept it. I bet it ended up in the trash cans that the raccoons now like to pillage.

"It took me forever to figure out a routine that worked," I say, tugging on another curl. Pointing at one of the options in her meticulously thought-out notebook, I say, "Let's try this one."

She consults the arrangement I chose before moving around the silent shop, picking out individual flowers from vases and galvanized buckets. "Do you want something traditional?" she asks, her hand hovering over red roses. "Or maybe something a little more modern and flirty? Not quite as on theme."

I feel a smile lift my face. "Nontraditional is perfect."

Finley moves around the shop like she could do it in her sleep, carefully choosing a flower before adding it to the bundle or putting it back in the vase if she doesn't like how the combination looks. She seems to forget I'm here, lost in her own little world of flowers and color, and I can't help but watch, transfixed. I don't think there's anything in my life that consumes me as wholly as it seems flowers do for Finley. It's sort of beautiful to watch someone so clearly in their element.

My eyes fix on the wall where, painted in forest green letters, is a Ralph Waldo Emerson quote. "Love is like wildflowers; it's often found in the most unlikely places." It makes something snag in my chest, those words. They're so simple yet beautiful, and it makes me appreciate the name of the store even more.

Finley steps in front of me, holding out a beautiful bouquet. It's nothing like I would have imagined—greens and pinks and oranges instead of reds and whites and pinks—but it's perfect.

"I love it," I say, a smile tugging at my lips.

Her face brightens, sunshine on a summer day. "Good, I'm glad. Just email and let me know how many you need, and I'll make sure to have them done. I won't be able to deliver that evening because June is in a musical at school, but I can do it that morning if that works for you."

I knew about the musical because Jodi also won't be able to attend the auction, although she will be helping all the way up until the event.

"That morning works great," I tell her, beginning to pull my gloves back on.

Finley watches me silently, a wrinkle forming between her brows. "Wren, can I ask you something?"

My eyes catch and hold on hers, and it feels so much like looking into Holden's eyes, although softer, more curious.

"Sure," I say with a shrug.

"You and Holden." She says this more like a statement, and I find myself breathless, waiting for her to continue. "The rumors aren't true, right?"

My head tips to the side as I examine her. Short blond hair, engaging hazel eyes, smattering of freckles across her tan nose. "No, they're not true. We're just friends."

Truth be told, after that weird encounter on Saturday morning, I feel the ground between us is more unsteady than ever. For a few short moments, it was as if the world was blotting out around us, and it was just his hands in my hair, his fingers on my skin. It didn't feel *friendly* at all.

She makes a noise in the back of her throat, moving back behind the counter without another word.

"Couldn't you have asked him that?" I ask before I can think better of it.

Finley shrugs, her creamy sweater slipping off one of her shoulders. "Sure, but he probably wouldn't have answered. He rarely opens up to anyone."

I've noticed this. It seems that for every layer of Holden Blankenship I peel back, there's another behind it, reinforced with steel. I'm starting to wonder if it's possible for anyone to know the real him. If he would ever let anyone close enough.

It's probably foolish of me, but I'm self-aware enough to admit that if he ever did, I hope it would be with me.

Eleven
- HOLDEN -

It's been two days since the call with Mia, and I'm still fuming. I haven't told anyone about the promises she made to June because I know my mother would tell me to confront her and Finley would tell me that I should cut off their communication. I don't need anyone to tell me these things. It's not like they're not in the back of my mind constantly, taking up space and hanging on like weights dragging me down.

If I'm being honest, it's not the anger with Mia that's eating at me. It's the imprint on my mind of the look on Wren's face when she left. I was harsh with her, I know that. It's just that, where Mia is involved, I don't always react with the most grace. And I took out that frustration on Wren.

Which is why I'm pacing the length of the tiny cabin instead of working, my eyes drifting to the window every few seconds, waiting for the telltale dust to stir in the dirt driveway that signals her arrival.

As if my thoughts conjured her, I see a slip of yellow in the corner of the window and then a plume of dirt rising into the chilly air, followed by the exhaust fog from her tailpipe.

Maybe I should try to look busy, not like I've been standing here, waiting for her to arrive, but I don't have it in me to pretend. There's that gnawing feeling in the pit of my stomach that feels a lot like guilt, and I'm desperate to make things right. I'd rather have her snark and pestering than her silence.

The front door squeals open, and I make a mental note to grease the hinges. Wren enters, a wrinkle forming between her brows as she notices me standing in the middle of the living room, no tools or work around me.

"Holden—"

"I'm sorry about Saturday," I say, cutting her off.

She blinks, surprise coloring her delicate features. One shoulder lifts in a shrug, making the soft cashmere of her sweater slip over her collarbone. "It's fine, Holden. You don't have to explain yourself to me."

"No, I do." I palm the back of my neck, warm under the weight of her stare. I feel like she can see straight down to the depths of my soul, where it's dark and cold and empty, that little piece of myself that I've hidden from everyone.

Wren leans against the now drywalled arch separating the kitchen and living room, one ankle crossing over the other. She's silent, waiting for me to continue. I wish I had the words to tell her how much that means to me. The women in my life have always talked over me when I struggled to put my thoughts into words, even if they meant well. It's like they think that I don't know what I'm feeling, so they try to help me get there. What I've never been able to explain is that I always know exactly how I'm feeling, I just don't know how to express it.

Maybe Wren knows this from all those months we spent texting, when she would respond immediately and I would take long minutes to send back my reply. Regardless, she *knows* something my own family and my ex-wife have never been able to figure out.

It makes that cold piece inside me warm, even if ever so slightly. As if there's a splash of sunshine breaking through the layers of grime, sending sparks of light dancing in the dark corners.

"Mia makes me crazy," I say finally, a little surprised at the words. Despite everything, I've always tried to respect Mia in front of my family, if only for June's sake. It's not like I don't feel the way my mom and Finley and even Grey feel about her. It's just that I don't want to sour June's idea of her mom. She may constantly fall through on her promises, but June still holds her on a pedestal, bragging to all her first-grade friends about how her mom lives in Paris, working as an artist.

So I normally don't allow myself to say the things I think about Mia out loud. But Wren feels…safe. And I haven't felt safe with a woman outside my family in a very long time.

Wren nods, just a slight dip of her chin, waiting for me to continue.

I grip the back of my neck once more, hard enough to feel pain. "She makes all these promises to June and never follows through, and then June is heartbroken and sobbing and I don't know how to make it better for her." My voice catches. "It *destroys* me to see her like that."

"I'm sorry, Holden," Wren says, and I think her voice sounds thicker too.

I swallow against the lump forming in my throat, unable to look her in the eyes that have gone soft and misty, seeing way too much. "So when she called on Saturday and promised to come to June's recital…"

"You freaked?" Wren asks.

My gaze snags on hers. "I freaked. And I took it out on you. I shouldn't have. I'm still," I pause, "getting used to this whole friend thing."

One corner of her mouth twitches upward, making the faintest dimple pop in her cheek. "Take all the time you need."

A breath heaves out of me, a weight being lifted off my shoulders. "I'm probably going to be an ass sometimes."

"Eh," she says, shrugging, her collar slipping even more with the movement, exposing creamy, freckled skin. "What else is new?"

I watch her as she looks away from me, taking in the changes to the space. I spent last week hanging up drywall and installing baseboards. It's amazing how much just that can change the look of a room. Now, it feels smaller, more intimate and cozy.

"It looks really good," Wren says, her gaze returning to mine. For some reason, this makes an unfamiliar sensation bloom in my chest.

"Thanks," I say, clearing my throat. "I'll install the new doors next. Those are on hold at the hardware store, right?" At her nod, I continue. "Then we'll have to choose flooring and countertops to go down next. Did you ever decide on floors?"

Twin splashes of red appear on Wren's cheeks, and she pushes off the wall, heading into the galley kitchen, where I've been attempting to install the builder-grade cabinets, although I kept getting distracted and ended up spending most of the morning pacing, waiting for her to arrive.

I follow her in, leaning a hip on the one cabinet I did get attached to the wall.

"You know," Wren says, spinning around to face me, her fingers trailing along the rough edge of one of the cabinets.

"Jimmy was going to let me shadow him while he worked. Teach me how to do some of this stuff so I could do a lot of it on my own in the next flip."

My eyes snag on hers and hold. "Is that so?"

"It was going to be a lot of help to me," she says, letting the words hang in the space between us.

I know what she's getting at, wanting me to do the same that Jimmy was going to do for her, but for some reason, I can't bring myself to offer it so easily. On one hand, it would be the *friendly* thing to do, and I probably owe her for snapping on Saturday. On the other, the thought of her here, spending all day alone with me...doesn't sound as unappealing as it should, and I don't know what to make of that.

I'm not sure when my feelings for Wren became so jumbled, but I do know that when I look at her now, my first response isn't irritation. It's almost...affection. Sure, it's the same kind of eye-rolling affection I feel toward June when she trades her carrots for gummy worms at lunch, but it's affection, nonetheless. And then there are the feelings that are nothing like what I feel for my daughter, something warmer and more electric, a buzzing beneath my skin and a pulsing awareness that hasn't been on my radar in so long it's practically alien.

Instead of offering to let her shadow me, I choose to focus on that splash of cherry red on her cheeks from earlier, the reason I trailed her in here. "So why haven't you picked out flooring?

Or countertops?" We spent the second half of our trip to the hardware store looking at samples of countertops that Oliver either had in stock or said he could get in quickly, knowing Wren's short timeline.

The flush returns, brighter this time, making her freckles pop against her skin, and she avoids my gaze. "I guess if we're being honest, then there's something I should tell you too."

Her voice is soft and almost dejected, barely above a whisper. It makes something in my chest twist and ache, enough that I have to press my fingers there and rub.

"I exhausted my savings buying the cabin, and renovations have been more costly than I expected. I can afford it." She says this last part quickly, meeting my eyes for the briefest instant before returning to a spot on the floor. "But I have to be frugal, and I'll probably need to choose the cheapest materials."

I think of the warm oak flooring I picked out at the hardware store and the way she turned it down without even really considering it. At the time, I thought she was being difficult, trying to push my buttons like usual, but now I can see the slight panic and embarrassment she was trying to hide. I can't help but wonder how many times I've misunderstood her. I want to sit down and examine every interaction we've had over the last four years in a new light.

"We can work with that," I tell her, and her eyes swing up to meet mine.

"Really?" She sounds hopeful and a little desperate, and it makes that ache in my chest a little more prominent.

"Yeah, of course. We have to work inside your budget, Wren." I say this with a softness I've always held back from her, and she looks surprised. "How about I go back to the hardware store and look at some cheaper samples and send you what I think would work?"

Her finger sweeps along the exposed rough edge of the counter. "Are you going now?"

"I'll probably finish installing the baseboards first and then go."

When her gaze meets mine again, her cornflower blue eyes are hopeful, the dark blue ring around the edges looking even more prominent in the fading afternoon light slanting through the window above where the sink will go.

"I could stay and help and then go with you to the hardware store." Even though it's a statement, she phrases it like a question, hope clinging to the edges of her words like dew on morning grass.

We're back at a crossroads. If I say yes now, she'll be back as often as her schedule allows, putting in the work on this place right beside me. A few weeks ago, just the thought of that would have made a headache begin to form at the base of my skull, but now my skin hums with an awareness I'm finding hard to ignore.

"Yeah, Wren, you can stay."

Finley is at my mom's when I arrive to pick up June. The three of them are in the kitchen, aprons on, and June is licking brownie batter from a whisk, chocolate smeared across her face. There's even a little on the ends of her hair, which should be really fun to try to wash out tonight.

"Making brownies, huh?" I ask, walking into the kitchen. They all look surprised to see me, caught up in something they were laughing at, and my heart swells a little in my chest. Sometimes I think June is missing out by not having her mom here, but other times, I see that she has my mom and Finley filling in the gaps the best they can, and I think maybe everything will be okay.

June smiles up at me from where she's sitting on the countertop next to a mostly empty mixing bowl. "Brownie batter is good."

"And has a risk of salmonella," I say, swiping it from her hand and taking a lick for myself before handing it back. It's too sweet, but the look of pure delight on her face that I would indulge in something usually off-limits makes it worth it.

"I'd like to have brownie batter for dinner tonight," she says, and a laugh rumbles in my chest.

Ruffling her messy hair, I say, "I'm sure you would, June Bug, but we're going to have to pass on that."

"We can have brownie batter for dinner on Friday," Finley says. I raise my brows in her direction, but she just shrugs, tucking a lock of smooth blond hair behind her ear. "I thought me and Junie could have a girls' night."

"Can I, Daddy?" June asks, flashing me her best puppy dog eyes. For a moment, they almost remind me of Wren's, with the pale blue and the darker ring around the iris.

I ruffle her hair. "Sure, June Bug, you can have a girls' night. As long as you eat real food," I say, attempting to sound stern.

She nods enthusiastically, but I don't miss the wink she tries to give Finley when she thinks I'm not looking.

Finley's mouth tips in a smile. "Now you can have a free night off to spend with your girlfriend."

I feel warmth creeping up my neck. "She's not my girlfriend."

Mom's head snaps up, her knobby knuckles still covered in a faint dusting of flour. "She's not?"

Finley looks between us, a pleased expression coloring her features, and the warmth in my neck slips higher, suffusing my cheeks.

"No, she's not," Finley finally says. "Wren told me."

Mom's face wars with confusion and shock, and maybe even a little disappointment. Finley has been after me to start dating for years, but even though Mom is more subtle, she wants to see me happily married again more than she lets on.

"Wren told you what?" June asks, her eyes darting between the three of us, all standing stock still in the middle of the kitchen.

Lifting June from the counter, I take the whisk she managed to snatch again from her little sticky hands and gently nudge her toward the hallway. "Go wash your hands, June Bug. When you come back out, we need to get home for dinner."

After she scampers down the hall, leaving a chocolatey handprint on the corner of the wall, I turn around to face my mom and sister. They've both got their arms crossed, and they look so similar standing there that I almost want to laugh. Finley is the spitting image of Mom, in looks if not in personality. Where Mom is loud and chaotic and always on the go, Finley tends to be more reserved like me, her humor leaning toward dry and sarcastic, unlike Mom's easy charm. I can tell Mom's nature wears on Finley sometimes too, although we love her for it.

Right now, though, they are mirror images of one another, and I swallow, trying and failing to stand my ground.

"What do you mean Wren told you we aren't actually together?"

I hadn't really made a conscious decision not to tell Mom and Finley the truth about Wren and me. It just wasn't a conversation I really wanted to have, and if it got them off my back about finding a soulmate and mother to my future children, great. So I wasn't hiding it from them, but I am a little shocked that Wren would tell Finley the truth when she told my mom the opposite.

"She came into the shop to work on arrangements for the Galentine's Auction, and I asked her about it," Finley says, her shoulders lifting in a shrug.

"But she told me they're together," Mom interjects.

I let out a sigh. "We're not together. I just told Charlotte we were to get her off my back."

"And that worked?" Finley asks, sounding a little surprised.

"Yeah," I say. "I guess. She hasn't tried asking me out again."

Disappointment sits heavy in the lines of Mom's face. "I was so excited for you two."

I feel a stab of guilt in my stomach, but I remind myself that I don't have to do what they want of me just because it makes them happy. For the last four years, I've had to tell myself this. June is my responsibility, and although I'm very grateful for their help, I have to do what I think is best for her. And same for myself.

"I wasn't meaning for the rumor to spread around town," I tell Mom. "I didn't expect Charlotte to tell anyone."

Mom rolls her eyes. "Of course she told everyone."

"Wren said the same thing," I mutter under my breath, but of course, Mom hears, and her expression perks up.

"So you are talking with Wren?"

I shrug. "Well, yeah, I'm renovating her cabin."

"But you're getting along?" Mom asks, equally skeptical and excited. I know where she's going with this, and I don't like it. I'm feeling jumbled up enough about Wren without her butting into it. If she finds out about the app, it's all over.

"Barely," I say, although this doesn't feel like the whole truth. Or even most of it, if I remember the moments on my porch with my hands on her skin, beneath her hair, or when I opened up to her about Mia today, something I haven't done with, well, anyone, really. That doesn't feel like *barely* getting along, but I can't tell them that.

June returns to the kitchen, saving me from Mom's next comment. Her hands are clean, and she even managed to get most of the chocolate off her face, although there's still a little smudge on her cheek. My lips lift into a grin at the sight of it.

"Ready to go, June Bug?"

She gives me a gap-toothed smile. "Can we take some brownies home?"

My bed feels especially empty tonight, the sheets cold to the touch, and for the first time in a very long time, I almost wish there was someone here with me. A warm body I could reach for. Delicate curls I could wrap around my finger. I can picture it when I close my eyes, red curls like the fire licking up my spine, spreading through me until I'm warm all over, my skin flushed and hot underneath my blankets.

My phone buzzes on the nightstand, startling me from the dangerous track of my thoughts, and I reach for it quickly, needing to cool down.

The name on the screen doesn't do anything to help.

> **LikeStrawberryWine:** You up?

I swallow thickly, kicking the blankets to the foot of my bed to cool my skin, and sit up so my bare back is resting against the headboard before I respond.

> **user6872:** Finley says no good ever comes after a text like that.

> **LikeStrawberryWine:** I knew I liked her.

> **LikeStrawberryWine:** But don't worry, I'm not trying to seduce you.

I don't know why, but those words don't hold the same comfort they used to, especially not now when I'm aching and wanting and feeling a little unhinged.

> **user6872:** Who said I don't want to be seduced?

I seriously have no idea where that response came from, but I typed it and sent it before I could second-guess myself. My heart races in my chest, my blood pulsing in my ears, and I have to force myself not to respond with a "jk," mostly because I've never said "jk" in my life.

My phone vibrates with an incoming text before I can spiral.

> **LikeStrawberryWine:** You did. Many, many times.

Before I can type back a response, another text comes in.

> **LikeStrawberryWine:** But you're always allowed to change your mind.

I stare at the words on the screen until they go fuzzy, imagining Wren in her own bed just a couple hundred feet away. I wonder if her heart is racing too, or if this is just a typical Monday for her. If she sends flirty texts to someone other than me.

Something knots in my gut at that.

But still, I don't respond yet, thinking about the lines I've drawn in the sand over the last few years and whether I'm actually ready to cross it yet. I don't know if Wren is the person I want to cross it with. At least, I tell myself that, even though crossing that line has never even entered my mind until all of this started with her.

I don't think this is a decision I should be making now, in the state I'm in. Not when the thought of being seduced by Wren Daniels seems so bright and effervescent that everything else seems dull and gray. Not when there's a drumbeat of wanting pulsing beneath my skin so strongly that I'm feeling reckless.

I can't afford to be reckless.

> ***user6872:*** **I'll keep that in mind.**

In fact, I don't expect I'll be able to think about anything else.

Twelve

- WREN -

"You know, I saw on HGTV—"

"If I have to hear about HGTV one more time," Holden says, "this whole shadowing arrangement is over."

I let out a long sigh, my breath causing the curls hanging around my face to flutter. "But the *Property Brothers*—"

"I'm not a Property Brother." Holden cuts me off again, standing to his full height after making sure the kitchen cabinet is firmly attached to the wall. He towers over me in the tiny space, that little wrinkle forming between his brows, and it suddenly feels as though the air is thinner, like standing in the fire tower atop The Mountain, wind rustling all around.

No, Holden most definitely is *not* one of the famous remodeling brothers. He's something else entirely, with his dark hair slipping from his messy bun, his beard trimmed a little closer to his cheeks, like he recently shaved, his skin covered in sawdust and glistening with sweat despite the chill in the cabin.

He looks a little unruly, like I've come to realize he always does when he's working, and it's become a lot distracting. I keep finding my eyes drifting to the curve of muscle beneath the straining fabric of his flannels, the bottom lip he tucks between his teeth when he's concentrating, the faint, barely there freckles that dot against his strong nose, the column of his throat that I've never really paid attention to on other men before.

Something about Holden Blankenship has become more than a little appealing to me, and I'm not really sure what to make of it.

"What are you staring at?" Holden asks, snapping me out of my thoughts.

I realize I've been focused on that smooth slope of his collarbone peeking out of the unbuttoned collar of his rust-colored flannel, but I can't tell him that.

"Nothing," I say, giving the cabinet a shove. It doesn't budge, which I guess is a good thing. I've spent every afternoon this week shadowing Holden as he works on the cabin, and he's even shown me how to do a few things, although that tends to take more time, so I try not to distract him, since we're on a tight schedule. We've made a good bit of progress this week, though, and I'm starting to get the vision for the place. It's not what I would have designed for myself, and the layout isn't necessarily ideal, but it's functional, and that's really all that matters in a short-term rental.

Holden tosses his tools into the bag at his feet, sighing and rolling his shoulders. They make a soft popping noise, and I can almost see the tension seeping out of him. It's an oddly intimate thing to watch, and I force myself to look away.

Clearing my throat, I ask, "You and June have fun plans tonight?"

"No, she's having a girls' night with Finley." He finishes packing up the last of his tools and leans against the cabinet, arms crossed over his chest. "I was thinking about going to Matty's if you wanted to come."

I stare at him for a long moment, noticing the way the hair falling out of his bun waves gently at the ends. He looks good standing here in the waning golden light slicing through the windows, and suddenly, I remember our text conversation from last week, when he made a comment about wanting to be seduced. I can still feel the way my body heated, spreading out from my middle until I was warm all over, my head a mess of all the ways I could imagine getting under his skin in a completely new way.

"Matty's sounds good," I say, not missing the way my voice comes out raspier than I intended.

If Holden notices, he doesn't say anything. Pushing off the cabinet, he grabs his tool bag and heads for the front door, his boots clomping against the floor. We picked out flooring samples in my price range and picked them up yesterday afternoon, so they're ready to be installed next week. They aren't what I would have chosen for myself, a gray-toned vinyl plank, but they were inexpensive and they're durable, if Holden and Oliver are correct, so they'll work. I give the stack a nudge with the tip of my boot as we head out the front door.

It's not snowing tonight, just cold, and my breath clouds in the air as we step out onto the front porch. The golden glow of the porch light only illuminates five feet into the dense forest surrounding the cabin.

Holden stops on the porch, swiveling to make sure I lock the door behind me. Apparently, no teenagers will be sneaking into this cabin anymore.

"I'm locking it, I'm locking it," I huff, my hands shaking in the cold since I didn't bother to pull on my gloves.

Holden makes what I can only describe as a grunting noise behind me.

My trembling, frozen hands drop the keys, and they land with a clatter at my feet. Before I can reach down for them, Holden has set his tool bag on the ground and has snatched them up. Then his arm comes around me to slide the key into the lock. His body dwarfs mine, blocking out the light. I can feel the warmth radiating off him and seeping beneath my skin.

He finishes turning the deadbolt, but stands still, not backing away. When I glance over my shoulder at him, his eyes are focused on the curve of my neck, where goose bumps pricked against my skin the moment we opened the door to the harsh evening wind. My breath catches in my throat as Holden's free hand tugs at the collar of my jacket, his fingertips brushing my skin, until it's no longer exposed to the cold.

His eyes connect with mine. "You need a warmer coat."

Surprisingly, his voice doesn't hold its usual gruffness. It's soft as silk, smooth as expensive whiskey, rich like decadent hot fudge. I feel it down to the tips of my toes.

"Noted."

His boots scuff against the floorboard as he moves away, and a wave of cold air rushes into the place his body vacated. Picking up his discarded tool bag, he asks, "See you at Matty's?"

I nod. "See you at Matty's."

I've never noticed how loud Matty's can be, or how dim the lighting, until I'm sitting at a table with Holden Blankenship, achingly aware of the shrinking space between us as we lean in to hear each other over the din of music and voices.

"It's the end of January," Holden says, and my eyes fasten on the way his throat bobs as he takes a sip of his beer.

"Christmas spirit is all year long."

Holden's eyes narrow, amber glinting in the light. "You just like to mess with me." His voice is a match to sandpaper, lighting a fire beneath my skin. "Admit it."

"I like to mess with you," I say, my hands tightening on my glass, humming with contained electricity.

Holden leans in as the music grows louder, the live band matching the energy from the crowd. I can't help the way my eyes drift over the planes of his face to settle on the full curve of his bottom lip.

"Why?"

I take my time letting my gaze trail back up to his eyes, pausing to focus on the dark beard covering his jawline, the dusting of freckles across his nose, the curve of his high cheekbones, the little wisps of hair escaping from his bun.

I press my thumb to the space between his brows, just a brush of the pad to the skin. "You get this wrinkle right here," I tell him. "I like it."

The words hang in the space between us, and time stands still as I wait for him to respond, to see if this new, intangible thing between us is going to die like embers in the grate or catch on the tinder and blaze to life.

"I—"

Out of the corner of my eye, I can see the front door to Matty's open. Charlotte walks in with Adam Brunner, one of the few single firefighters in town.

"Charlotte's here," I say before I can think better of it, before I realize I've cut off whatever Holden was going to say.

Holden's body stiffens, and he swivels around to follow my line of sight. When he sees who she's with, his shoulders relax. "She's with someone," he says, relief in his voice.

To my surprise, *I* don't feel relieved by this, because there was a chance to pretend, to push the limits, and now it's dissolved. I don't really want to examine why I want that chance so badly. Because this is *Holden*, and I guarantee that this burgeoning attraction I'm feeling toward him is entirely one-sided.

It doesn't stop me from saying, "We should probably keep up the pretense anyway."

Holden turns around to face me, eyes intense and assessing once again. I don't know if I hope he can read me or not. I wish I could read him, because I feel like since we sat in here a few weeks ago, shocked to find out we were more than just neighbors who don't get along, every interaction has been a mixed signal, a green light followed by an immediate red, a push forward and then a pull back.

I'm craving an open highway in the dead of night, no one else around for miles.

Holden finishes off his beer, never pulling his gaze from mine, and heat coils low in my stomach, spreading to the tips of my fingers, the arch of my ears, the space behind my knees. Pushing back from the table, he says, "Let's play pool."

Instead of leading the way, he motions me forward, and I startle when his hands find my hips, guiding me through the crowd of people toward the dim corner where the darts and pool tables are. The warmth of his hands seeps through the wool of my sweater, and with every gentle press of his fingers to move me around a table or person, that heat turns into a pulsing ache beneath my skin, a buzzing hum of awareness at his body behind mine.

Holden stops us in front of the empty pool table, his front brushing against my back, his weight leaning heavy into mine as he reaches for the rack. When he speaks, his breath warms that spot on the back of my neck where my collar has slipped again, and I can't help but shiver at the memory of his hands there. "Are you any good at pool?" he asks, voice just above a raspy whisper. He doesn't have to yell this close, his lips pressed to the shell of my ear.

"Yes, actually," I say.

His fingers tighten on my hips. "Charlotte doesn't know that."

My breath staggers in my chest, my heart pounding against my ribs so hard I wonder if he can feel it with the way his body is pressed up against mine, not even a sliver of space between us.

"Then you should probably show me," I say, and I swear I feel that rarely present smile lift against the curve of my ear.

"Guess I will."

He backs away, and I have to grip the edge of the table to continue standing upright, my fingers digging into the green velvet until my knuckles turn white with the pressure. I don't turn around to see if Charlotte is watching. I don't want to know, and I don't want Holden to either. I'm terrified that if she's not, he'll bring this all to an end. It feels dangerously real, and I want to push my advantage for all its worth.

Holden pulls striped and solid balls from the pockets, rolling them in my direction, and I catch them with trembling hands before dropping them into the rack. I swear I feel his eyes on me in the moments my focus is elsewhere, hot and heavy and lingering, but every time I look up, he's looking into the next pocket.

When the last of the pockets has been emptied, he goes to the wall where the cue sticks are hanging, and I push onto my tiptoes, leaning over the edge of the table to push the rack into place.

I feel Holden before I hear the cue stick settling against the table, the solid line of his body bending over mine, nudging the rack the last inch my short arms couldn't manage before lifting it away from the balls, leaving them in a perfect triangle on the table. "Got it," he says into my ear, rustling the fine hairs at the base of my neck.

He pulls me up with him, a hand pressed to the space between my hip and waist, finger flexing in the thick material of my sweater.

Surprise hums through me when I look back at him and find a smirk playing at the edges of his lips, a playful look I would have bet the cabin I'd never see on his face. It does something to me, that knowing smile.

He holds out the cue stick in front of us, his body still pressed against the back of mine. "*This* is a cue stick," he says, voice teasing.

"Is it really?" I ask. "My gosh, there's so much to learn. I'm so grateful to have a big, strong man like you to teach me."

He grips my waist a little harder, leaning in until his lips are pressed to my ear once more. "You might be going a little overboard."

"What can I say? I'm a zealous lover."

Holden grunts in my ear, putting space between us as he moves around the corner of the table. He points the cue stick at me. "I don't know about that, Red, but you're trouble. That's for sure."

Thirteen
- HOLDEN -

The grin that Wren gives me proves my point. I feel it pierce straight through the steel barrier I've been building up around my heart since Mia left, snagging on the tender flesh beneath. Wren Daniels has the potential to be my downfall, but damn it all to hell, I want to see where she'll take me anyway.

My palms still itch, imprinted with the memory of her curves beneath my hands, the soft wool of her sweater bunched beneath my fingers. It took everything inside me not to tug on the pesky fabric and see if her skin feels as soft and warm as I've been imagining it would.

If you would have told me six weeks ago that I'd be fantasizing about Wren Daniels, I would have laughed, but I can't deny the pinprick of electricity zinging up my spine as she follows my path around the table and comes to stand beside me.

"You're going to have to show me how to do this," she says, her voice low and smooth, made for darkness and tangled bedsheets. We both know she's lying but don't pretend to want to do anything else.

I nod, moving behind her, my hand finding that same spot on her hip once more. It settles in the perfect little curve between her waist and hip, like it was meant to be there. I think I hear her breath catch, and I wonder if she can feel my heart beating, if she knows how long it's been since I've had a woman this close, since I've *wanted* a woman this close. If I think about it for too long, I'll freak myself out and retreat. But I don't want to retreat right now, not when she makes me feel safe to explore this again. Not with Wren. With Wren, I want to keep moving forward and see what happens.

My hand folds around one of hers, positioning it around the cue stick. She follows my unspoken directions with ease, probably because she doesn't actually need my help, but despite that, it doesn't feel like pretend. It doesn't feel like we're trying to put on a show for Charlotte, who may have even left by now, because from the moment I walked in here with Wren, I haven't noticed much else. No, it doesn't feel like pretend. It feels like an *excuse* to do what we've been dancing around since that first night here, just feet away, perched on stools at the bar.

"You want to hit the white ball," I say into her ear. "The cue."

Wren nods, her hair catching in my beard.

"Then, whichever ball ends up in a pocket, that's yours."

"I'm going to be stripes," Wren says, and a smile twitches my lips.

"You can't pick before they go in, Red. Or you can, but if you knock in a solid, I have one less to deal with."

Her eyes meet mine with a simple twist of her head. We're so close I could press my mouth to hers, taste the lips that have been haunting my dreams and leaving me waking up frustrated and wanting every day for weeks.

"I won't knock in a solid," she says, confidence in every note of her voice.

It makes me want to do it, kiss her and see if she tastes like the strawberry wine she was drinking at the table. I've never been a fan of wine, especially not fruity wines, but I think I'd like it on her. I think I'd like anything if I tasted it on her lips. Brownies, butterscotch syrup, caramel cheesecake, powdered sugar.

With her gaze still fixed on me, Wren slides the cue stick back and pushes it forward, sending the cue ball crashing into the ones lined up at the end of the table. They scatter, and I pull my eyes away from her long enough to watch them slide across the green velvet.

She was right. Two striped balls end up in pockets, but not a single solid follows. They all roll to a stop on the table, and she stands, flashing me a wide smile.

That's all it takes for my control to snap. That smile that I feel right in the center of my chest.

Grabbing Wren's hand, I tug her toward the hall where we hid from Charlotte last time. She's still got her free hand wrapped around the cue stick.

"Holden," Wren yells loud enough for me to hear her over the music. "Where are we—"

She cuts off as I pull her down the hall, stopping in the same spot we did last time. My hand at the small of her back is the only thing stopping her from thudding against the wall.

"Wren," I breathe, my mind in shambles now that we're away from the crowds of people. The din of music quiets in this little hidden away nook. I'm sure someone will come down here to use the restroom at some point. In a town full of busybodies, I should probably care, but I can't bring myself to. Not when Wren's got her bottom lip tucked between her teeth. Her cornflower blue eyes are wide as she stares up at me, that ring of dark blue around the irises drawing me in like a moth to flame.

Gathering my thoughts, I ask, "What are we doing?"

Wren's breath fans against my lips, and I want to sag into her, but I stop myself, planting a hand on the wall beside her head.

"Aren't we pretending?" she whispers.

I search her face, looking for any indication that she's telling the truth. There's a constellation of freckles over every inch of her skin, and I want to trace them with my fingers. Her bottom lip is full, her top dipping in a deep cupid's bow. This close, I can tell she has the longest eyelashes of anyone I've ever seen. They're just a pale red, and white blond at the tips. She's an amalgamation of features that make her into something stunning, precious, and utterly unforgettable, but I can't tell if she means what she's saying.

The truth sizzles beneath my skin, begging to be let out, and there's only a moment of hesitation before I give in.

"I'm not."

Wren's face softens into something like surprise before it changes, her eyelids growing heavy, her breath stopping completely. She blinks once. "Me neither."

That's all it takes.

My last vestige of control snaps like a worn-out rubber band, and my hand dives into those curls that have been driving me mad, pulling her close enough to fuse her lips to mine. The pool cue clatters to the floor as Wren drops it and fists her hands in the collar of my flannel, erasing the last bit of space between us until we line up perfectly.

I won't lie and say I haven't thought about kissing Wren before. When I'm staring up at my ceiling at night, cold and tired and lonely and wanting, it's practically all I can think about. I've imagined how it would happen, whether it would be soft and slow or frantic and hot, how she would taste, how she would feel.

Nothing could have prepared me for the real thing. For the press of her curves against me. For the taste of her lips. For the way she responds, leading the kiss even though I was the one who started it.

If there was ever a doubt in my mind that Wren wanted me, she's obliterating it.

A hard groan escapes me when Wren sinks her teeth into my bottom lip, and I drop my hand from the wall, placing it behind her thigh, hauling her up against me. Her legs wrap around my waist, bringing her face more level with mine, and I take the advantage, gripping her hair tighter and angling her head better.

She lets out a soft moan, and my tongue slips inside, tangling with hers. I was right. She does taste like strawberry wine, although mixed with the taste of my beer. My skin flushes hot with the knowledge that she's going to taste it for the rest of the night.

I pull my mouth away long enough to trail open-mouthed kisses along her jaw, down the smooth line of her neck to where her scent is the strongest, like she sprayed her perfume *right there*. I want to memorize that scent, imprint it on the back of my mind to remember when I need a pick-me-up.

I can't imagine anything feeling better than this. Better than Wren Daniels sighing my name in my ear, scratching the back of my neck with the tips of her fingers, tugging my mouth back to hers.

I'm not sure how much time passes, but the kiss goes on and on, changing tempo from something hard and rough to languid and seductive, like a lazy Saturday morning in bed, with long, lingering touches and twisted sheets and all the time in the world.

"Holden," Wren murmurs against my lips, her fingers scratching against my scalp before moving down the length of my neck and across my shoulders.

When I don't respond, she pulls back. I follow, trying to close the distance between us once more, but her laugh fills the gap, making my eyes spring open.

Her lips are kiss-swollen, her cheeks and neck red from the scrape of my beard. She looks like every dream I've woken up from over the past few weeks, and I want to pinch myself to make sure it's real.

"Holden," she says again, a smile curling up one side of her mouth, making that faint dimple crease her cheek. "Your phone is vibrating."

I finally notice the buzzing in my pocket, pressed against her thigh.

"Sorry, I better check this," I say, slowly lowering her to the ground, soaking in the way her body slides against the length of mine. I brace one hand against her hip when she seems a little unsteady, and she flashes me another heart-melting smile as I fish my phone from my pocket and swipe it open.

"She's okay," Finley says on the other line, and my heart, which has been beating erratically for the last few minutes, slams to a stop in my chest. "I think June's got a stomach bug. She's been complaining of a tummy ache and just threw up." Finley pauses. "Twice."

I back away from Wren, pushing my free hand through my hair. "Why didn't you call me the first time?"

"She had a bunch of sweets, and so I thought it was that at first," Finley says, and at my loud sigh, Wren's brow wrinkles, and she signals, asking if everything is okay.

I nod, focusing on the conversation.

"Anyway, I was going to call you after I got it all cleaned up, but then she threw up again, and so I don't think it's just from the sweets."

"No," I say, walking down the hall toward the bar again, Wren at my heels. "There's a stomach bug going around her class. Her teacher emailed about it a few days ago."

"So it wasn't the sweets?" Finley asks, her voice ringing with relief.

I shake my head even though she can't see me. "No, it wasn't the sweets, although you know she's not supposed to have much. I'll be right there."

Hanging up, I grab my coat from where I left it draped over the chair at the table and pull out a couple of bills from my wallet to drop on the table.

When I spin around to head for the door, Wren is there. Guilt slams through me, because I had almost forgotten about her with everything going on with June. I just made out with her in the bathroom hallway at Matty's, and I was going to bail without even a goodbye.

This is why I don't date. Not because I'll compromise where it comes to June, but because I *won't* compromise, and there's no room for anyone else. I've made it so there's no room for anyone else.

"Is June okay?" Wren asks, worry etched in every line of her face. In the brighter lights of the main room of the bar, she looks even more disheveled. Her corduroy skirt is twisted, hiked up higher on her thighs than it was before we disappeared down the hall, and there's a rip in her tights, where my fingers dug into them. Her usually wild curls are even wilder, mussed from my hands, and her lips look thoroughly...kissed.

"She's got a stomach bug," I say, clearing my throat. It's hard to look at her like this, knowing how she tasted and felt against me. Seeing the clear evidence of my mouth and hands on her body.

Knowing I can't do it again.

Not after I almost walked out of here without even acknowledging what we did, June not only my first priority, but my *only* priority. No one deserves that, especially not Wren. She's too good for the shattered remains of my heart. All that's left is only able to care for one little girl who is too young to know the grip she has on it.

"Oh no," Wren breathes. "Do you need anything for her? Ginger ale, saltines?"

My heart crumples a little more in my chest, grating into fine dust sure to blow away on the next big breeze, because I don't know what I did to earn Wren's concern. I don't deserve it.

Palming the back of my neck, I say, "No, we're good. I've got to go, though."

Wren moves out of the way, motioning toward the door. "Yeah, of course. Go. I'll talk to you later?"

I nod, backing in the direction of the door. "Yeah, Wren, I'll talk to you later."

Fourteen

- WREN -

I'M TOO WIRED TO go home, my heart still ratcheting in my chest, my skin still tingling in all the places Holden's calluses scraped against. Despite Holden saying he and June didn't need anything, I could see that he was frazzled, focused on getting her home, and so I decide to load up on supplies and take them over there anyway.

My phone rings as I make my way out of town, toward one of the bigger suburbs, since everything in Fontana Ridge shuts down after sunset.

It's Rae, and I smile as I swipe it open. "Hey, Rae. It's been a while."

My sister lets out a long sigh. "Too long. We've been crazy busy around here. How are things in the Ridge?"

"Quiet," I say, turning on my blinker to merge onto the highway.

"Are you out driving? It's after nine there. Everything but Matty's is closed."

I hadn't realized how long Holden and I had been at Matty's after we finished dinner, sitting at that little table in the corner, talking about everything under the sun. I don't even let myself contemplate how long we were in that hallway, how many town busybodies could have come down there looking for the bathroom. If they did, I don't think either of us would have noticed.

"Yeah," I say, clearing my throat, trying to get the images of Holden Blankenship kissing a line down my throat out of my head. "I was at Matty's. I'm heading to Smithville to go to the store."

"You're driving all the way to Smithville to go to the store?" Leland asks. Rae must have me on speaker.

"Hi, Leland."

"Hi, Wren." His voice sounds louder now. I can imagine him leaning into Rae on their tiny couch to position himself closer to the phone. My heart aches a little at the thought, just like it always does when I think of them so far away but never alone since they have each other.

"So why are you driving to Smithville, baby?" Rae asks.

I hesitate, unsure how much I want to share. This thing between Holden and me feels precious, fragile, but if there was anyone to tell, it would be my sister and brother-in-law, hundreds of miles away. It's not like they're going to show up at Smokey the Beans tomorrow and share the news over coffee with Myra and Melissa.

"I was out with Holden," I say slowly.

There's a rustling on the other end, like Rae is sitting up straighter. "Your neighbor Holden?"

"Remember," Leland says, "he's not just her neighbor. They've been talking on that app for months."

A smile touches my lips, because I'm so insanely thankful for them, for this little slice of privacy that I have in them, because I can tell them anything, and no one will know.

"Yes, yes," Rae says. "I remember now. Continue."

I flip my turn signal on to take the exit to Smithville. The road ahead grows brighter with the city lights, unlike Fontana Ridge, which is only illuminated by the moon and stars and occasional streetlight barely bright enough to break up the dense darkness coating the trees.

"Well, things between us have been..." I pause, looking for the word. "Different, I guess. I don't know how to explain it, really. We still drive each other crazy most of the time, but we also..."

"Drive each other crazy," Rae fills in, her voice taking on a suggestive quality, and I hear Leland's rich, deep laugh through the phone.

A hot blush steals up my beard-burned cheeks. "Yeah," I agree. "And tonight, after we finished working on the cabin, he asked if I wanted to grab dinner at Matty's."

"Please tell me you ended up necking in the hallway."

Laughter rockets out of me because, more than anything, I wish Holden's huge body was stuffed into my passenger seat right now, his hand on my thigh, his warm, quiet chuckle filling the tight space with me at hearing my sister use the term *necking*.

"Actually, yes," I say through my laughter. "We did."

"Baby, please tell me you're serious right now." In my mind's eye, I can see Rae shooting up off her couch and pacing the three steps she can make in either direction in her living room.

"I'm serious," I tell her.

She lets out a soft sigh. "Was it so hot? He looks like he knows what he's doing."

"What's that supposed to mean?" Leland asks, and I know my pacing suspicion was correct, because his voice sounds far away again.

Rae sighs, sounding exasperated. "Leland, don't sound toxically masculine. You can say a man looks like he knows what to do in bed without losing your man card."

"I'm not toxically masculine," he shoots back. I have to press my lips together to keep from laughing. "I just want to know what gives someone the look. Do I have the look?"

"Eh," Rae and I both say, and Leland makes a defensive noise on the other line.

"It doesn't mean you *don't* know what you're doing," Rae assures him. "You definitely, *definitely* do."

I ask, "Do I need to be here for this?" I'm not liking the direction of this conversation.

"Yes," they answer in unison.

Rae says, "You look like a college professor."

"I *am* a college professor."

"Yes, but college professors are hit or miss on this scale," Rae explains. "They all look like *they* think they know what they're doing, but only some of them actually do."

"What other college professors are you sleeping with?" Leland asks, and this time I do laugh, loud and long, unable to hold it in any longer.

I can imagine Rae waving her hands wildly, trying to make her point. "No one. This is just common knowledge."

Leland lets out a miffed sigh. "So what kind of man looks like he knows what he's doing?"

"Mr. Darcy," I answer easily.

"He looks like a nineteenth century college professor," Leland says.

There's a noise on the other end, like Rae is settling back on the couch to make her point. "It's not really his looks. It's the hand flex."

"Ah, okay. I get it now," Leland says, his voice brightening with understanding.

When Rae and Leland met ten years ago, Leland, like most men, was not versed on the 2005 *Pride & Prejudice*, but the three of us spent his first visit to Fontana Ridge locked up in Mom and Dad's living room, watching the movie, pausing every few minutes to give our commentary.

"So Holden looks like the hand-flex type?" Leland asks.

I dig my nail into the little hole he left in my tights, where his fingers gripped my thighs hard enough to tear the delicate fabric, and my skin goes hot at the memory. "He definitely does."

"I'm so happy for you, baby," Rae says. "So why are you going to Smithville?"

I steer my car into the big box store parking lot and shut off the engine. "His sister was watching his daughter, June, and she called to say that June was throwing up, so Holden had to leave to get her. I thought I'd drop off some ginger ale and saltines. Electrolyte drinks. Disinfectant wipes. You know, the essentials."

Rae lets out a soft sigh. "That's so sweet of you."

Something warms inside me, thawing the unease. "You think it's okay? He said he didn't need anything, but he was frazzled and rushed." I've never dated someone with a kid before, and I know how protective Holden is of June, so I don't want to overstep or insert myself where I'm not wanted. But I also can't just go home with all this energy still crackling beneath my skin. I have to *do* something, and I want to do something for him and for June.

"No, it's perfect," Rae assures me.

"Good," I say. "I better get off here so I can get everything I need."

Rae says, "Let us know how it goes, okay?"

"Will do."

We hang up, and I sit in the darkness of my car, the lights in the parking lot casting shadows through the interior. Fingering the rip on my thigh once more, I decide to get another pair of tights while I'm in here. I'm going to keep these, though, a little memento of this night. Gasping breaths and flexing hands. Strawberry wine and sour beer. Kiss-stung lips and the scrape of a beard on sensitive skin. Passion and tenderness and that feeling of free-falling into something new.

My hands shake when I pull into my driveway an hour later. Holden's truck is parked beside his house, and dim lights pour through the cracks in his curtains. I don't know why I'm nervous to see him, except that two hours ago, he had me pinned against the wall, his mouth on my neck, his hands in my hair and on my thighs. I wanted to see what he looked like when he came undone, and I got it. I don't think I'll be able to forget the memory of his hair ruffled and coming out of that ever-present bun, his cheeks stained pink from desire, his hazel eyes turning gold in the diffused lighting of the hallway, shadows playing across the planes of his face.

Climbing out of the car, I brace myself against the cold, remembering how Holden's hands felt at the back of my neck, tugging up my collar. I really *should* get a warmer coat, although I can barely feel it now. Warmth floods through me, stealing up my chest and cheeks as I climb Holden's front porch steps, bags in hand.

Softly, I knock on the door, then hear footsteps making their way across the house.

When the door swings open, Holden looks even more disheveled than when I saw him last. He's pulled his hair into a haphazard bun, and he's stripped his flannel off, leaving only a fitted white tee beneath. It's wet, plastered to the planes of his chest, and I can't help the way my eyes dip to examine it.

"Wren?" Holden asks, his brow wrinkled. "What are you doing here?"

I hold up the bags, plastic rustling. "I thought you might need supplies."

Relief colors his features. "June just threw up on the couch. I got most of it cleaned up, and she's in the bathroom, waiting for the shower to heat up. I need to get back to her."

I nod, motioning him forward. "Of course. I'll just put these on the counter."

He holds my gaze for a fleeting moment, and I can't quite read his expression. His jaw tightens as he nods. "Thanks, Wren."

Turning, he disappears down the hallway, jogging in the direction of what I assume is the bathroom. I follow him inside, shutting the front door behind me with a soft click. His house is much like I imagined—dark wood, sleek countertops, minimal decor—but as I drop the bags on the kitchen counter and turn around to examine the living room, surprise spreads through me in increments. The wall behind the couch is painted a warm, golden yellow, the exact shade of the accent wall in my own living room. It's a splash of sunshine in the otherwise minimalist landscape.

I can see evidence of June everywhere. Her artwork is taped to the refrigerator, and there's a pile of friendship bracelets stacked on the counter. I recognize them from the ones Holden wears on his wrist, a new one each day like he rotates through the many she makes. There are little pink shoes stacked by the door, and from what I've seen of wild, untethered June, I can imagine Holden following behind her, straightening them after she discards them in a haphazard heap. Holden even has some of her projects hanging on the wall, along with candid pictures of June and of the two of them.

Something about this house makes my chest ache in the same way that listening to Leland and Rae does. Like I'm being confronted with an essential thing that I'm missing and have ignored thus far. I can feel it right beneath my breastbone, hollow and spreading.

Turning back around, I pull out the disinfectant spray and wipes and move through the dining area that separates the kitchen and living room. The couch is a soft, supple brown leather, thankfully, which means that Holden had easy clean-up earlier. I go ahead and wipe everything down before consulting the back of the spray can to make sure it's safe to spray on leather. Then I set to work spraying all the surfaces.

When I turn around a few minutes later, Holden is standing at the end of the hall, eyes focused on me. He's still wearing that unreadable expression, his jaw in a tight line, dark circles making purple half moons beneath his eyes.

"I didn't think you'd still be here," he says, watching me.

I hold up the spray can and disinfectant wipes. "Thought I'd disinfect."

Holden palms the back of his neck, exhaustion written in every line of his body. Guilt pricks me, because when I get home, I can go to bed and sleep easy. Holden will probably end up on the floor in June's room, one eye open, waiting to see if she will get sick again. I have the overwhelming urge to offer to help, even though I know he's not there yet, *we're* not there. We made out once in the hallway of a bar, even if it was the single most intense experience of my life. I can't offer to take a shift watching over June, to let him sleep, knowing his day was as physically taxing as mine, but every part of me wants to be able to do that, to take something off his plate and let him be the one to be taken care of. I get the sense that he never gets that treatment.

"Is there anything I can do?" I ask, and when his eyes meet mine, they're raw.

"Wren," he sighs, moving into the living room, although it feels as if the space between us is growing. "About before..."

That's when I finally decipher the look on his face. Regret. It makes dread curl in my stomach. The taste of strawberry wine and beer go sour on my tongue.

"Oh," I say, backing up a step, the backs of my knees knocking into his sofa and unsettling my balance.

Holden reaches out, as if on instinct, and holds me steady, his hand finding that same spot it claimed on my hip all night before drawing back just as quickly.

Regret turns to remorse, settling deep in the lines bracketing his eyes. "Wren, I'm sorry," he says.

I wave him off. "It's fine."

"No," he says, voice firm, tiredness clinging to his words. "No, it's not fine. I just—" He cuts off, sighing heavily, tension tightening his shoulders. I can see them clearly through the transparent fabric of his damp shirt. "I'm a mess."

I allow myself to trace the planes of his face, the tiredness clinging to him like a pesky cold you can't shake. The dim lights catch in the first hint of grays at his hairline, the premature lines in his forehead, the ones surrounding his mouth, even though I rarely see him smile.

He's right. He is a mess, but it doesn't make him any less beautiful standing here in his living room in a damp T-shirt and faded jeans, the muscles in his arms flexing as he balls his hands into fists and releases them over and over again.

"My life is a mess," Holden says, voice raw and tired. "I just don't have room to add anything else right now." He pauses again, eyes locking on mine. They look more brown than green or gold in this light. "*Anyone* else. No matter how badly I might want to."

I wish I didn't understand where he was coming from. I wish I hadn't walked in here and seen the trash can next to the couch for a sick June, the pile of clean laundry waiting to be folded on the armchair in the corner, the overfull calendar amid the finger paintings on the fridge. His life is full and messy, and there isn't room for me in it. I just wish that was easier to swallow, that it didn't hurt so much.

Nodding, I say, "I understand."

His eyes soften, some of the tension leaving his shoulders. "You do?"

"Yeah, Holden," I say. "I do."

He lets out a sigh, and it echoes in the quiet room. "I've never really wanted it before, you know? But I do now."

That hurts worse, burrowing beneath my skin. "Right," I say, barely above a whisper. "I better go."

I think he sees the pain in my eyes. I think I see it reflected in his. I think tonight wasn't meant to be a one-time thing. I think things could have gone much differently if not for that phone call. I think a lot of things, but none of them get me anywhere.

"Wren," Holden says when my hand lands on the doorknob. "Are we okay?"

I spin around to face him and force myself to nod. "We're okay."

"Friends?" he asks, and the word has never sounded so disappointing.

"Friends."

Fifteen
- HOLDEN -

It's been a week since the kiss with Wren, and I still can't get it out of my head. I can still feel the silky smoothness of her tights beneath my fingers, taste the strawberry wine on her tongue, hear the noise she made in the back of her throat when my lips ghosted across the slope of her neck.

It's made it fairly difficult to focus at the cabin when she's just a hairsbreadth away from me as I show her how to install floorboards and countertops, or when I watch her across the room, screwing door knobs into place on the newly painted doors.

And although we agreed to remain friends, it's obvious that something has changed between us. I'm afraid we've crossed a bridge we can't turn back on.

"Daddy," June says from her booster seat in the back of the truck on the way to Mom's for family dinner.

I meet her eyes in the rearview mirror for a second before returning my attention to the road. "Yeah, June Bug?"

"I wish Mommy could come to the musical." She sounds so dejected that my chest hurts.

That's another thing that's gone wrong this week. Mia, of course, couldn't attend June's musical like she promised, and June has been practically inconsolable all week. I've spent the last three nights sleeping on the floor in her room after she's woken up crying, my heart shattering into a million little pieces every time she squeezes my hand in her sleep.

"I wish she could too, honey," I say into the darkness of the truck. "But I'll be there and so will Grandma and Aunt Finley."

"What about Uncle Grey?" June asks, pushing her feet into the back of my seat.

A smile touches my lips. "Uncle Grey has to go to Wren's auction that night."

"Oh, yeah," she says, and a broken piece of me feels like it's stitching itself back together at the way her tone perks up. "Uncle Grey told me he's going to find his wife at the auction."

Laughter rumbles in my chest. I can't wait to bring this up at dinner tonight. "Is that so?"

"Mm-hmm. I bet she's going to be pretty."

I steer the car around the final curve in the road before reaching Mom's driveway. "I'm sure he will be glad to hear that."

"But not as pretty as Aunt Finley," June says quickly. "No one is as pretty as Aunt Finley."

The truck rumbles to a stop in Mom's driveway, and I shut it off before turning in my seat to face June. "I don't know, June Bug. You might give Aunt Finley a run for her money. You look a lot like her, you know."

June's pale blue eyes brighten. "You think?"

I boop her on the tip of her nose. "I know. You look like Aunt Finley and talk like your Mommy and act like…"

The words catch in my throat, and I don't let myself say them aloud. Because it's Wren I'm thinking of. Wren, with her easy smiles and ability to jump into life without deliberating over the consequences. Wren enjoying the little moments because they seem just as important to her as the big ones. Wren poking my buttons to see me smile. Wren letting me sort through the mess in my head in peace. I see all of my favorite traits in Wren reflected in my little June Bug. I think if she grows up to be anything like Wren, I'll be lucky.

June scrunches her nose. "Who do I act like?"

"You act like you, June Bug," I say softly. "Now let's go inside and have dinner. If you eat all your veggies, I might just let you have dessert."

A girlish squeal erupts from the back seat, and I press my lips together to hold back my smile, climbing out to catch June before she jumps from the back of the truck. Her little hand fits into mine, and she hops down, the red cowboy boots she's been insisting on wearing lately kicking up dust beneath her feet.

June shoots off like a rocket before I even have her door closed, and I take my time meandering inside, letting the cool air kiss my skin. It feels a little warmer today, like the first hint of spring, and it seems like the last rays of sunshine hung on just a little longer. It almost makes me sad. The town comes alive in the spring, but I like the quietness of winter.

A car pulling into the driveway disrupts the silence, and I turn around, not sure who to expect since Grey's and Finley's cars are both already parked out front. Surprise shoots through me when I see Wren's yellow Beetle coming to a stop. She looks equally shocked to see me, although it is *my* mother's house.

"Hey," Wren says as she climbs out of the car, her strawberry blond curls catching in the wind and drifting around her face.

I shove my hands into my pockets. "Hey, what are you doing here?"

Her head dips toward the back seat, brow wrinkling in confusion. "Your mom is supposed to be helping me with the party favors for the auction."

My own face mirrors hers as bewilderment settles over me. "Tonight?"

"Yeah, she—"

"Wren," Mom says, her voice carrying from on the porch. She's got her arms wrapped around her middle against the cold, her feet tucked into fuzzy slippers. "Come on in."

Wren and I catch each other's glances for a moment, unspoken words passing between us. It feels as intimate as it does unfamiliar. I've forgotten what it feels like to have a secret conversation with someone with only a look, the kind of easy camaraderie that comes from knowing someone well. I don't know how I feel that the person is Wren.

Wren looks like she wants to say something, but Mom just turns in her fuzzy slippers and disappears inside the house, leaving us no choice but to follow. Wren walks ahead of me up the stairs, and my eyes follow the sway of her hips, unable to forget what they felt like beneath my hands.

I shake the thought away and close the front door behind us, shutting out the cold air. Wren's eyes dance up to mine again, holding for a brief moment before she continues down the hall and into the kitchen, where country music is playing softly over the speakers.

Wren's voice carries as she says, "Hi, everyone. Jodi, I didn't realize you'd have company."

Stuffing my hands into my pockets, I head for the kitchen, ready to listen to whatever excuse my mom decides to make up. Wren might not see this obvious setup for what it is, but from the looks on Finley's and Grey's faces, they do.

I turn to see Mom waving a hand in dismissal. "I must have gotten the times mixed up. I was planning for you to come after dinner, but since you're here…"

Wren's gaze catches on mine, and I can see the exact moment she realizes what Mom is up to. "Oh, Jodi, I couldn't."

Mom pats Wren on the cheek. "Nonsense, sweetie. Food is all ready. I insist."

What follows is an awkward shuffling around as we fill our plates with Mom's homemade baked mac and cheese, roasted veggies, and fried chicken. Despite Mom trying to fill the heavy silence, tension clings to the room like dew on grass. Other than Mia, I've never brought someone home for family dinner. Neither has Finley nor Grey, even though Finley has been dating Gus for months.

We make our way to the table, where Mom has pulled an extra chair up next to mine. Wren's eyes connect with mine as she takes in the setup, and she tries for a smile, but it looks forced. I hate how awkward things have been between us since the kiss, how the friendship we'd formed feels snuffed out, just smoke from the flame that used to exist. We still talk at the cabin, although our messages have become entirely focused on the renovations, and she still badgers me constantly, but it feels *different*, and I don't like it.

Wren's knee bumps against mine under the table, and she quickly scoots it away, but I can still feel the imprint of it.

"So, Wren, how are things going for the auction?" Finley asks, swatting Grey's hand away as he tries to snatch a roll off her plate.

Some of the tension seems to leave Wren. It's funny to me, because I'm most uncomfortable when the focus is on me, but Wren seems to breathe easier now that she has something to say.

"It's good," Wren answers. "It's getting a little hectic now that we're getting into crunch time, but I like being busy."

"I like being busy too," June says proudly, grinning up at Wren. Something in my heart softens at the sight.

Wren smiles down at June, her eyes crinkling at the edges. "I hear you have a musical coming up. Are you getting excited?"

The smile melts off June's face, and the sound around the table quiets, everyone freezing. Wren stiffens at the change, and I can practically feel her panic.

"I don't want to do the musical anymore," June says.

Dread and guilt sour in my stomach. It feels like a sucker punch to the gut, and if there was anything I could do to make that sadness lingering in my daughter's eyes disappear, I would move heaven and earth to do it.

Wren glances up at me, and I can see the same look in her eyes, even though she doesn't know the situation.

Clearing my throat, I say, "June was really excited for her mom to come to the musical, but she had to cancel at the last minute."

Mom makes a noise, and I don't have to look to know her jaw is set, angry tears forming in her eyes.

Wren turns to June, gaze soft, and reaches across me to give her hand a squeeze, her arm brushing against my stomach. The sight of June's tiny, tanned hand wrapped in Wren's pale, freckled one makes my heart pinch painfully.

"I'm sorry, June Bug," Wren says. The nickname coming from her does something to me, making my chest constrict further. "I bet you're still going to be the best person on the stage."

"Maybe," June mumbles, her bottom lip stuck out in a pout, fat tears clinging to her lashes.

Wren's hand tightens on June's before she lets go. "I know so. You want to know why?"

June looks up at Wren, eyes wide. "Why?"

"Because you're going to be the only one with someone cheering for you from all the way across the world."

The tension inside of me pops like a balloon at June's smile, a quick, wide thing that feels like watching a shooting star streak across the night sky. Wren smiles too, that one that's been missing all week. Seeing the two of them like this makes me soft and warm all over.

I give Wren a grateful look as she sits back in her seat, returning to her meal. She shrugs like it's no big deal, but it's not to me. To me, it means June might not cry herself to sleep again tonight. To me, it means my little girl might once more be excited about the musical she's been counting down to for weeks. To me, it means June is happy.

And anyone who makes June happy is someone I want around.

"How you feeling, June Bug?" I ask as we turn into the school parking lot. It's already starting to fill up, and the musical doesn't even start for another hour and a half.

June meets my eyes in the rearview mirror, a wide smile on her face. Since family dinner with Wren at Mom's house last weekend, which became much more relaxed after Wren's pep talk to June, my little girl hasn't cried once about Mia not being able to come. She even told Olivia all about how her mom was going to be watching her from all the way in Paris. Mia never confirmed to video call to watch the musical, but I plan to record it for her anyway.

"I'm excited," June says, practically bouncing in her booster seat. Her hair is a mess, and I'm hoping one of the volunteers for the dress rehearsal will be able to convince her to let them deal with it, because I had no luck.

After shutting the engine off, I say, "Good. You're going to be my favorite one up there tonight. I've got a present for you."

June lights up like a Christmas tree. "Really?"

I nod and tell her to hold on before climbing out of the truck and opening her door. She's already got her seat belt off, shimmying in her seat, and I can't help but laugh. Reaching into my pocket, I pull out a beaded bracelet tiny enough to fit on her little wrist. After she went to bed last night, I cracked open her bracelet-making kit and put this one together.

June sounds out the words. "Across the world." Her eyes meet mine, bright in the darkened interior of the cab, only lit up by the golden streetlights in the parking lot.

"You've got people rooting for you all across the world tonight, June Bug," I tell her, hoping she doesn't understand what the catch in my voice means. I don't know how I'll ever thank Wren for the mantra she's given June Bug and me. Realistically, I know Mia probably doesn't even remember what's going on with her daughter tonight, but June doesn't need to know that. All she needs to know right now is that she's got people all across the world who love her.

I slip the bracelet onto her wrist, moving it around with my fingers so I can trace the letters once more.

June throws her arms around my neck, holding me tight. "Thanks, Daddy."

I squeeze her back, inhaling the watermelon scent of her shampoo. "You're welcome, June Bug. Now, let's get you inside."

After dropping June off with the other tiny thespians, I make my way across town to pick up Mom and Finley. After seeing the state of the parking lot, I'm glad we planned to do it this way. Trying to find three parking spots there would have been a nightmare. When I pass the turnoff to head toward Misty Grove, I can't help but think of Wren. I hope that all is going well at the Galentine's Auction. I've barely seen her all week, spending most of the afternoons at the cabin working alone since she had a million last-minute tasks to accomplish. I haven't wanted to admit it to myself, but there's an ache in my chest. I can't deny that I *miss* her. Despite how crazy she drives me, I miss the sound of her voice, the cadence of her laugh when she's gotten under my skin, the way her nose crinkles when she's happy and her eyes squint into slits.

I miss Wren, and I have no idea what to make of that.

When I told her my life was a mess and I didn't have the capacity for more, I wasn't lying. There's a pile of laundry in my living room that's been sitting there for two weeks, and if

Mom hadn't dropped off dinners after June's late rehearsals this week, we wouldn't have had vegetables in days. I've fallen asleep reading the same page from the book on my nightstand every night. My life is hectic and messy, and there's no room for anything else, but I can't deny that I want it.

That I want *her*.

I shake the thought away as I pull into Mom's driveway. I don't need her to see me moon-eyed over Wren or she will never let me live it down, and I'll never know another moment of peace.

Finley and Mom make their way out of the house, bundled in dress coats and thick tights. Despite being the middle of February, the weather has only warmed marginally, and tonight is cold and icy with a freeze warning in effect.

They climb into the truck, and I notice Mom is on the phone, nodding at whatever the other person is saying. "Good to hear, hon. Hope you all have the best time tonight. I'm sorry I can't be there to help out." She nods again. "Okay, bye, Wren. Good luck tonight."

Mom hangs up and turns to give me a wide smile. "That was Wren."

I roll my eyes and back out of the driveway. "You don't say."

Truth be told, I want to ask how she sounded, if she said she was nervous about tonight, but I don't dare ask my *mother*.

"She said everything is going as planned."

I can feel Mom watching me, waiting for a reaction, so I work my best not to give into one. My fingers flex on the steering wheel, though, and tension I didn't realize I was carrying leaches out of me.

"Good," I say, keeping my focus on the road.

Finley pipes up from the back seat. "So what's going on between you two?" Her face is illuminated by her phone screen, and she doesn't bother looking up. I'm glad, because I don't know if I could handle her scrutiny as well as Mom's.

"Nothing," I say, but the answer feels wrong somehow. "We're just friends."

If you would have told me six months ago, or even six weeks, that I would be friends with Wren Daniels, I wouldn't have believed it. But she isn't who I thought she was. She's unexpected in all the best and most surprising of ways. She certainly takes up more real estate in my mind than I care to admit.

"I don't know," Finley says as I turn onto the highway, hoping to avoid some of the traffic in town heading to the school and auction. "There was a vibe between you two."

"What is that supposed to mean?" I ask.

"It means that this whole *friends* thing smells like bull—"

"Finley," Mom cuts her off. Then she turns to me. "But I agree."

I slow to a stop behind a line of cars on the four-lane highway, the red glow of taillights disappearing around the bend in the road. "There's nothing going on between us," I say, but I can't help but remember the way she felt against me in the hallway at Matty's, how she looked in my living room, disinfecting my couch after June got sick, how tender she was dealing with June's sadness, how I lie awake at night replaying all these moments over and over again until sleep drags me under. Wren certainly doesn't feel like a friend.

"But—" Finley says.

"Can we just drop it?"

Mom and Finley let out identical annoyed huffs of air, but they don't press it, so I turn on the radio, which is still playing holiday tunes two months later. I'd change it if it wasn't the best of the three stations we get out here in the middle of the mountains. I can't tell you how many times I've listened to the radio preacher when the music station decided to play reggae.

"What is going on?" I ask, leaning forward to try to catch a glimpse around the curve in the road, but it's useless, shrouded by mountains and trees. Anxiety starts to curl in my gut as I glance at the glowing clock numbers. The show starts in less than an hour, and we still have to park and find seats.

The car in front of me switches into park, and it only heightens my anxiety as I watch the numbers on the clock move higher and higher, the minutes until the show ticking away. Finley and Mom are chatting nervously, but I barely hear them. All

I can think about is June looking out into the crowd and not seeing me.

Up ahead, a police officer is making his way down the line of cars, stopping to talk for a moment with each one. The closer he gets, the more the feeling of dread spreads through me until I'm cold all over.

I roll down my window as the officer nears, hoping I'm wrong.

"Evening, sir," the officer says. "A tractor trailer carrying oil overturned up ahead. It blocked off the lanes on both sides of the highway and spilled oil everywhere, so it's probably going to be a while before anyone can get moving. Do you have plenty of gas? It's a cold one tonight."

I nod numbly, my mind already racing.

"Thank you, sir," Mom murmurs from beside me, but I barely hear her.

The window hums as it rolls up, and I think through my options. June is on the other side of town, blocked off from me, Mom, and Finley.

"Grey," I say aloud, reaching for my phone. "He's on the other side of town, at Misty Grove. I need to call Grey."

Sixteen

- WREN -

I ALWAYS GET JITTERY the day of an event, and this one is no exception. So far, everything has gone according to plan, which is practically unheard of when it comes to event planning. All my volunteers, Jodi excluded, arrived on time, the caterers have been cooking in the event barn's kitchen, and Finley dropped off the floral arrangements a few hours ago. The barn looks like a magical dream. Twinkle lights hang from the rafters and look like stars peppering the night sky. Tiny candles float in votives, giving the room a warm, golden glow, and the columns are draped in swaths of tulle.

In less than twenty minutes, the bachelors will come out for the meet and greet with the auction attendees. The first of the guests have arrived, filling the barn with the cadence of voices over the soft music the band is playing in the background.

In short, it's perfect.

That is, until I see Grey. The look on his face tells me something is very, very wrong. My first thought goes to June and Holden, and dread sinks like a weight in my stomach, buckling my knees.

"What's wrong?" I ask the second he's near enough, trying to keep my voice down so I don't alarm the attendees filtering in through the barn doors.

"Holden just called me," he says.

I'm shocked at how calm and steady his voice sounds when my heart is pounding in my chest.

Worry creases the lines beside his eyes, but he keeps his composure as he explains. "There's an accident blocking the highway, and Holden, Jodi, and Finley can't get to June's school for the musical. He was calling to see if I could go."

The words settle on me, and now that I know everyone is safe, I can clearly think through all my options. Grey's face is plastered on a poster on the other side of the room and in the event programs, along with the rest of the bachelors. I've already heard talk around town of him being a hot commodity. He's sure to bring in a lot of money for the fundraiser. But on the other hand, June can't be left alone. I can still clearly picture the tears in her eyes at the dinner table last week, the way my heart shattered in my chest at the sight of it.

"I'll go." The words spring out of me before I've even fully come to the conclusion in my head. "You have to stay here for the auction, but my volunteers can take over." I meet his eyes, my voice more steady now. "I'll go."

Grey watches me for a long moment, and I get the feeling I've just passed a test I didn't even know I was taking. His expression softens. "Yeah, you should go. I'll tell Holden."

I'm nodding, thinking through everything I need to get done before he's even finished speaking. I need to find Stevie. She can take over, and the rest of the volunteers have been doing this for years. They know what they're doing.

When I turn around, Stevie is already there. "You need me to take over?"

"Please," I answer. "I wouldn't go, but it's..."

A soft smile touches her lips. "I know. I can handle it."

With that, I head for the doors, checking the clock on my phone. I only have fifteen minutes to get to the school and find a seat before the show starts. I should probably call Holden, let him know I've got it under control, but I don't have time. I'm not going to let June perform for one second without someone in that audience rooting for her.

I make my way to the school in record time, and although parking is a mess, I manage to find a spot at the drugstore across the street. Then I rush inside before the curtains draw. The lights are just going down as I slide into a seat near the back.

I hope June won't search for Holden at the front and notice he's missing.

My phone buzzes in my lap. It's a message from Holden on the app, because for some reason, neither of us has wanted to use each other's numbers.

> **user6872:** Wren, I can't thank you enough.

My eyes fasten on the front as June and the other background performers take the stage. Her smile is wide, and I see no one managed to tame her hair. It's a wild mess of blond curls. It makes me smile, because even in costume, she looks exactly like herself.

I snap a picture and send it to Holden.

> *LikeStrawberryWine:* **Glad to be here!**

Swiping out of the app, I put my phone on Do Not Disturb and open the camera, knowing Holden won't want to miss a thing. My heart is still racing, adrenaline pumping through my veins, but something inside me relaxes as I watch June on the stage, the happy smile never leaving her face. She's something special. Holden didn't have to thank me for coming, because I feel lucky to be here.

By the end of the show, my cheeks hurt from smiling at June's antics on the stage. She may have just been a background performer, but she stole the show. I wish more than anything that Holden could have been here to see it.

As the crowd begins to disperse, I quickly send the video to Holden and then head toward the backstage area to find June. Despite how happy I am to be here, a sinking feeling sits heavy in my gut as I think about having to tell her that Holden isn't. I'm scared she'll fall apart like she did at the dinner table, and I don't know if I can handle that.

I find June as she's exiting backstage with a few other background performers and...Charlotte. Her eyes catch on mine before drifting down to June.

"Holden called," she says when I get close enough, her voice low so June can't hear. "He said you'd be taking June home if he didn't make it in time." I don't miss the way her voice feels full of meaning. For the first time, I want to tell her that the thing between Holden and me isn't real. Or at least, it wasn't, and I'm not so sure now.

"Wren!" June yells, finally noticing me. A lump forms in my throat when her skinny arms band around my knees, almost knocking me over. "Where's Daddy? Did you come with him?"

Bending to my knees to get on her level, I meet her eyes. "June, I'm so sorry, but your daddy got stuck in really bad traffic and couldn't make it."

Confusion and surprise wash over her face. I'm a little amazed at how clearly her childish features show the emotions. "He didn't see me?"

"No," I say, reaching for her hands and giving them a squeeze. "But I recorded the whole thing for him and sent it to him so he could watch it in the car while he's stuck in traffic." I pause, watching her face for any hint of tears, but she's taking the news better than I expected. "He's so sad he couldn't be here."

June watches me for a long moment before asking, "What about Grandma and Aunt Finley?"

My shoulders feel heavier. "They're stuck with your dad too, June. I'm sorry."

"But you got to see me?" she asks, and the words catch me off guard as much as the hope in her voice.

I nod and squeeze her hands three times, just like my mom has always done for me. "Yeah, June Bug. You were amazing."

Her mouth splits in a gap-toothed grin, and she puts her wrist right in my face. "That's because I have people cheering for me all across the world."

I wrap my fingers around the beaded bracelet on her wrist, tracing the letters of the words I told her last week, my throat clogging with emotion.

"Daddy made it for me," June says proudly.

An image of Holden, hair pulled back in a messy bun, firelight dancing across his skin as he hunched over this little bracelet after June went to bed, fills my mind. It's so clear it almost feels as if I were there.

"It's beautiful," I tell her, my lips forming a wobbly smile. Her grin widens, and I give her hands three more gentle squeezes before standing back up to my full height. "Let's get you home, June Bug. I've got a present for you in the car."

Twenty minutes later, after securing a booster seat from Mrs. Heeter, who was here to watch her grandson and told me I was free to borrow it, June and I pull into her driveway. The lights illuminate the front porch, spotlighting the package there. It's probably the replacement light fixture I ordered for the bathroom at the cabin. I had it delivered to Holden's house again, even though he accidentally broke the last one. I probably shouldn't have risked it, but I also wanted to force him to come over and knock on my door.

June has already climbed out by the time I open my door, the extra flower arrangement I stole from the auction clutched in her hands. When we got to the car, I told her every performer deserves flowers, and she beamed brighter than the streetlamps. I don't think anyone has ever looked at me with that much admiration before. It felt heavy and warm and out of breath all at once.

As we climb the stairs, it hits me that I don't have a key to Holden's house. "June, I don't have a key to get in."

"Oh," June says, handing me her flowers. "I know where Daddy hides it."

This feels like information I shouldn't be allowed to know, but my mind is also running with prank ideas I could employ with a key to Holden's house.

June crosses the front porch to the wooden bench, which she shoves aside before I can move to help her. Then she presses her foot into a floorboard that pops up, revealing a golden key that winks under the porch lights.

"June," I say as she hands the key to me. "Your dad tends to go a little overboard."

I have to press my lips together to keep from laughing when she props her fists on her hips and says, "Don't I know it."

Fitting the key into the lock, I push it open and flip on the light switch. The place looks just like the last time I was here, a mixture of clean and chaos, the remnants of both the people who live here stark in contrast. Holden's plain black coffee cup rinsed in the sink. June's sticky pastel purple plate with half a piece of unfinished french toast on the counter. Holden's work boots lined up by the door, June's discarded in a colorful heap beyond the entryway, like she walked straight out of them and kept on going.

It feels intimate being in their space, seeing the evidence of their life. And strangely, there's an ache in the middle of my chest, something that feels like longing, as I look at it. I can almost imagine my plate in the sink next to Holden's coffee cup, my shoes kicked off next to June's.

My phone buzzes in my pocket, and I shake the thought away, reaching for it, expecting a message from Holden. It's a response from Stevie instead, assuring me that everything is going well. When I made it to the school earlier, the auction all but disappeared from my mind. It wasn't until after I'd gotten June buckled into the back seat that I remembered to check in.

I type out a message and then turn to June, who has already discarded her shoes and carried her bouquet into the kitchen.

"We need to put these in water," I tell her, rifling through the cabinets. "Do you have a vase?"

She shrugs, climbing into one of the barstools. "Daddy just puts the flowers Aunt Finley brings him in one of the big jars in that cabinet."

I follow the line of her finger to the cabinet she's pointing to and find a sixty-four ounce wide-mouth canning jar interspersed with others of varying sizes.

"Perfect," I say, carefully pulling it from the cabinet and turning to fill it in the farmhouse sink. Everything about

Holden's house is nicer than mine, although the decor isn't what I would have chosen. That is, except for the sunshine yellow wall in the living room.

Nodding in that direction, I ask, "Did your dad paint the wall that color?"

June turns to look at the living room, noticing the wall I'm referring to, and a grin splits across her face. "Me and Daddy did it together. I wanted it to look like your house."

Her words hit me square in the chest, and surprise spreads through me in increments, leaving no square inch untouched. "My house?"

"Like your yellow wall," June says, as if this should be obvious. "It's my favorite."

"How do you know it's yellow?" I ask, shutting off the tap. I put the flowers in the jar, arranging them until I'm happy with the way they're positioned.

"Oh!" June says, and points to the window above the sink. "You can see into your house through that window. Sometimes Daddy will shake his head while he's washing dishes when he sees you dancing in your living room. But I like your decorations. They're so colorful."

I turn, glancing out the window above the sink, and sure enough, Holden left this information out when he told me about being able to see into my house. I imagine during the day or at night, when my blinds are open, they have a clear shot of all my lonely shenanigans. For some reason, though, the thought doesn't rankle like I expect it to. It almost fills me up, making me warm all over, like laying out in the sunshine on the first warm day of spring, knowing that while I've been all alone in my house and June and Holden have been alone over here, we've had each other in some way, making each other laugh even if we weren't actually together.

Tears prick at the backs of my eyes as I move away from the window, catching sight of the clock on the stove. It's late. Later than I assume June usually stays up. Blinking back the unexpected tears, I say, "How about we get ready for bed?"

June surprises me by not putting up a fight. Instead, she just jumps down from her stool and heads for the hallway. I follow after her, and she leads me into her bedroom. It's an explosion of light green and pastel yellow and blushing pink and soft lavender. It feels like stepping into one of the wildflower meadows at Misty Grove in spring.

"Do you need help with anything?" I ask as she pulls open her drawer, a mess of pajamas stuffed haphazardly inside. My eyes snag on the wild mess of her hair. "Want me to brush your hair for you?"

June's gaze meets mine in the mirror. "No, I don't like brushing my hair."

A smile curves my lips, because I can't count the number of times I said the same thing as a kid. "Not even when you shower or take a bath?"

She shakes her head. "Sometimes, but not usually."

"What stuff does your daddy put in your hair after you shower or take a bath?"

June's nose crinkles. "He doesn't put anything in it."

"Ah," I say, finding the root of the problem. "Well, what would you say if I gave you some stuff to use in the shower and after you get out that will keep your hair from getting so tangled? Could I brush it out for you then?"

Skepticism is written on every smooth line of June's face, but eventually she shrugs. "Okay."

"You go brush your teeth, and I'll run over to my house and get it, okay?" I ask, and June nods, looking a little more excited.

My phone buzzes with another message from Holden as I let myself into my cottage.

> **user6872:** Everything going okay? We're still not moving.

After grabbing the hair products from my bathroom and stuffing them in a plastic grocery bag, I text him back.

> **LikeStrawberryWine:** Everything is great here. June told me about how you can see into my living room. Guess

> **I should stop walking through there naked...**

I send the message before I can think better of it, before I can remember he's sitting in a car with his mom and sister, who are notorious for trying to set him up, but I can't bring myself to care. Really, I just hope it will make his lips twitch in that little half smile, the one I see in my dreams when I'm tangled up in my bedsheets, praying I don't wake up just yet.

> **user6872: Wouldn't that be a shame.**

I smile to myself as I make my way back over to Holden's, plastic bag of hair products in hand. When I open the front door, June is standing on a barstool that she must have dragged across the kitchen, trying to reach into one of the upper cabinets. She stares at me, eyes wide, before her mouth splits in a mischievous grin.

"What are you doing, June Bug?" I ask, closing the door behind me. From here, I can see the neon orange jack-o'-lantern bucket inside the cabinet, presumably full of old Halloween candy.

"Daddy lets me have candy before bed," she says sweetly, her little hand inching closer to the bucket.

I nod, humming in the back of my throat, pressing my lips together to keep from smiling. "Is that why you waited until I left to get some?"

"I didn't think you'd be able to reach it."

Kicking my shoes off, I make my way into the kitchen and easily slide the plastic bucket from the cabinet, peeking inside. Sure enough, it's full of candy. I pluck one of the pieces out and hand it to her. "Our secret."

Her smile widens, and she looks incandescent, like a beam of sunshine breaking through the curtains on a lazy Saturday morning. "Thanks, Wren."

"Now, let me show you what I brought for your hair."

The plastic bag crinkles as I set it on the counter, opening it to reveal a myriad of curly hair care products that I've painstakingly curated over the years through trial and error. There's shampoo and conditioner, mousse and curl cream, a lightweight gel and a detangling spray, a wide-tooth comb and a specific type of brush that makes brushing through the tangles almost painless. It's my Holy Grail.

June watches me pull out the products with wide, curious eyes, munching on her mini chocolate bar.

"First things first," I tell her. "We're not going to go near your hair with a brush until after you wash it."

"Really?" June asks, looking surprised.

I have to hold back my cringe. Of course Holden wouldn't have known that curly hair breaks when dry brushing, but I hate that because of that, June has a phobia of brushing it.

I nod. "You're going to wash it with this first. Just a little bit in your hand," I say, pointing to the shampoo, and then demonstrating how much product she should use. "Then you're going to use this stuff and let it sit in your hair for a little bit while you wash your body. Then you can rinse it out."

Her forehead crinkles in concentration as she listens to my instructions.

"If you forget one, it's okay. The important part comes when you get out and I put all this stuff in there," I say, pointing to the array of products spread out on the counter.

"Okay," June says, and I motion down the hall.

"How about you go get your pajamas, and I'll put these in the bathroom for you?"

June leads me down the hall to the bathroom, and I flip on the light switch as she goes to her room for pajamas. This bathroom is all June—shades of lavender and yellow and light green. My heart squeezes in my chest when I see handwritten notes taped to the mirror in what I assume is Holden's handwriting.

One is curling at the edges, like it's been here the longest, holding up under the steam of many showers. It says, *You are loved, June Bug.* Another newer one, taped with pink tape, says, *Across the world.*

My throat clogs with emotion at the evidence of a man who loves his daughter more than anything else in this world.

Although I understood where he was coming from when he said he wasn't in a place to date before, I can see even more clearly now what he meant. June is everything to him.

June slides to a stop in her socked feet right outside the door, flannel pajamas in hand. "I'm ready," she says, out of breath, like she was racing to see how quickly she could follow my instructions. It brings a smile to my face.

"This one first," I say, raising the shampoo again and then the conditioner. "And then this one."

She nods eagerly, and then that lump is back in my throat when she throws her arms around my thighs, dropping her pajamas in the process. I smooth my hands down the untamed mess of her curls, something sparking and warming in my chest.

"Thanks, Wren," she says and lets go. "Be out in a minute."

I step back, leaning against the opposite wall as she closes the door, my heart feeling tender and fragile in my chest, like she's holding it in the palm of her hand. I think I understand Holden a little better for it. If I feel this raw after one hug from her, I can't imagine how he must feel just looking at her, a piece of himself out in this big, scary world.

The shower kicks on, and I push off the wall, planning to return to the living room and wait for June to finish, but then an open door at the end of the hallway catches my eye. It's not the room June went in, so unless it's the guest room, there's only one other option, and my curiosity wins out.

Holden's room is exactly what I would have expected after getting to know him these last few months. Though it's nothing like what I would have guessed before that. I would have thought it would be cold and impersonal, modern with minimal touches and probably navy sheets.

Instead, it's warm and inviting, all dark wood and soft, luxurious bedding. His massive bed takes up most of the space, and while there's a nightstand on one side, a stack of books piled atop it, there's a chair where the other one should be, a matching deep, leather armchair to the one in the living room, and if that isn't a sure enough sign that he's had no intentions of bringing someone into his life and space, I don't know what is. Maybe that should make me sad, but really, there's a soft tenderness seeping through me, a thankfulness that he would let me in even just the bit he has.

The shower cuts off, and I startle, unaware of how much time I've been standing here, lost in my thoughts. I flip off the light switch and head for the kitchen, waiting for June to finish up. My eyes catch on the bar cart in the corner, and a smile touches my lips as I imagine Holden crafting a cocktail after June goes to sleep, waiting on my nightly messages on the app. I wonder if he ever noticed that they started coming earlier and earlier in the evening, that I would come home early from parties or dinners at my parents' house so I could snuggle on my couch and send a message to my anonymous friend.

June comes out of the bathroom a few minutes later, her hair dripping onto the soft fabric at her back. When her hair is wet, it's even longer than I could tell before, hanging down to the small of her back.

The excitement has waned from her face, replaced with a wary skepticism.

"I promise I won't hurt your head," I tell her when her eyes meet mine.

She sighs, a sound much too old for her six years. "Okay."

Motioning to the couch, I take my bag of products with me, the plastic rustling. "You sit on the ottoman, and I'll sit behind you on the couch."

When we're in our respective spots, I ask, "You want to watch a movie while I do this?" The distraction of the TV always helped me when my mom had to tackle my hair as a kid.

June nods eagerly, reaching for the remote, and I set to work, applying the detangler to her hair first. We're both quiet as I go through my hair care steps, not even pausing to think since it's become second nature to me. I take extra care on detangling, working through the tiny knots that have formed and trying to stay in tune to any flinches or tension she may have.

But surprisingly, June gets wrapped up in the cartoon movie on the screen, and I do too. Before I know it, I've finished with the entire process, and her hair is tangle-free, so I set to work braiding it into two french braids to hopefully keep it from getting tangled again while she sleeps. It's a trick my mom discovered when I was around June's age. I was unable to keep still even when I was sleeping, and all her hard work detangling would be ruined again by morning.

"All done," I say, and June spins around, surprised.

"Really?"

I tug on one of her braids. "Yeah, Bug. These will keep it from getting all tangled again while you sleep."

Her fingers touch the braid, and a smile breaks across her face. "That wasn't so bad."

I can't help the laugh that rumbles out of me. "Well, good. I'm glad. I'll let your daddy keep all this stuff to use on you, and I'll get some more for myself."

Her nose wrinkles. "Can you come show him how to do it?"

"Sure," I say, the smile still playing on my lips. It falls when she climbs off the ottoman and into my lap, snuggling against me. I let my hand trail down the smooth expanse of her arm, breathing in her little girl scent mixed with the smell of my hair products. She's so warm and soft and trusting, and I feel that responsibility like an aching weight in my chest.

My arm tightens around her, and she settles more fully against me. "Thank you, Wren."

"Anytime, June Bug."

Seventeen
- HOLDEN -

I think I'm going to die in this truck. We've been stuck here for five hours, the highway shut down on both sides, unable to move. That alone would be frustrating, but being trapped in a car with my mom and sister, knowing I just missed out on my little girl's first performance, is making my skin itch.

Up ahead, the stark red glow of brake lights pierces the darkness, and adrenaline surges through me. My hands tighten on the wheel until my knuckles turn white in the dim interior of the truck.

"Oh, we're moving!" Mom says, interrupting her monologue on...something. If I'm being honest, I tuned her and Finley out hours ago, instead focusing on the anxiety and nausea roiling in my gut.

I shift the truck into gear, feeling antsier than I have all night. Wren has been texting me updates all evening, keeping me apprised of what she and June are up to, and with every single one, I want to be home more.

I can't believe Wren dropped everything. I can't believe she left her event to show up for June. She owes June and me nothing, but she did it without question.

It makes me want to get home to her just as much as June. I don't know what to say or how to thank her, but I need to see her, to clear this lump in my throat enough to try to express my gratitude.

Tonight, Wren Daniels has been better to us than Mia ever has.

That's the only thought running through my head as I drop my mom and Finley off at Mom's house and turn around to make the drive home. Wren's house is dark, only visible when my headlights slice across it, but my house is lit, warm, golden light seeping through the gaps in the blinds, the porch light casting shadows across the yard. Something in my chest tugs at the sight.

Cold whips at me, but there's a warm buzzing beneath my skin as I climb out of the car, my boots clomping on the cracked walkway leading to the house. For the first time since getting stuck in traffic tonight, the anxiety and the frustration melt away, replaced with an emotion I can't quite name.

My hands shake as I fit the key into the lock and let myself in. The TV plays softly in the living room, but my eyes catch on the shoes in the entry, Wren's boots kicked off next to June's. I expect Wren to sit up on the couch or June to bound for me, but it's quiet except for the TV, and as I make my way into the living room, I see why.

June is stretched out on the couch, her matching flannel pajamas twisted around her body, her head resting in Wren's lap, mouth ajar as she sleeps. Wren is curled protectively toward her, one of her hands curved around June's shoulder like she fell asleep smoothing it up and down her arm. June's hair is tied back in neat braids that Wren must have used some kind of magic to talk her into.

Everything inside me softens as I watch them, my feet rooted to the floor. There's a lump in my throat, thick and heavy, and an ache in my chest so strong that I have to press my palm there to try to ease it.

I must make a sound, because Wren's eyes flutter open, catching on me staring at her. They're soft from sleep, and her lips curve in the barest of smiles. I can picture her waking up next to me on a lazy Saturday morning, her skin drenched in morning sunlight, giving me that same smile as I tug her close.

Suddenly, that's what I want to do more than anything. It's a need so visceral that my body aches with it. With the need to touch her. With the need to feel her. With the need to thank her for showing up when she didn't have to. With the need to tell her how important she's become to me without my permission. With the need for *her*, in any way I can have her.

June stirs in Wren's lap at the movement, her own eyes fluttering open, and Wren's hand smooths down her arm just like I imagined it doing earlier. The movement wrecks me even further because it looks so natural, so instinctual, and that single movement feels like a piece I didn't even know was missing clicking into the puzzle.

"Daddy," June says, her sleepy eyes clearing as she notices me. She sits up, and I'm moving to her, scooping her up, and holding on tight.

"I'm so sorry I wasn't there, June Bug," I say into her neck, breathing in the scent of her. It's different this time. There's no watermelon shampoo. Instead, she smells faintly like Wren.

Her little arms wrap so tightly around my neck that I can hardly breathe, but I don't loosen my grip. "It's okay, Daddy."

"Wren sent me a video. Maybe we can watch it together in the morning?"

Her braids scrape against my beard as she nods.

Finally, I let my eyes move up to Wren's. They're soft, filled with a tenderness I haven't seen before, and it makes that ache in my chest grow stronger.

I mouth, "Thank you," and her lips curve in a small smile, her dimples barely indenting.

June yawns and nuzzles into my chest, her arms starting to slacken, and I smooth a hand over her back. "You ready for bed, June Bug?"

She doesn't answer, and I turn my head to press a kiss to her cheek, breathing in this new scent of her mixing with the old one.

"I'm going to put her down," I say to Wren. "Wait for me?"

Surprise colors her features, but her smile deepens, like she's pleased, and the ache in my chest travels lower. She's so beautiful it hurts, all mussed hair and sleepy eyes, wrinkled dress and stockinged legs. The memory of my fingers gripping her thighs until I broke through her last pair of tights flashes through my mind, and I want to do it again and again until she doesn't have any left.

Turning on my heel to stop the direction of my thoughts, I make my way down the darkened hall to June's room. I could make this trek blindfolded with her in my arms. It happens so often that it's muscle memory. But I've always returned to the living room alone. There's never been anyone waiting for me. No one I wanted to get back out to.

June's arms tighten around my neck as I lay her down, a soft squeeze of a hug that feels like a squeeze around my heart as well. I don't know how I'll ever deserve this sweet little girl, how she's mine.

I press a kiss to her forehead, tugging up the blankets around her chin, and she snuggles into them. Silently, I back out of her room, watching the way the moonlight casts shadows over her skin, the braids in her hair.

The door shuts with a soft click, quiet enough to keep from waking June, and my attention shifts to the woman in my living room, a tug in my stomach pulling me toward her.

I find Wren in the kitchen, rinsing a mug in the sink. Her eyes meet mine and hold, a pretty blush staining her cheeks. She looks so *right* here in my kitchen, and I have the overwhelming urge to ask her to stay. To be here when June and I wake up for Saturday morning pancakes. To back me up when June asks for chocolate chips *and* whipped cream *and* syrup. To steal a kiss when June isn't looking. To keep driving me nuts with those tights and that smile and the way she pulls laughter from me, even when life feels hard.

Maybe I should ask. Maybe I should thank her. Maybe I should *think*. But I don't. I've spent so much time thinking, and it's gotten me nowhere.

Not when right where I want to be is with *her*.

So I don't ask. I don't speak. I don't think. I just move across the kitchen, closing the distance between us, and claim her mouth with mine.

If she's surprised, she doesn't act like it. She responds immediately, her arms coming around my neck, her nails scraping against my scalp, her lips slanting over mine.

She tastes like hot chocolate and feels like every dream I've had over the last month. She's soft everywhere I'm hard, and my hands find that perfect spot on her hips, fingers digging in.

Wren breaks away, her breath coming in heaving gasps that make the hairs around my face billow. Her eyes are saucers, holding mine. "What are we doing?"

My hands tighten on her hips, and one corner of my mouth quirks. "If that's not obvious, then I need to work on my technique."

There's a beard burn on her jaw, a redness I want to trace with the pads of my fingers. I can see every freckle standing out starkly against the creamy whiteness of her skin. She looks wild, like always, and for the first time in a very long time, I want to let go and be as reckless and uninhibited as she looks.

Her hand moves from my nape, sliding across the bare skin at my collar, and it prickles beneath her touch. "I guess I mean *why* are you kissing me?"

She doesn't meet my eyes when she asks, and her hands don't stop moving, playing with one of the buttons at the hollow of my throat.

I feel her touch everywhere. The actual spot where her hands brush against skin, but also in the pit of my stomach, the backs of my knees, the top of my scalp. I feel *her* everywhere, in all the ways I was never sure I would feel someone again.

Which is maybe why the words come so clearly to me. "Because you make me want to kiss someone again. You made me trust you enough to want to kiss you. You made me feel safe enough to...try with you."

Her eyes soften, her body melting into me. "Oh."

It feels like a reversal, me speaking this much and her giving me a one-word answer. It makes my lips tug up in a smile.

"Oh?"

Her smile transforms her face, a ray of sunshine breaking through the clouds. "Yes, oh."

I lean in, unable to breathe with the space between us, my lips dragging across the slope of her neck, not quite a kiss, just a brush of my mouth trailing up to her ear. "If that's the only thing you're going to say," I whisper, my voice a harsh rasp. "Then I'm going to give you something to say *oh* about."

She clears her throat, another soft "Oh" falling from her lips.

With that, I slide my hands down the curve of her hips, curling under her thighs and lifting, until she lands on the counter, her thighs bracketing my waist.

I press a kiss against the shell of her ear, and she shivers, a full body shudder that I feel in every place we touch. It's electric, a pounding beneath my skin. I think I could feel her against me every day for the rest of my life and never get enough of it.

Of her. Her soft, sweet scent. Her enticing, unruly strawberry curls. The thousands of freckles I want to trace like constellations in the sky. The lips that drive me mad in so many ways.

I want all of her, and this is just the first taste.

When my teeth scrape against her neck, she lets out another "oh," urging me on, and my hands tighten on her hips, pulling her closer.

"Thank you," I say into her skin, and she scrapes her nails against my beard.

"For what?"

I sigh into the hollow of her throat. "For tonight. For showing up for June. You didn't have to do that."

She backs up, moving away until she's no longer a peachy blur, until I can see every curve and freckle and blue hue of her eye with complete clarity. "I wanted to, Holden. You don't need to thank me."

There's a lump in my throat, cutting off my words, because I can see she means it. I'll never understand why we were too much for Mia yet just the right amount for Wren. It will never make sense to me that Mia couldn't make it work but Wren stepped in so effortlessly. I won't get it. But I'm so thankful for it.

Suddenly, not kissing her feels like torture, like holding my breath underwater for too long until everything in my body is screaming at me to go back to the surface, to get air. Wren is like that for me. She's the thing I've deprived myself of until everything inside me is rebelling at the distance between us.

I don't wait any longer to press my lips to hers, to give into what I want more than anything. And Wren doesn't hesitate to give it right back. We meet each other move for move, as if this isn't only the second time we've done this, as if we've been doing this forever. She feels like pancakes on Saturday morning and family dinner on Saturday night and late-night movies on the couch, like all the familiar, comforting things in my life wrapped in one. Yet also wholly new. And I want to find out every single thing—what makes her gasp, what makes her throw her head back, what makes her shiver against me—until she's no longer a mystery, until she's as permanent and imprinted on me as the tattoos on my skin.

I slide my tongue along the seam of her lips, taking advantage when she gasps against my mouth. When her hands find my hair, tugging until the hair tie falls out somewhere around my feet, my hands tighten on her hips, pulling her closer to the edge until there's no space left between us.

Wren makes a noise in the back of her throat, one that's going to haunt every single one of my dreams for the rest of my life, taunting me, and I pull back, resting my forehead against her, trying to quell my desire. She's so responsive, her mouth following mine as I back away. It almost snaps my control, seeing her so mussed and undone like this, her dress bunched up around her hips, her hair messy and untamed.

"You look stunning." The words slip out of my mouth, unfiltered, but I can't bring myself to regret speaking without thinking when that breathtaking blush steals into her cheeks again.

"You look," she says, and then pauses, catching her bottom lip between her teeth.

I reach up, tugging it free. Her jaw is red from my beard, her lips bee-stung, and I can't help the surge of masculine pride that sings through my veins.

"I look what, Red?"

Blue eyes meet mine, startling in their intensity. "You look like how I've always wanted to see you," she says.

I squeeze her hips. "What's that mean?"

She trails her finger along the inside of my arm, starting at the wrist and moving her way up. We both watch the progress until she smooths over the curve of my shoulder, slipping her hand behind my neck. Her skin is warm against mine, and so, so soft. I want to know if she's this soft all over, if she's got freckles everywhere.

"Undone," she says simply, holding my gaze. The word sends another jolt through me, desire so strong I feel weak in the knees. It's been too long since I've touched a woman, but

I'm glad I waited for her, that it's her body beneath my hands, that it's her lips I can still taste against my own.

Maybe that's what makes me extend the offer so easily. Because it feels right to trust her with another part of my life when she's proven to be safe enough to have this piece.

Eyes never leaving hers, I say, "Come to breakfast tomorrow. June and I always make pancakes on Saturdays."

Her brows arch high on her forehead, and I know she understands how important this is, how big of a step this is for me.

"Are you sure?"

I should be nervous. I should feel worried about letting someone into June's life. I should be afraid of getting my heart broken again.

But not with Wren.

"I'm sure, Red. Have breakfast with us."

Eighteen
- WREN -

"He wants me to come to breakfast."

"Is that a euphemism?" Rae asks, her voice sleepy, as though I woke her up with my call. Glancing at the clock on my bedside table, I realize that with the hour time difference between us, I probably did. She's lucky I didn't call the minute I woke up. I barely slept all night, my mind playing all the details of yesterday evening in great detail.

I sigh. "No, it's not a euphemism. He actually invited me over to breakfast. With June."

"Why would he do that?" Rae asks, sounding a little more alert now.

I flop back against my pillow, saying the one thing that I haven't been able to stop thinking about since the moment it happened. "He kissed me. Like really, really kissed me."

"Do tell," Rae says, definitely more awake and interested now.

"Yes, please do," Leland yells in the background, sounding half-asleep and irritated at the wake-up call.

It makes a smile twist up the corners of my lips. I spend the next few minutes recalling the events of last night, pausing to answer Rae's questions, and, halfway through, Leland's as well. Despite his grumbling, he's as invested now as she is, just like I knew he would be.

"So you mean to tell me he pinned you against the counter and kissed you?" Rae asks.

I hum in the back of my throat, remembering how it felt to have him against me, his lips slanting over mine. I thought maybe our kiss in the hallway at Matty's was a fluke, driven by heightened emotions and an intense awareness of each other, combined with the risk of someone finding us. But last night, we were alone, just us. There was no one to perform for. And we still fit together like we were made for each other. Like finally finding the key that fits into a door that's been locked for too long.

It ruined me for anyone else, and I've spent all night terrified he'll tell me it was a mistake again.

"Yeah," I respond a little breathlessly. "That's exactly what he did."

"Wow," Rae sighs.

I nod, even though she can't see me. "Yeah."

"How was your evening with June?" she asks, and I'm a little surprised by the change in direction.

Despite my surprise, I smile, sinking further into the cushions as I remember her little body curling up against mine, the way she snuggled into me, so full of trust. I've never had someone rely on me and have such easy faith in me before. It was scary, having all that directed at me, when I felt so undeserving. But it also made me ache with a mix of pride and longing. Something entirely unfamiliar yet also exactly right.

"She's amazing, Rae. You'd love her. She's sweet and sassy and just so fully herself, you know?"

I can almost hear the smile in Rae's voice. "Sounds like you when you were little."

Holden has made similar comments the past few weeks, though not in such a direct way. It's been more like a comment about my sweet tooth or the way I pester him. It feels like honey in my chest when Rae says it, though. Like a secret, hidden desire I wasn't even aware I had.

"She's something special," I say, and I mean it. Glancing at the clock once more, I see I need to get up and shower so I can make it to breakfast. "Rae, I've got to go."

"Call us and give us all the details," Leland shouts, and my lips tip up in a smile. I'm really thankful my sister married someone as good as him.

"I will," I promise and end the call, staring up at my ceiling once more, the events of last night playing through my head again.

I can still taste Holden's lips, smell that woodsy, earthy scent that's so specific to him. I wanted to sneak into his bathroom last night and see if it was a body wash or if he just smells like that because of his job. I can still feel June's hair slipping through my fingers as I braided it, hear her breaths even out as she fell asleep against me.

Last night seems like a dream, the kind that opens your heart up to an ache that wasn't there before, an unknown desire. Even though it was all so new, it felt familiar, easy in a way I wouldn't have expected. Getting June ready for bed, being woken up by Holden, being wrapped up in his arms when we were finally alone.

I've known for a long time that I want *someone*, a partner. I just didn't expect him to come with someone else. Holden and June are already a family, but last night felt like I fit seamlessly into it. I don't know if today will be the same, but suddenly, I want it more than anything. I want to fit.

My hands shake as I prepare to knock on Holden's front door. I don't know what to expect from him, how he'll react to me in the light of day. How I'm supposed to act around June. I know he's so protective of her, and I don't know if he feels entirely comfortable letting me into his life with her.

The door swings open before I have a chance to knock, and a head of blond curls comes barreling out toward me, smacking into my legs. Tiny arms grip my thighs in a vise-like grip.

When I look down, June is smiling up at me, her front two teeth missing. "Good morning, Wren."

And just like that, my reservations die, replaced by a spreading warmth that blocks out the morning chill. Bending down, I scoop her up, and she moves her arms around my neck instead. She smells like my shampoo, and I notice her curls today are significantly more tamed from the overnight braids.

"Good morning to you too, June Bug."

"Daddy said we can have chocolate chips in our pancakes," she says, and a smile pulls at my mouth.

Setting her down, I ruffle her hair. "Can't wait."

June's little hand wraps around mine, tugging me toward the kitchen, and my heart hammers as she pulls me closer to Holden. I don't know how he's going to react after last night, if he's going to regret it again, or if he's going to give me one of those smiles that I feel in the tips of my toes and the pit of my stomach.

My eyes snag on Holden's immediately, like there's a tether between us, drawing us together. The anxiety roiling inside me disappears the moment I see that half smile, the one that makes his beard twitch. It's almost invisible, but I know how to look for it now. I wonder how many times I missed it before, when I thought he was scowling or angry at my antics. I wonder if it was there, if he found me as interesting as I've always found him.

"Morning, Red," he says, and it's like he whispered it straight into my ear. I can feel it *everywhere*. A hot blush races across my skin, stealing up into my cheeks, and I can see the moment he notices by the way his eyes heat and how his smile grows into something bigger and fuller than I've seen before.

"Ready for pancakes?" he asks.

June tugs on my hand, snapping me out of the trance I've fallen into in Holden's warm hazel eyes. "With chocolate chips, just like you promised."

Holden looks down at his daughter, his expression going soft and tender. "With chocolate chips."

I've never noticed how expressive his face is if you know how to look for it. He's always seemed distant and aloof to me, and I marvel at the way I'm able to read him now after such a short amount of time.

"I'm making something for you," June says, pulling my attention back to her.

Something warm seeps through me at the statement. "For me?"

June nods eagerly and gives my hand another tug toward the counter. She climbs up into one of the barstools, and I sit in the one beside her, eyes fastening on the clear box of beads on the countertop.

"It's a bracelet," she says, lifting up a piece of clear, stretchy string, threaded with colorful beads. Blue eyes fix on mine, bright as the early morning sunshine streaming through the windows. "Can you tell me how to spell your name?"

When I glance at Holden, he's watching us, that same soft expression playing on his features. Turning back to June, a smile on my lips, I say, "Of course. *W* is the first letter."

Her little fingers begin digging through the section of letter beads, and I let my eyes trail to Holden, where he's pouring pancake batter into a skillet on the stove. It's been months since I've seen him without a flannel, and I've never really noticed the thick cords of muscle in his arms, the way they flex and move when he's doing something as simple as flipping a pancake. Every single one of his movements is sure and precise. I can't help but admire that about him. Everything I do is rushed and disorganized, but he moves in a way that feels efficient and deliberate. I wonder what it would feel like to have all that intensity focused on me for longer than a handful of moments.

Just the thought sends a shiver up my spine, warmth pooling in the space behind my belly button.

"What comes next?" June asks, finished with threading the *W* onto the string.

I turn my attention to her. "*R*."

Holden finishes making a stack of pancakes and scrambles eggs while I spell out my name for June and watch as she puts the final beads on my bracelet. She catches her bottom lip between her teeth as she focuses on tying it off, just like I've noticed Holden does when he's focusing at the cabin. They're so different, their looks and mannerisms, but I like that I can see this similarity in them, and I want to discover more.

"Table, June Bug," Holden says, nodding in the direction of the scarred oak table in the dining nook.

I hold my wrist out, my heart squeezing as she slips the bracelet onto it.

"Does it fit?" she asks, looking up at me with wide, concerned eyes.

Truthfully, it's a little big, and I'll have to remove some of the beads and make it tighter when I get home so it doesn't fall off, but I give her a broad grin. "It's perfect, June Bug."

I'd do almost anything to receive the smile she gives me in return, the kind you feel like a kick in the stomach, so good it hurts.

My nerves come back as we sit around the table, and I remember that Holden invited me into a family tradition. I don't know this for certain, but I have a pretty good idea that he's never done this before.

"Whipped cream or syrup, June Bug?" Holden asks.

"Both."

Holden narrows his eyes in her direction, holding her gaze until she sighs, as if this is a regular argument between the two of them. I have to press my lips together to keep from smiling when she finally relents and chooses syrup.

Turning to me, Holden asks, "Whipped cream or syrup?"

I let loose the grin. "Both."

Beside me, June giggles, bright and loud, and I want to bottle the sound up and keep it for bad days. Holden's knee finds mine beneath the table, pressing against me until my focus narrows down to that one point of contact.

"Syrup," I finally say, hoping neither of them notices that I sound a little more breathless than before.

I expect Holden to move his knee away when he slides the syrup in my direction, but he keeps it there, pressed up against mine, as we eat our breakfast, June and I munching on stacks of chocolate chip pancakes and a small helping of eggs, Holden choosing eggs and no pancakes.

It feels remarkably easy, like a seamless fit, at least for me, and every bit of me wants to know what's going on in Holden's head. He's stoic, although I catch that twist of his lips beneath his beard, see the sparkle in his eyes as he watches me with June. But he keeps his knee against mine, and when he finishes his breakfast and pushes his plate away, his hand wraps around my knee, warm and big and making every nerve in my body come to life.

"Can I go outside?" June asks the second she finishes her pancakes. I have a feeling it's not the first time she's asked this morning.

Holden nods in the direction of her room. "Socks, shoes, and coat."

Her chair squeaks against the wood floor as she bounds out of it, scrambling down the hall to her room. The second she's out of eyesight, Holden releases my knee. I'm momentarily distraught at the loss of contact, but then his hand finds mine on top of the table.

Goose bumps prick along my skin as his calloused fingers smooth over the inside of my wrist, spinning the bracelet around until the letters are on the inside, resting against my pulse point.

"She was really sweet to make this for me," I tell Holden, that tender feeling swelling inside me as I remember the way she focused so intently on it. I don't know how I've earned her attention or admiration, but I'm grateful for it, nonetheless.

Holden's eyes meet mine, sending a bolt of fire down my spine. "She likes you," he says. I don't miss the huskiness of his voice, the way he sounds a little surprised but not unhappy about this development.

I nod, trying to focus on his words and the look in his eyes rather than the feeling of his skin on mine. "I like her," I say simply.

June comes bounding down the hall once more, and Holden pulls his hand away slowly, almost as if he doesn't want to let go.

"I'm ready," she yells in the way all kids are unable to speak at a regular volume.

Holden lets out an aggrieved sigh that I know isn't real because of the twitch of his beard. It really makes me wonder how often that same sigh he's given me hasn't been genuine, how often he was smiling at me when I didn't know it.

I know something now—I want all his hidden smiles.

"Put your plate in the sink, June Bug," Holden says, pushing up from his seat with his own plate. He snags mine before I can get it, and my heart stutters when he winks. "Guests don't have to clean, at least not the first time."

I want to ask if this means I'll be invited back next Saturday. I should probably be alarmed at how desperately I want that after such a short amount of time. It can't be healthy how attached I'm growing after two kisses with Holden and one night hanging out with June. But I can't bring myself to care.

Maybe I'll make a fool out of myself and beg to be a part of their lives. It feels worth it.

The clatter of dishes dropping into the sink pulls me out of my thoughts, and I push up from the table, following Holden and June to the back door. I didn't bring a jacket, and when Holden realizes this, he pulls one of his off the hook beside the door and drapes it over my shoulders. It's huge and deliciously warm and smells so much like him that I have to tell myself not to snuggle inside and sniff deeply.

I'm probably going to take it home with me, though.

June yanks the door open, running out onto the back porch and down the wooden stairs to the fenced-in yard. In the summer, they're outside almost every night, and I've often seen Holden lounging in one of the Adirondack chairs, a glass of something amber and most likely expensive in his hand. He's always looked peaceful out here on this back deck in a way that intrigued me, made me want to venture across the yard separating us and see if he'd let me into his little haven.

And this morning, he does, slipping his hand into mine and leading me to the two chairs facing the backyard. I feel his gaze heavy on me as we settle, the cold wood seeping through my pants. But I feel warm under his perusal, my skin heating in all the places his eyes linger.

When I finally give in, letting my eyes drift to meet his, there's a warmth in his stare that feels like sitting too close to a fire but not wanting to move away from the flames.

"So, I was thinking," he says slowly.

My gaze snags on the way his tongue darts out, wetting his lips. I can't help but remember the way it felt sliding against my own last night and wonder when I'll get to experience that again.

"We should go on a date."

"A date?"

Holden Blankenship doesn't seem like the dating kind. I wouldn't have been surprised if he just kept inviting me to Saturday morning breakfasts or occasional movie nights on the couch with June until I'd fallen so madly in love with him that I couldn't see straight.

I don't know how I'll be able to keep myself intact on a *date*. If I want him this badly after long days working at the cabin or stolen moments when June isn't around, I don't know what I'll do with his full attention fixed on me for an entire night. Just thinking about it makes goose bumps prickle along my skin and something warm and liquid settle in my stomach.

"In two weeks," Holden says.

My thoughts screech to a halt. "Two weeks?"

A knowing smile tugs at his lips, something devious, and I decide I'm ordering a slew of supplies for the cabin and sending them to his house to get back at him for looking so smug.

"June has two birthday parties and a swim lesson next weekend. And weeknights are too hard," he says, shoulders lifting in a shrug.

And really, this makes sense, but it doesn't keep the disappointment from souring in my gut, because now that he's brought up a date, I want it more than anything.

Leaning forward until his lips brush my ear, sending a shiver down my spine, he whispers, "I'll make the wait worth your while."

Then his lips drag across the slope of my jaw, not quite a kiss but full of intention that has my toes curling in my boots.

"Two weeks," I say.

He nods, sounding a little less pleased and a little more desperate, mirroring the way I feel. "Two weeks."

Nineteen
- HOLDEN -

Two weeks have never felt so long. There's almost nothing I hate more than a child's birthday party, but especially when it's the thing keeping me from spending time with Wren.

Wren. I don't know how she came to take up so much space in my head, but she's taken up residence and I don't see her moving out any time soon. I've barely seen her except for the couple of hours every day that she manages to steal away to the cabin. She's already busy planning the next event at Misty Grove—a spring fling the first weekend of May. Even then, we barely have time to quit working so we can make sure to hit her deadline, only a month away.

But today is Saturday, and I just dropped June off at Finley's for the night. So I have Wren all to myself.

I steer my truck into her driveway, gravel kicking up beneath my tires, anticipation building beneath my skin. I want to touch her without feeling like we're wasting our precious work time at the cabin, kiss her without listening for the pitter patter of June's feet running down the hallway.

Wren has her Christmas lights on, the different colors winking at me as I climb out of the truck and up her porch steps. But instead of annoying me, they make my lips tip up in a smile. Earlier this week, a slew of packages arrived on my doorstep, and I wasn't even angry. It gave me an excuse to go next door and press her up against the doorframe so I could steal a kiss.

The door swings open before I have a chance to knock and my heart stutters in my chest when I see Wren. Her hair is piled atop her head in a messy bun, curls falling out to frame her face. The grin she gives me is pure sunshine. She looks like a dream I don't want to wake up from.

"You clean up nice, Red."

Her smile widens, full to bursting. "You don't look half bad yourself. I rarely ever see you in anything but flannels and T-shirts. Where are you taking me dressed like that?"

I look down at my outfit—black jeans and a charcoal gray button-down that always feels way too starched when compared to my usual perfectly worn flannels. The sleeves are rolled, though, and I like the way her gaze catches on the tattoos covering my forearms and lingers there when she thinks I'm not watching.

"Someplace that required a reservation."

Her eyes widen, a little smirk kicking up her mouth. "Bet you hated having to call a restaurant and make a reservation."

I press my lips together to keep from smiling. "They even wanted to know how many people were coming. Like it's any of their business."

Her smile stretches further. "The nerve of some people."

I let my eyes trail down her body, taking in the simple dress she's wearing, a deep emerald-green corduroy that stands out starkly against her skin, her sheer black tights that make my palms itch, and her thick-soled boots.

"You look good, Red," I say, wondering if she heard the way my voice dropped.

"You said that already."

Leaning forward so my lips are against the shell of her ear, I say, "Deserves mentioning twice."

She shivers, goose bumps pricking against her skin. I want to skim the pads of my fingers against them, get lost in the scent and feel of her. But I make myself pull back. If I press her against the doorframe and let my lips find hers, we'll never make it out of this cottage. And that just won't do, because I have plans for Wren Daniels.

"C'mon, Red. Let's get out of here."

On the drive out of town, Wren talks, and I'm content to listen. Mia used to get upset when I didn't have much to say back to her, but Wren doesn't pressure me to come up with small talk. She asks questions, ones that feel easy to answer, but she never asks for more than I give her. I don't think she'll ever know how good that feels, how it makes it less difficult to open up and speak my mind. I've never had a woman in my life do that for me, give me all the space and time I need to answer.

It's the last weekend in February, and the first hints of spring are making an appearance. Tiny wildflowers sprouting up in the mountains, sunshine lasting longer and longer into the evening with every passing day, birds chirping in the mornings. It feels like a time for new beginnings, and as my eyes slide over to Wren, who's laughing at one of her own jokes, I can't help but think maybe this is one.

"Hey," I say as we near Asheville. "Do you mind if we stop in on one of my projects to check out the progress? It should be about finished."

Wren sits up straighter in her seat, excitement coloring her features. "Absolutely. Let's see what I can expect when my cabin is finished."

A laugh rumbles through my chest. "It's just a little bigger than yours."

"I wish my cabin was bigger," she says with a sigh. "It was all that was in the budget, though. And even then..."

I haven't asked her about her finances since that day in her cottage when she cried on me, her tears seeping through the fabric of my flannel. Mostly, I've just chosen the cheapest materials available that are still decent quality, and that haunted look hasn't returned to her eyes.

"Can I ask you a question?"

Wren shifts in her seat, turning to face me. "Why did I buy the cabin if I didn't have the budget to fix it up?"

My lips twitch at her bluntness, because truly, that's probably how I would have asked, and I think she knows that. "Yeah."

"I think you've figured out that I sometimes jump into things without thinking them all the way through."

"Like joining an anonymous dating app in a town this small?"

A smile stretches across her face. "It worked out for me, didn't it?"

"I don't know, Red. You're dating a single dad whose wife left him to move to a city she'd never even been to." I don't mean for the words to slip out the way they do, but as soon as it happens, I regret it. Silence hangs heavy in the cab of the truck, and I hate myself for bringing the easy conversation to a screeching halt.

My hands tighten on the wheel as the silence stretches. When she finally speaks, her voice is a thick rasp. "You really think that's all you have to offer?"

The words are a shock to my system. I don't know why *that* response rocks me to my core, but it does. I feel heat licking at my sternum, a sharp prick at the backs of my eyes, a lump in the base of my throat.

At my silence, Wren shifts in her seat, her hand wrapping around the crook of my elbow. I can feel the warmth of her skin seeping through the fabric, and it grounds me probably more than it should. I don't know how I went from being annoyed by her mere months ago to needing her touch to reassure me. I can't say that I regret it, though. Maybe that should scare me, but it doesn't.

"Holden," Wren says slowly, soft and honeyed. "You're good right down to your bones. You may be grumpy or prickly sometimes, but it has nothing to do with what's in here." She pokes at my chest, right above where my heart is beating wildly. "You're the best dad June could ever ask for, and you stepped right into my life and picked up all the broken pieces I'd scattered everywhere. You didn't deserve how she treated you."

Words stick in the back of my throat, thick and heavy. Mom and Finley and even Grey have always talked about what an awful person Mia is, how she was so selfish to leave, but they've rarely ever mentioned that I was worth staying for. Until now, I didn't realize it was something I needed to hear.

"You know what you are, Holden?" Wren asks, just a whisper against my neck where she's leaning into me over the console. I don't answer, but I don't need to. "You're like our little spot off the beaten path. You have to work to find it, but when you do, it's breathtaking."

We're on a winding country road leading up to the cabin in the mountains, but it doesn't stop me from pulling the car over right here. It doesn't stop me from unbuckling Wren's seat belt and hauling her over the console and into my lap so her knees cradle my hips. A sharp gasp seeps out of her when my hands slip around her neck, threading into her hair before I pull her lips down to mine.

The thing I love most about Wren is that she always takes whatever I throw at her. I just swerved off to the side of the road and pulled her into my lap and kissed her, and she didn't miss a beat, her lips sliding against mine like this was her idea, her hands smoothing up over my chest before dipping below the collar at the back of my neck.

She fits against me like she was made for me, and my head spins at the contact, at how long it's been since I've been touched like this. I want to breathe her in like she's my last breath of oxygen before the world goes dark.

My hands smooth down her sides, finding that spot on her hips where they fit perfectly, the fabric of her dress bunching up beneath my palms. I want to tug it up, feel her skin against mine, but I hold back, slowing the kiss down until we're less frantic, our teeth no longer crashing, our moans no longer filling the quiet cab. The kiss turns leisurely and gentle, like a lazy morning twisted up in bedsheets, and when the thought takes shape in my mind, I want it more than anything.

I want Wren in every way. Stolen, needy minutes in the cab of my truck, unhurried hands in my bed on a Saturday morning, soft, quiet nights on my couch, wrapped in a blanket with the TV playing a movie we've long since given up watching. I want all the small and big moments with her.

I break the kiss, my forehead resting against hers, our breaths sounding loud in the quietness of the truck. I can feel every intake of her breath under my palms, every exhale against my cheeks. Suddenly, I feel overwhelmed that I get to exist with her, that somehow, in all of time and space, we turned out to be neighbors, we became friends on an anonymous app, and we ended up in my truck, breathing the same air.

Just the thought of getting to exist with someone as pure as Wren makes my heart ache in my chest.

"What was that for?" she asks, her hands slipping out of the collar of my shirt to slide down over my rapidly beating heart.

I like that she can feel it there, beating for her, that maybe she feels as connected to me as I do to her in this moment.

"I'm just glad you exist."

Even in the darkness of the cab, I can see the quicksilver glint of her smile stretching across her face, feel the happiness in the change of her body, the way she sits up straighter, her eyes glinting in the moonlight. "I'm glad you exist, too, Holden Blankenship."

Twenty

- WREN -

"You did all this?" I can't help the wonder in my voice as I look around the cabin. It's massive, making my little place in the woods look like a tiny home, and the entire color palette is shades of warm neutrals. It's not what I would have chosen for my own house, but it's lovely just the same. The layout, however, is my dream. All tall ceilings and large floor-to-ceiling windows overlooking what I'm assuming is a stunning view of the mountains beyond.

Holden leans up against a wood pillar below the loft, arms crossed over his chest as he watches me move around the space. "Don't sound so surprised."

I glance over my shoulder at him, my heart rate ratcheting up just looking at him. I'm not sure how things changed between us, just that I'm glad they did. Something inside me snapped at the broken, hollow sound of his voice in the car when he was talking about Mia. I couldn't fathom how someone as *good* as him would ever doubt his worth. I have to wonder, though, how many people have really told him otherwise since she left and how many people have solely focused on June's wellbeing. It makes me want to spoil him, which he will probably never allow. But it's my mission anyway.

"I don't want to leave," I sigh, trailing my fingers over the white marble countertops, wishing I could afford something even half this nice for my little cabin in the woods.

Holden stands up straighter, dropping his hands to his sides. I can't help the way my eyes trail the movement, my skin heating just remembering how they felt on my body, the reverent way he held me. I've never been touched the way he touches me.

"Why don't we stay, then?" he asks, jolting my attention back to his face.

My nose scrunches in confusion. "Stay?"

He shrugs. "I've got a blanket in the truck. We could order food. Hang out here."

"A blanket in the truck? I see where you expected the night to go."

He rolls his eyes, pushing off the pillar to cross the distance separating us. Every part of my body tingles in awareness. "It's for June, smartass. She gets cold in the car sometimes."

"Likely story," I say as he gets close enough for his hands to find the spots on my hips that feel like they were made just for him. It's a little crazy to think about how, mere months ago, I'd never been touched by him, and now there are spots on my body that feel cold or empty when his hands aren't there.

"What do you say?" he asks, hazel eyes earnest, fingers tightening on my hips. "We can do the whole restaurant thing if you want. Or we could eat on the back porch and look at the stars."

The corners of my lips lift, a smile that feels like it's being pulled directly from the center of me. "That sounds perfect."

"It's a real shame you ordered the gnocchi," I say an hour later, seated beside Holden on the double camp chair he found in the bed of his truck, our legs tucked beneath a shared blanket.

His eyes slant toward mine, wary. "Why is that?"

"Because if you had gotten spaghetti, we could have done *Lady and the Tramp*."

A sigh leaves him, and a smile curves my mouth. "I'm not doing *Lady and the Tramp* with you."

"But you'll do it with someone else. Wow, and here I thought I was special."

"I'm not going to share a spaghetti noodle with *anyone*." He says this firmly, like it's the end of the conversation, but I'm just getting started.

"What about pushing a meatball toward me with your nose?"

"Wren."

"But you have such a nice nose," I continue.

"I don't have a nice nose. I have a nose, period."

"You shouldn't talk about yourself that way," I say, tugging the blanket up a little higher on myself to keep out the chill.

His gaze moves in my direction. "You're frustrating."

"Vexing, remember?"

"I prefer frustrating."

I flash him a smile, leaning into his shoulder. "You like me, though."

"There's no proof of that," he says.

"I have a hickey on my collarbone from when you snuck over with the baby monitor a few nights ago." I was sitting on my couch when there was a knock on my door. Holden was on the threshold, a baby monitor secured to his belt, and my ovaries kicked into overdrive. I sat on my counter, and we ate ice cream from the carton. I remember he tasted like vanilla bean, and that even though his mouth was cold, his hands were warm on my waist. That stolen moment with him felt better than free time with anyone else.

"That so?" he asks, not turning toward me, but in the warm yellow illumination of the porch light, I can see the satisfied curve of his lips.

My elbow finds his ribs. "Don't look so pleased with yourself."

"I'm not pleased," Holden says, but his beard twitches again.

"You absolutely are, you Neanderthal."

Holden pounds his chest with his fist. "Wren, mine."

He's joking, but I can't help but like the sound of that.

I drop my empty takeout container onto the porch by our feet and lean onto his shoulder, looking up at him. He looks good like this, his hair tied back in a messy bun, eyes focused on the darkness above and beyond, his body soft and relaxed in a way it rarely is.

"Can I ask you a question?"

Holden glances down at me, hazel eyes deep and warm in the glow of the porch light. "Should I be worried?"

"Why didn't you delete it? The app. You said Finley signed you up for it without asking, but you could have just deleted it."

He returns his focus to the darkness in front of him, but I don't feel him tense, so I don't think the question bothered him. I wonder if he knows how expressive his body language is, even when his words aren't.

It's quiet for a few moments, only the sounds of the trees rustling in the wind. I've noticed that Holden has a lot to say when given the opportunity, that he's not as reserved as he seems. Finally, he answers, "I don't know. Maybe I wanted to see what would happen."

"Did you expect...this?"

His arm comes around me then, wrapping me in his now familiar scent—sawdust and woodsy soap, like he doesn't bother with cologne—and his chin rests on the top of my head, his beard catching in my hair. "No, I couldn't have imagined something like this, Red."

"I wish we had some strawberry wine," I say into his chest, my words muffled.

His body tenses. "I forgot. I have some in the truck."

I sit back, staring up at him. "You keep strawberry wine in your truck?"

"Not until recently," he says, pushing up out of the chair and disappearing into the cabin. Something in my chest warms and spreads watching his shoulders fade from view, going to his truck to get my favorite beverage, something he would never drink if he had another option. I wonder where he was when he saw it and thought to buy it, if he was shaking his head as he did it, calling it bitch juice as his lips twitched beneath his beard, a smile fighting to take shape.

I wish the rest of the world could see the ooey gooey center beneath his tough exterior, but I also like that I'm one of the select few who knows it's there, buried beneath a gruff attitude and a thick beard that hides his smiles.

Holden's boots clomp on the wooden porch boards as he returns, bottle of pinkish wine in hand. Instead of sitting back beside me, though, he picks me up.

I squeal, wrapping my arms around his neck as he lowers us into the camp chair, settling my legs across his lap. "You could have just asked, you know," I say into his neck.

I feel more than hear the rumble of his laugh. "Where's the fun in that?"

"You hate fun."

He flashes me a look that makes my skin heat. He's so close I can see the different shades of greens and golds in his irises. "I like fun with you, Red."

After peeling the plastic from the cap, he jimmies his truck key into the cork, wedging it firmly before slowly pulling it out.

"I see you got the fancy stuff."

"Ten dollars at the market."

A smile curves my mouth. "You shouldn't have splurged on me like that."

The cork gets stuck, and he drops the keys. "Anything for my girl." And then he bites the cork, pulling it the rest of the way out before spitting it on the porch.

It's probably the hottest thing I've ever seen in my life.

He takes a long swig, his throat working with the movement, and I stare open-mouthed. His face scrunches as he pulls it back, handing it to me.

"Way too sweet."

I blink at him. "Do you practice that in the mirror?"

His brow wrinkles. "What?"

"Nothing," I say and take the bottle from him. It's sweet and better than the six-dollar bottle I usually buy. Of course he's ruined me for strawberry wine too. I'll never be able to drink my budget bottle again, and when I buy this kind, I'll always remember how he looked pulling the cork out with his teeth and taking a drink like a dying man.

My heart stops when his tongue darts out to lick a drop of pink liquid from his bottom lip.

"What?" he asks again, no doubt catching me staring.

I swear he doesn't know how attractive he is, and it makes me want to throttle his ex-wife for ever making him feel anything less than desirable.

I lean in, pressing my lips to the spot where that drop of wine lingered, tasting it. Time slows, like the universe is stopping just for us, the earth halting on its axis.

Holden sighs into my mouth, his hands tightening on my hips before he pulls back, placing a kiss to my nose. "Let's watch the stars, Red."

Maybe with someone else I'd feel rushed, frantic, but with Holden, sitting with his arms around me, our eyes fixed on the wide expanse of sky above us, I feel like we have all the time in the world.

"I like it here," I say, watching a star streak across the inky blackness.

"Me too, Red."

"The view at my place is better."

He laughs into my hair. "You can't see the view."

"I can feel it."

His sigh ruffles my curls, but I know he's not exasperated with me, even though he wishes he was. "The view at your place *is* better."

"Maybe we could pick this cabin up and transport it to my property."

"Maybe I'll just build you one like it."

A smile into the sky. "I'd like that. I might need a little more money."

"Someday," he says, his breath warm on the back of my neck.

"Yeah, someday."

"Until then, I'll take sitting here with you on a camp chair in the dark."

I turn my face into his, feeling his beard scrape against my cheek. "It's a pretty good first date, huh?"

"It doesn't really feel like a first date." His words are a soft rumble, seeping into my skin and penetrating my heart.

"No, it doesn't," I agree. It feels like the first of many. Like a last first date.

Twenty-One

- WREN -

Wildflower season starts the first weekend of March at Misty Grove, and I've never in my life missed an opening weekend. As a kid, I'd come with my parents, and as a teen, I'd meet Stevie and her cousin Hazel here and we would pick wildflowers until our baskets were full. Then we'd pluck the petals off to find out if our crushes loved us back. For the last few years, I've been working at the farm on the first weekend, coordinating vendors and food trucks, taking photos for social media, greeting the guests with Stevie's parents.

I've never been quite as excited for wildflower season as I am today, watching June's face light up as bright as the sunshine overhead when she sees the fields of wildflowers.

"They're beautiful," she says in as reverent a tone as a six-year-old can muster. Her hair is braided away from her face today—my doing—and every one of her freckles stands out on her little tanned face. She makes my chest hurt.

"I think so too, June Bug." I tell her, squeezing her shoulder.

"Eh, it's okay," Holden says, but I can see his lips twitch, catch the sparkles of sunlight in his eye.

June spins around, her face gone hard. Her hands land on her hips, and I have to fight the urge to laugh. "It *is* pretty, Daddy," she says sternly.

Holden scoops her up, and she squeals. "Hard to notice the flowers when I've got the two prettiest girls in town with me."

We haven't told June about us, probably because we haven't really talked about it ourselves, but we've spent most evenings together for the last week. It was mostly me coming to their place for dinner, although one night they came to watch a movie on the tiny TV in my cottage. I'm not sure whether June knows we're *together*, but she seems happy to have me around, and although I think Holden and I expected the adjustment to be hard, it's been fairly seamless.

I don't know how I'm supposed to feel about the ease with which I've integrated into their lives, but I know my heart is full to bursting and that every second with them feels like finding something I didn't know was missing.

"Okay, fine," June says with a roll of her eyes, wiggling until Holden lets her down. "Can we pick some flowers now?"

"Go for it, June Bug," he says, giving her a pat on the head. She takes the basket I extend her way before scampering off to the field.

It's busy today, dozens of people showing up for the first weekend, so we stick close but let June do her thing, stopping to smell each flower she plucks before putting it in her basket.

When I look up at Holden next to me, his eyes are focused on her, soft and tender, a little smile in the curve of his lips. He's always attractive to me—when he's working at the cabin, sweat glistening on the cut of his muscles, when he's pinning me to the couch after June goes to bed, hands and lips branding my skin, when he's trying not to find me cute, holding back a laugh until his chest rumbles—but he's never better looking than when he's looking at June. Everything about him softens, his hard edges dulling, the stiff set to his lips never failing to lift in that tiny smile that makes me melt. He's hard to look at like this.

"My mom wants you to come to family dinner tonight," Holden says, jarring me from my staring.

"What?"

That smile is back on his face, but this time, it's knowing, teasing. "Mom wants you to come to family dinner."

A horde of butterflies takes flight in my stomach. "But we're not..." I trail off, not sure where I want to take this sentence.

His brow wrinkles. "We're not what?"

My eyes flick to the wide-open blue sky above us, wishing that the words would disappear on a gust of wind like the pollen in the air. Swallowing, I try to think of how to explain myself. "We're not together?" It comes out more like a question than a statement, and Holden's confusion deepens in the lines of his face.

"What do you mean we're not together?" There's an edge to his voice that I don't recognize. It's not angry, more like hurt, and it wrecks me a little.

I kick my boot in the dusty earth beneath my feet, avoiding his gaze. "We've never talked about what we are."

It's true. Our relationship has always been very undefined. In the beginning, we were neighbors who annoyed each other, and then we were friends who knew everything about each other but our names. For a while after, we were a strange mix of both while we also dealt with the foreign, budding attraction between us. Then we became what we are now, something that feels deeper and more intimate than any other relationship I've ever been in, something words can't adequately describe.

"Wren, look at me," Holden says. When I do, his expression is earnest, the way he looks at June when he tells her she's beautiful or smart, like he wants what he's about to say to stick.

Holden holds my gaze as he says, "I thought I'd made it fairly obvious that I'm not a casual sort of man. I knew when I kissed you in my kitchen after the musical that it meant commitment." He pauses, watching me. "At least for me it does."

It's warmer today, the first hints of spring making an appearance, but it's nothing compared to the warmth spreading through me at his words, the kind that feels like it's seeping into my bones. Altering me in a forever sort of way. It's like how you can cut down a tree and count the rings to see how old it is. If you were to open up my soul, the time and date of this moment would be etched there.

"That's how I feel too," I say, holding his eyes. They're more green right now, out here in the fields.

"Good," he says, turning his attention back to June. "Then you'll come to dinner."

I have to press my lips together to hold back my smile. "Does this mean I'm your girlfriend?"

Holden grunts, just like I knew he would, and crosses his arms over his chest. I can't help the way my eyes catch on the tattoos below his rolled-up sleeves. I've noticed he wears them like that a lot more since I mentioned it to him that first night at the bar.

"Girlfriend doesn't feel like the right word."

I look up at his face to find him looking back at me, a softness in his gaze that feels like warm honey. "What am I, then?"

"You're mine."

"Will you sit next to me at dinner?" June asks, tugging on my hand as we make our way up the front porch steps to Jodi's house. I've been to family dinner before, but *this* feels different, and my stomach is full of butterflies. They settle a little when Holden's palm finds the small of my back, his fingers drawing little circles there as he opens the front door, letting us in.

"Of course, June Bug," I say, giving her hand a squeeze. I was worried about how June would react to me showing up in her life, disrupting her routines, but she's welcomed me with open arms. My favorite part of the day has been in the evenings, when I end up at their place and she asks me to braid her hair before bed. I've even been trying to teach Holden, although he's abysmal at it.

Jodi appears at the end of the hallway, a wide smile on her face. She doesn't fail to notice my hand in June's or Holden's at my back, and if possible, her smile stretches further. "You're here."

"Same as every week, Mom," Holden says, tone dry.

Jodi ignores him. "You look lovely, Wren."

I glance down at my outfit, a long flowy white skirt and an oversized sweater paired with my boots. I considered changing after the day in the fields with Holden and June, but this felt comfortable and it helped to ease my nerves. I shouldn't have worried, though, because Jodi looks *delighted*.

"Thanks, Jodi. Can I help with anything?"

She beams, eyes landing on Holden's, and I can almost hear her saying that Mia never offered to help. I haven't spent a lot of time around Holden and his mother together, but I've been around Jodi enough to hear her complain about Holden's ex-wife.

"You and June can help Finley and me," she says. "Give Holden a little break."

"I can help," Holden interjects.

Jodi rolls her eyes. "I know that well enough, son. I'm just not asking you to."

I think I hear Holden mutter something like *women* under his breath, and it takes everything inside me not to laugh. I shoot him a glance over my shoulder and catch the twitch of his lips beneath his beard.

We follow Jodi into the kitchen, where Dean Martin is playing softly over the speakers, and Holden makes a beeline for the back porch after Jodi motions for him to get out of the room.

"Hey, Wren," Finley says from where she's stirring something in a deep pan on the stove. It looks like some kind of creamy veggie pasta, and my mouth waters just looking at it. Her short blond hair is pulled back in a stubby ponytail and she's got no makeup on today. Finley is one of those people who looks even prettier without makeup, with naturally sun-kissed skin and candy apple cheeks. I want to be her when I grow up.

"Hey, what can I help with?"

"You can toss the salad," Jodi says. "I was just finishing cutting up a tomato for it."

"Can I help?" June asks, her little hand still folded in mine.

I grin down at her. "Absolutely. You'll probably need to show me how to do it. I'm not sure if I know how."

The look she gives me is brighter than sunshine on a summer day, and when I look back up at Jodi and Finley, they're watching us with soft expressions on their faces that I can't quite decipher.

As June and I add the remaining ingredients to the salad and toss it with a homemade dressing that I learned from Stevie, Finley and Jodi pepper me with questions about work and the cabin, although they're careful not to bring up Holden and me. I'm guessing it's more for June's benefit than mine, but I'm glad for it. I don't know how to explain how I feel about Holden in a way that doesn't feel cliché. Like the end of a sappy rom-com movie when everything feels right and perfect, although they *just* got together.

That's how I feel all the time.

"Hello, ladies," a male voice says from behind us, and I turn to see Grey. "And Finley."

Beside me, Finley rolls her eyes and turns back to the dishes she was rinsing in the sink, ignoring him.

"Where's Holden?" he asks.

"On the back porch," Jodi answers. "Will you tell him dinner is ready?"

A few minutes later, we're all sitting down to dinner, June on one side of me, Holden on the other, his thigh pressed against mine under the table. Despite my nerves, everything about it feels *natural* and right. I don't know whether I should be elated or anxious about how easy it feels to slip into this family.

"Wren said she thinks you'll be able to finish the cabin in time?" Jodi asks, looking at Holden across the table as we all dig into dinner.

I was right about the veggie pasta. It's a pasta primavera with a creamy Alfredo sauce that has been making my mouth water for the last fifteen minutes while we finished up making dinner.

"Looks like it," Holden says. "We're probably going to have to work extra for the next three weeks, but I think we should be able to finish by the deadline. Plus, June has graciously agreed to help."

"Daddy said I can paint," June says proudly from beside me.

"Is that right?" Jodi asks, grinning at June. "I bet you're going to be a big help."

June nods. "I think Daddy and Wren need some help. They're so tired after working all day. They always lay on top of each other on the couch and take naps after they think I've gone to bed."

Holden chokes on his drink, and I can feel red singeing its way up my neck as three sets of knowing eyes swivel to us, identical smirks on their faces.

"Sounds exhausting," Finley says dryly.

"That's my favorite way to nap too," Grey pipes up.

I think I'm melting into my chair.

"Anyone need anything?" I ask, my chair squeaking against the floorboards.

"Not Holden, from the sounds of it," Grey says, grinning at me maniacally.

I flash him what I hope is my best glare, but he just smiles wider, laughing this time. Groaning, I grab my empty glass from the table and disappear into the kitchen. "I'm getting a refill."

A moment later, Holden appears beside me, leaning against the kitchen counter, arms crossed. He looks remarkably unfazed, and I have to believe this family is very familiar with teasing. It makes me feel a little better, since mine is the same way, but embarrassment still burns hot in my belly.

"Are you okay?" Holden asks.

I let out a little sigh. "Yes, just embarrassed."

"No need to be embarrassed."

Glancing up at him, I say, "I just want them to like me."

Holden's brows raise on his forehead. "You've known them your entire life."

"Not like this."

Holden holds my gaze for a long moment, like he can see right to the depths of my soul, where his name is etched. "They love you, Wren."

"How do you know that?"

He doesn't hesitate. "Because they know how I feel about you."

There's a sunrise inside of me, peeking over the horizon and lighting up all the dark spots until it's all light everywhere.

"Hey," Grey calls from the dining room. "Are you guys *napping* in there too?"

Holden rolls his eyes, pushing off the counter and extending his hand toward mine. I place my palm in his rough, calloused one, and his fingers wrap around mine immediately. Leaning down, he presses a kiss just below my ear.

"C'mon, let's give them something to talk about when we leave."

Twenty-Two

- HOLDEN -

"How did I end up doing all the work with two helpers here?" I grumble, my arms burning from painting, and turn to face Wren and June. They're sitting on the floor of the cabin, beads and strings strewn all around them.

Wren sighs. "Holden, we're busy."

"Yeah, Dad, we're busy," June parrots, and a bright smile spreads across Wren's face.

I wish I could stay annoyed with them. It's proving harder and harder to be frustrated with Wren. I've even grown to love the way those damn Christmas lights look in the moonlight. And when she had a package of cabinet hardware for the cabin delivered to my house last week, I was just excited to have an excuse to see her.

I'm a sap.

"My arms are killing me," I mutter under my breath. I hate painting. It always makes my arms and lower back hurt, and then I hate myself for turning into an old man overnight.

"But you look great doing it," Wren says, flashing me a wink. I have to press my lips together to keep from smiling. If she knows her teasing makes me happy, she'll never let me live it down.

"Wren, does your name start with *R*?" June asks. "I can't remember what you told me before."

"It actually starts with *W*," Wren answers, and my heart squeezes at the sight of them together. Wren is good with June in a way that feels natural and easy.

June nods, pushing around the beads spread out on the floor before her, her bottom lip trapped between her teeth. When she finds what she's looking for, she strings it, then goes looking for another bead.

We work in silence, me painting, them making bracelets. Even though I complained, I like seeing them together, and I like having them here with me, even when we're not talking or doing something together.

My girls.

"All done," June says proudly, holding up the finished bracelet. It's got red, yellow, and brown beads on it, along with three white letter beads.

"What's it say, June Bug?" Wren asks.

"H, J, W," June says. She points to me. "Holden." Then herself. "June." Then Wren. "And Wren. And I matched the beads to the color of our hair."

Wren's eyes meet mine.

"That's really pretty, baby," I say to June. "Why did you put all three of our initials on there?" I can feel my pulse in my throat, waiting for her to respond. June is getting attached, I can see that clearly. But for some reason, it doesn't trigger the anxiety I would have guessed.

Because it's *Wren*.

June looks at me, confusion written on her features. "Because Wren is your girlfriend. Isn't she?"

Wren's watching me, no doubt trying to figure out how I'm taking this. So I let my eyes drift to hers for a moment, holding her gaze. She visibly softens, and something inside me warms knowing I was able to do that with just a look.

"If she was, June Bug, how would you feel about that?"

June's focus shifts between Wren and me. "I love Wren," she says simply.

Those words crack me wide open, because I'm worried I might feel the same way. That somehow my bright-as-sunshine next-door neighbor has wormed her way so far into my heart and my daughter's heart that thinking about life without her feels like missing a limb.

"So you'd be okay with it?" Wren asks softly, and when my eyes catch on her, I can see the nerves holding her body taut.

June crinkles her nose. "Of course."

Maybe I was wrong when I told Wren she's mine. Because looking at my daughter now, at the way she's staring at Wren with wide, trusting eyes, I know Wren is *ours*.

Wren and June have the windows down in my truck, the chilly early spring evening air pouring in, their belting voices singing Taylor Swift pouring out. I can't even bring myself to be annoyed, and I have a stupid, sappy smile on my lips the whole way home from the cabin.

That is, until I pull into the driveway and see an unfamiliar rental car parked ahead with a very familiar frame leaning against the hood.

Mia.

My blood runs cold at the sight of her, and I hate the way my heart stops the moment June sees her and yells, "Mommy!" She's unbuckling her seat belt and sliding out of the truck before I can even turn the engine off.

Beside me, Wren is tense, her eyes meeting mine over the console before dashing out the windshield to focus on the woman in my driveway. My ex-wife. "So that's Mia?"

I swallow, staring at the woman I once knew so well. "That's Mia."

I climb out of the truck, needing to get to June, before Wren has a chance to respond. Later, I know I'll feel guilty for abandoning her, but June is my first priority right now. The passenger door closes a moment later, when I'm finally standing in front of my ex-wife, but I don't hear the crunch of gravel of Wren coming to my side. Instead, I see a flash of strawberry red hair disappearing across the lawn separating our houses.

Before I can call for her to come back, Mia says, "Well, look who it is." Her voice is low, husky, something I used to find attractive, but that now grates on my nerves. It's nothing like the light, musical tone of Wren's voice.

"Hi, Mia."

June is wrapped around her legs, and Mia bends down to scoop her up. "How's my girl?"

At one point, hearing Mia say that would have been everything I'd ever wanted, but now it feels like ice freezing in my veins, because I know June is only *her girl* when it's convenient for her.

"I've been painting," June says proudly, pointing to the sage green paint stain on her knee from when she and Wren finally came to help me. It feels wrong that just a half hour ago, the three of us were laughing and painting together, and now Wren is in her house alone, and June and I are here with Mia.

"Oh yeah?" Mia asks, brows shooting up high on her head. "What were you painting?"

"Wren's cabin."

Mia's eyes dart in my direction before returning to June. "Who's Wren?"

A smile stretches across June's face, bright as a summer day. "Daddy's girlfriend."

"Is that so?" Mia asks June, but she's looking at me now, and I can't quite read the expression there. I've never been able to read her, not the way I can with Wren. After the last few months with Wren, I wonder how I ever thought Mia and I could have worked. We're so different, but in all the ways that clash. We never brought out the best in one another. We've always been oil and water, unable to mix into something good.

"What brings you to town, Mia?" I interrupt before June can offer any more information.

From the look in her eyes, I know Mia sees my tactic for what it is, and I know this won't be the end of her questioning about Wren. As June's mother, she has a right to know about the people I'm bringing into June's life. But considering her past involvement, I can't understand why she would be concerned.

Squeezing June closer to her, Mia nuzzles her nose into the crook of June's neck and says, "Well, I felt so bad about missing Junie's musical last month that I decided to pay my girl a visit."

"It's okay, Mommy. Wren came."

For a moment, I almost think I see hurt flash in Mia's eyes, but it's gone before I can decipher it. "I'm glad, honey. Think we can convince your daddy to bring my bags inside?"

"You're staying with us?" June practically squeals.

Mia smiles wide. "Sure am." Then turning to me, she says, "As long as it's fine with your daddy."

My jaw clenches, my teeth screaming in pain, because of course I can't say no now that Mia has gotten June's hopes up. "Of course," I say through gritted teeth, and Mia's smile stretches further.

"Perfect."

"June Bug, it's time to start getting ready for bed." Actually it was time an hour ago, but Mia said it was fine for her to stay up a little longer. Of course, she's not going to be the one to get up with her at sunrise, either. Mia has always been a night owl and a late riser, so even when she still lived here, I had early morning duty. I used to think it worked for us, because I could go to bed early and she could take the late-night shifts when June was a baby and not sleeping through the night, but now that June is older, that dynamic doesn't work. I'm going to be dealing with a tired and cranky six-year-old in the morning while Mia is fast asleep in the guest room.

"But Daddy," June whines.

I cut her off with a hand in the air. "June, it's bedtime."

Mia looks between us, no doubt noticing the tension in my body, and says, "Come on, June, let's take a bath."

June's nose wrinkles. "I don't take baths anymore. I take showers."

A look of surprise flashes across Mia's face, but she pushes up off the couch and reaches her hand out to June. "Okay, a shower, then."

"Can you braid my hair after? Wren always does."

This time I'm sure I haven't mistaken the way Mia tenses. "I don't know how to braid, hon."

"Oh," June says, not noticing the change in the atmosphere. "Well, that's okay. Wren has been teaching Daddy. He can do it."

I clear my throat. "Sure thing, June Bug. Just go hop in the shower."

Mia looks between us. "Do you need help, Junie?"

"No, I'm good." And with that, she scampers out of the room, closing the bathroom door with a bang. Silence stretches, filled only with the sound of the shower turning on, and I can feel the way the space between us charges with unspoken words.

Finally, I look at my ex-wife. She's seated back on the couch we picked out together, staring down the hall where June disappeared, an expression I can't read on her face.

"What are you doing here, Mia?" I don't mean for the words to sound as harsh as they do, but my patience has worn thin.

Mia sighs loudly, her shoulders stiffening, and when she looks at me, that unreadable expression is gone, replaced with annoyance. "Do I need a reason to see my daughter?"

"When you haven't taken many opportunities to see her in the past, yes." Maybe it was too direct, but I'm sick of it. After seeing the way Wren constantly shows up for June and me when she doesn't have to, I can't stomach all the times Mia hasn't been there for us when she should have been. The time June broke her arm at three years old when she fell in the backyard. When I got pneumonia last winter and Mom had to stay with us for a week to help take care of June. The late nights, the early mornings. All the little moments where it should have been three instead of two. She's missed *so much*.

Mia stares at the ceiling, and I can see the exact moment the fight leaves her. "I miss her," she says, her voice soft and quiet in a way I've so rarely heard before.

"You're the one who left, Mia. We've always been right here."

Her eyes meet mine, the exact same blue as June's. "Your mom sent me the video of her musical. You know what she said?"

Probably something rude, but I don't say that.

"She said 'you should have been there.' Rich, seeing as how she missed it," Mia says with a roll of her eyes.

"We did everything we could to be there," I say, my voice steely. "You didn't."

Mia holds up a hand, cutting me off. "I don't want to argue about this. I just…" She trails off, avoiding my gaze once more, staring everywhere around the house but at me. I wonder what she thinks of the house I bought without her. She's been here before, a few years back, but so much has changed since then. There are no longer toddler toys and tiny shoes. Now there are stray friendship bracelet beads and a pile of clothes that look like they should be way too big for our tiny daughter stacked in the corner, waiting to be folded and put away.

"I watched that video and I hardly recognized her," Mia says finally.

"She's growing fast," I say, trying desperately to sound gentle when all I want to do is tell her she's missing seeing her daughter grow up.

Mia swallows. "I want things to be better between us. All three of us."

There's so much baggage there, I don't know how we will ever unpack it, especially with Mia halfway across the world, hours and miles away. But I refrain from saying that.

"What do you mean?"

"I don't like how things are with us, that I don't know my daughter, that I hardly recognize you."

I cross my arms over my chest. "I haven't changed."

Mia gives me a soft smile. "You have, Holden. You've changed so much."

My jaw tenses, all the words I've held back for years fighting to break loose. She doesn't have a right to say these things, to waltz back into our lives and act like she knows us. Like she *cares* about us, when she's spent the last four years proving otherwise.

She must recognize the look in my eye, because the smile falls from her face and she leans back on the couch, letting out a heavy breath. "How can I fix things?"

I stare at her, not knowing what she's meaning, exactly *what* she's hoping to change. Things with her and June? *Our* relationship?

"Fix what, Mia?"

She sighs. "I hate how things are between us."

"We're not getting back together."

Her gaze swings up to mine, surprise in every line of her face. "What?"

"I said we're not getting back together." My body is tense, my hands tightening on my biceps.

Mia blinks. "I don't want to get back together with you, Holden. I'm seeing someone in Paris. I told you this, like, six months ago."

Maybe she mentioned it during a phone call, but I don't remember it. Her relationship status has never concerned me. I'm more concerned with her relationship with her daughter.

"Good," I say finally.

"We were never right together. I don't regret leaving."

I expect that comment to needle me, to get under my skin and make me fume. But for some reason, it doesn't. For the first time, I don't regret her leaving either. Staring at her on our old couch right now, I know her leaving was the right thing, that we never would have worked even if she had stayed. I don't like the circumstances or the way she abandoned her relationship with her daughter, but I'm surprised to realize that I'm glad she was brave enough to leave *me*, to do the thing I probably never would have, no matter how unhappy we were.

"I just don't like this…tension between us," Mia says, waving her finger between us.

"Mia," I say with a sigh, having a hard time keeping myself in check now.

"What?" Her voice raises.

"You can't just walk out of our lives and expect things to be the same when you come back. It doesn't work like that. June and I are a family. We work every single day to be a family. And you're not part of it. You *left*."

Mia's jaw clenches. "Well, what if I want to be a part of it again? What if I want to figure out a way to do that?"

"From Paris?" I scoff.

She nods. "From Paris. I have a job there. I have a partner there. I have a *life* there, Holden."

"Well, we're *here*," I say, pointing at the ground to emphasize my point.

"And you don't need me here!" She's practically yelling now, her arms waving. "Look around, look at what you've built with her all on your own. I just want to be allowed to try to build something with her too, Holden." Her voice drops. "Can I do that?"

I stare at her for a long moment, her words bouncing around in my head. "You haven't wanted to before."

Mia swallows, and I expect her to look away, but she holds my gaze. "No, I haven't. I've been selfish."

In all my days, I would have never expected her to admit to that, to finally *see* it, and maybe that's what finally makes me realize that maybe she's serious about this.

"You have to stop promising her things you can't follow through on."

Mia nods, tucking a strand of blond hair behind her ear. "I know."

"And you need to call her when you say you're going to. Ideally at the same time every week."

"I can do that."

"I know you can't be here for everything, but you need to be here for some things."

She nods again, a dip of her chin. "I want to be. I want to start now."

I tap my fingers on my arms, watching her. "How long are you staying?"

Mia shrugs. "I don't know. I bought a one-way ticket. I have to be back for some projects in the next few weeks, though."

My jaw tightens again, because *of course* she would show up without a call and have no idea how long she's staying. But I have to remind myself that at least she's here, at least she's trying.

Finally, I say, "Okay."

"I'm going to do better," Mia says softly.

The shower turns off, and the room goes silent again. Pushing up off the couch to head to June's room for pajamas, I say, "We'll see."

I'm halfway down the hall when Mia calls, "Holden?"

Spinning on my heel to face her, I sigh. "Yes, Mia?"

Her blue eyes look a little cloudy. "Is Wren good to her?"

A knot forms in my throat, picturing all the little moments with Wren and June over the last few weeks, the gentle way Wren shows up for both of us. "Yeah, she's good to her."

Mia nods, looking a little sad but pleased, her lips pressed together. "I'm glad. June deserves that."

"She deserves her mom too."

Twenty-Three
- WREN -

I'M PULLING UP TO Stevie's Airstream when Holden calls. A sigh of relief escapes me, and some of the tension that's been coiling inside me since I walked away from him and June finally releases.

I accept the call with shaking hands. "Hey." The word sounds like a prayer, a breath of relief.

"Hey, Red," Holden says with a sigh, like he feels just as much relief at hearing my voice as I feel hearing his. "I missed you this evening."

"I missed you too," I whisper into the darkness of my car. And it's true. When I saw Mia, and then Holden seemed to disappear into his head, I wasn't sure what to do. The time she called when I was around, Holden asked me to leave, so I thought it was my best course of action. For the first time in weeks, I felt like an intruder.

I left, but that doesn't mean I was happy about it.

When I finally couldn't take looking out my windows and seeing the lights on behind his curtains, I called Stevie and asked her if I could come over. She said it was perfect timing because she'd just made way too many of her famous churros.

"Mia said she wants to be a part of June's life more," Holden says, and warring emotions battle for precedence in my mind. On one hand, I'm so glad for June. Yet another part of me is mourning the little taste I got of life with the two of them.

"How do you feel about that?" I ask, unable to read the tone of his voice. It's been so long since that's happened, and I don't like that either. I wish I was on his couch, his body warm against mine, instead of alone in the chilly darkness of my car on a back road in the woods.

He sighs again, a long, tired sound that makes me want to pull him close, massage the spot between his neck and shoulders that gets tight after a strenuous day of work. "I'm not really sure," he says finally. "I want her to be telling the truth, but I don't know if I can trust it. And I don't want her to drag June along again."

I make a humming noise in the back of my throat, acknowledging his feelings but allowing him to continue.

After a moment, he says, "She seemed sincere. More so than I've ever seen her."

"You've always done what's best for June, Holden. I have no doubt you'll be able to figure out what's best for her now."

Holden's silent for a long time, and I want to ask him where he's at, what he's doing. Where Mia is.

"You never give me advice," he says finally, and it takes me off guard.

"Do you want my advice?"

"Actually, I wouldn't mind it. But I like that you don't just give me your opinion without asking, that you give me time to figure things out for myself. You never try to explain my feelings to me." He clears his throat, as if the verbal dumping made him uncomfortable, and I have to wonder how often he says the things he's actually thinking out loud. Not his reactionary thoughts, but the emotions deep down.

"I think you're perfectly capable of explaining your feelings on your own," I say softly. "You don't need me to do it for you."

He's so quiet that I pull the phone away from my face to make sure he hasn't hung up. But he's still there, the seconds passing by on the darkened call screen. Finally he says, "No one has ever made me feel the way I do for you, Red."

Maybe it's the insecurity of seeing Mia, of seeing the three of them together, but the words slip out before I can think better of them. "Not even Mia?"

Heat steals up my chest and into my cheeks, and I want to snatch that question back, stuff it into the recesses of my mind where it should have stayed.

But Holden just laughs, that deep sound that I've come to love so much, that becomes less and less rare as the days go on. "Definitely not Mia."

"Can I ask you a question?" I ask, not hesitating so I don't chicken out.

"Yeah, Red," he says. "You can ask me anything."

"Why did you marry her?"

Holden sighs, sounding tired, and I almost feel bad for asking. But I have to know. "She was pregnant. It seemed like the right thing to do. Looking back now, I realize we all would have been a lot happier if we hadn't forced it. Marriage is a lot more than duty."

I'm quiet for a moment, then ask, "Have you figured out what it should be?"

"Commitment. Selflessness. The kind of love that feels like you're missing a limb when you're not with your person." He pauses, clearing his throat. "It was never like that with her."

His words settle down in my soul, where the ache of missing him is strongest.

"Wren, about earlier, why did you—"

A knock on my window jars me out of my call with Holden. I turn to see Stevie there, her long, wavy brown hair piled atop her head in a messy bun, a chunky cardigan pulled over a faded cropped tank, and soft-looking baggy pants covering her legs.

"Holden, I've got to go," I say into the phone. "I'm at Stevie's."

"Okay, Red," he says. "Talk to you tomorrow?"

"Talk to you tomorrow."

It's not until we've hung up that I realize I never asked how long Mia would be around, what it would look like for us with her here.

My car door squeals as I open it. Stevie scrunches her nose as I climb out, tugging her sweater closed against the slight chill in the air. "What are you doing out here?"

"That was Holden," I tell her, and she raises her eyebrows.

"What did he say about Mia?"

I let my gaze trail up to the wide-open sky above us, breathing in the pine-scented air. "I'm going to need a churro first."

A smile stretches across Stevie's face, and she loops her arm through mine, guiding me toward the Airstream. "That can be arranged."

This has been one of the longest weeks of my life. Mia is *still* here, which means that I haven't spent any evenings with Holden and June. Holden invited me to dinner one night, but I didn't want to intrude on Mia's time with June. I just didn't realize how much I would miss them, how hard it would be to be away from them. How much a part of my life they've become.

I've hated watching them sit around Holden's kitchen table at night while I'm in my cottage alone, so I've spent the last few nights at either Stevie's or my parents'. Holden told me that Mia booked a flight for tomorrow afternoon, and he invited me to family dinner at his mom's again, so I'll finally get to see them tomorrow night. I just have to fend for myself for one more night, and I intend to spend it having a picnic at the overlook. I haven't been there since that last time with Holden, and I wonder if it will feel different now that it's not just my special place. It's ours. I wouldn't have thought a few months ago that I'd be so happy about that.

There's a knock on my front door just as I'm about to leave, and when I swing it open, surprise hits me square in the face. Mia is standing on my porch, dressed in white slacks and a soft taupe cashmere sweater. She looks put together in a way I never will. Even her curls look shiny and tamed, unlike my wild tresses that chose today to completely rebel.

"Wren, is it?" Mia asks, smiling at me, although her eyes feel assessing.

"Yeah, and you must be Mia," I say, a little breathlessly. "I've heard so much about you."

Her smile tightens slightly. "Likewise."

My confusion must show on my face because she clarifies. "June talks about you constantly."

I clear my throat, awkwardness burning a hole in my belly, because while she says June talks of me, she's rarely mentioned Mia.

"She's a very special little girl," I finally say, and Mia's pinched smile softens.

"She is," Mia agrees. "May I come in? It's chilly."

I barely manage to contain my shock, but I do, moving back from the door to motion her inside. "Yeah, of course."

Mia moves into my tiny cottage, and I try to see it through her eyes. The mismatched dishes on the open shelving in the kitchen. The vintage rug with a strawberry wine stain on the corner from a tipsy girls' night with Stevie. The empty teacups on the scarred coffee table and the colorful blankets thrown over the back of the couch. The shoes I walked right out of discarded by the front door. My space looks especially eclectic when she's standing inside it.

"Would you like something to drink?" I ask, moving toward the kitchen, desperate for something to do.

"No, thanks."

I stop in my tracks, swiveling to face her, twisting my hands together in front of me. My bottom lip catches between my teeth as I examine her, trying to figure out what she could possibly be doing here.

"This is awkward," she says, a statement, not a question. Maybe that's what makes me feel comfortable enough to sigh and nod.

"A little," I agree.

Mia's eyes snag on my coffee table, and I follow her gaze to the stack of friendship bracelets June and I worked on at the cabin last week when we were supposed to be helping Holden. She stoops, picking one up and tracing the beads with her fingers.

"H, J, W," she says softly under her breath, and a knot of anxiety forms in my stomach.

"Mia, I—"

"You're good for them, you know," she says, meeting my eyes. "I've never seen Holden so settled and happy. And June…"

I don't know how to respond, so I don't.

"I'm glad they have you."

"I think they'd be glad to have more of you too." Mia's eyes connect with mine. The surprise reflected in them matches the surprise I feel at actually saying that aloud. Maybe it wasn't my place, but I can't help but see the effects of her absence on Holden and June.

She's silent for a long moment before saying, "I want that. Holden says I need to be more consistent if I want to be in June's life."

I don't know if she expects a response from me, but although I told her I think Holden and June would like to see her more, I don't feel it's my place to comment on her parenting. Even if I do think it leaves something to be desired.

Mia clears her throat. "Well, I just wanted to meet you before I leave tomorrow."

"Why?" I ask before I can think better of it.

She shrugs, looking at me like the answer should be obvious. "I think you're going to be around for a long time. I'm sure we'll see more of each other." She nods toward the front door and starts walking in that direction. As she lets herself out, she looks over her shoulder and says, "Come around more next time."

Twenty-Four

- HOLDEN -

I don't know how to feel about Mia leaving as we walk into the airport Saturday afternoon. On one hand, I'm sad for June. She's loved having her here for the last week, and I think it's been good for her. I only hope Mia doesn't drop off the face of the planet when she leaves again. I have a good feeling about it, though, after watching her with June this week. Something felt different.

On the other hand, I miss Wren, and despite inviting her to dinner and seeing her briefly at the cabin in the afternoons when she stopped in to help me work, we haven't spent much time together. Not having her around in the evenings with June and me has felt like something was missing. And although technically it should feel right to have Mia there, it didn't. Even if she does come back into June's life more regularly, her place is never going to be *with* us again.

That place is reserved for a woman with the wildest red hair I've ever seen, who drinks cheap strawberry wine and looks like sunshine when she smiles.

Mia comes to a stop just outside the security gate and turns to face us. I'm surprised to find her eyes shiny as she picks up June, hugging her to her chest. "I'm going to miss you, sweet girl," she whispers.

A lump forms in my throat as June wraps her little arms around Mia's neck. "I'll miss you too, Mommy."

"I promise to call more." Her eyes meet mine over June's head as she says it, and I nod with a dip of my chin.

Clearing the tightness in my throat, I say, "I'm going to hold you to that."

Yesterday, we talked about Mia's next visit. She told me she'd set aside some time in early September to come back, and although I'm not holding my breath, I'll be happy if she follows through with it. She even agreed not to mention it to June yet, in case her plans fell through. I think it hurt her feelings when I asked her to wait, but she seemed to understand. Things feel different, but I'm not taking any chances.

When she first told me about Mom sending her the video of June's musical and the message that she should have been there, I was angry at my mom for overstepping. But before I could even call her out on it, I started to see the good that was coming from it. Maybe that message was the push Mia needed. I should have stood up to her a long time ago, and it feels good to do so now. I hope she proves me wrong.

Mia sets June down, running a hand over the braids I put in her hair this morning. Her gaze snags on mine again. "You'll have to teach me how to do those next time, okay?"

My lips curve in a soft smile. "Sure thing, Mia. Let us know when you make it back, all right?"

She nods, her focus fixing on June once more. "I love you, Junie. Don't ever forget it."

June squeezes her hand. "I love you too, Mommy."

And with that, Mia turns around, her shoulders squaring, and heads for security. I don't expect her to look back, but when she does, her eyes are misty again. She gives us one last wave before funneling into the line.

June reaches for my hand, her little fingers wrapping around mine. "I hope she comes back soon."

I pick her up, hefting her onto my hip. She smells like Wren's shampoo and that distinctly little girl smell I'll miss when it's gone. "Me too, June Bug. Me too."

We stand there until we can't see Mia anymore, and then I squeeze my little girl tighter and say, "Let's get to Grandma's house. Wren's coming for dinner."

My heart expands in my chest when the sadness melts off June's face and is immediately replaced with a dazzling smile. "Really?"

"Really."

"I've missed her," June says as I set her down.

My lips curve in a smile, and I pat her back, echoing my words from before. "Me too, June Bug. Me too."

The rain is falling in heavy sheets, lightning brightening the sky, and I can't help but wish for good weather. I want long summer days with my girls, floating in the lake or running through the sprinkler, sitting on the back porch with the monitor after June falls asleep, watching the stars from the bed of my truck. I spent one week without Wren, and I don't intend to do it again. I'm becoming attached at an alarming rate, and I can't even bring myself to care.

I park beneath the carport to avoid the rain, and before we've even climbed out, Wren's little yellow Volkswagen turns in behind us. June squeals in the back seat, unbuckling and wrenching the door open. She hops out before Wren is even in park, running to the driver's side. My chest cracks wide open at the sight of Wren climbing out of the car, that wide, glittering smile on her face as she stoops to envelop June in a hug.

"Hey, June Bug. I missed you. How was your visit with your mom?"

"It was good," I hear June say over the sound of the rain pattering on the metal carport above us. "But I missed you a lot."

Suddenly, I have no desire to go into my mom's house and share my girls with the family. I want to take them back home and spend the night just the three of us, how it should be.

Wren's eyes connect with mine as she says, "I'm sorry I wasn't around so much. I promise I won't do that again."

I know Wren wanted to give June time with her mom, and that's well and good, but I want her by my side the next time Mia is around. I want her hand in mine as she listens to me when Mia starts to talk over me. I want her braiding June's hair at night and sitting on the couch with me when Mia takes over bedtime duty. Wren has fallen so effortlessly into our lives that her absence felt just as foreign as Mia's presence, and the next time Mia is here, we need to figure out a rhythm with the four of us to make it right.

"June Bug, how about you go inside and tell Grandma and Finley we'll be in there in just a minute?" I say, desperate for a moment alone with Wren without Mia's shadow hanging over us.

June's arms tighten around Wren's neck, enough to cut off her breath, one last time before she lets go and scampers inside, her little braids thumping against her back as she runs.

"Her braids look good," Wren says, her tone a little wistful, and my heart warms at the softness on her face as she watches my daughter. I think she's smitten. I just hope she's as smitten with me as she is with June. I know I'm a goner, that once suffocating four letter word desperately clawing to come out any time I'm in her presence.

The minute June disappears through the side door, I cross the distance between us, gathering Wren in my arms. She makes a soft *hmph* of surprise against my chest, but her hands don't hesitate to smooth up the planes of my back. It feels good to hold her.

"I missed you," I whisper into the curly mess of her hair, damp from when she must have run from her house to her car.

I can feel her soft chuckle. "I saw you every day."

"It was different," I say, and she nods into my chest. "I don't want you to back off when Mia is here, especially if she keeps her word and starts coming around more."

Wren pulls back, her soft blue eyes meeting mine. There's a hesitancy there, almost a hopefulness. "You don't?"

My hands come around her neck, thumbs gliding against the smooth skin of her jaw. I want to press my lips there, feel her soften against me like she does when it's late at night and we have to be quiet so we don't wake June. "No, I always want you around, Red. You belong with me and June. Always."

"Oh," she says, more of a breath puffing out against my lips than an actual word, and something inside me snaps at the feel of it. At that moment, I can't take not kissing her. I just have to hope June and my mom and sister aren't at the windows watching us. Right now, I don't even know if I care.

"Wren," I sigh, giving into the magnetic pull and pressing my lips to hers.

She responds immediately, her hands fisting in the collar of my flannel and tugging me closer. A groan rumbles in the back of my throat, and she smiles against it. Actually smiles. I love how much she smiles for me. I'll have all her smiles for the rest of time if she'll let me.

When I swipe my tongue along the seam of her lips, begging for entrance, she stops smiling, melting against me just like I knew she would. She tastes sweet, like strawberries and whipped cream, and I remember her excitedly telling me at the cabin the other day that some of the strawberry crop came early at the farm this year.

My every nerve stands on end as her hand slips into the collar of my shirt, stopping over my heart that's beating just for her. I wonder if she knows it, if hers is beating for me too.

I pull her tighter against me, wanting to feel her everywhere, and she gasps against my mouth. I could hear that little gasp in my ear for the rest of time and never tire of it. That little gasp is giving me all kinds of ideas about blowing off family dinner and dragging her home where we can be alone.

"Holden," Wren says, pulling back. Her lips are kiss-swollen, cheeks burned from my beard. She looks completely disheveled, and there's a primal surge of satisfaction in my chest knowing I'm the one who did that to her. "Your phone is vibrating."

"How do you know it's my phone?" I ask, smirking, and she shoves my chest, trying not to smile. Pulling the phone from my pocket, I see Grey's name on the screen. "It's just Grey."

"Answer it."

"I'd really rather be doing something else."

She sighs. "Holden."

"Fine, fine," I grumble and slide open the call. "This better be important, Grey."

He sounds out of breath, and I think he's running. My nerves go on high alert. "It is."

"Where are you? Are you on your way to dinner?"

"I'm on shift tonight. There's a fire, Holden."

My heart stops in my chest. "Where?"

"Wren's cabin."

Twenty-Five

- WREN -

The truck is silent except for the sounds of the heavily pounding rain and the furiously swiping windshield wipers. My heart is in my throat and my hands are squeezed so tightly in my lap that my knuckles are white and popping.

A fire. At my cabin. The cabin I've spent my entire savings and the last few months of my life working tirelessly to get ready for guests that will be here in *two weeks*. I managed to get the cabin listed on the town rental websites and booked up even though the renovations weren't finished, and now I'm regretting that, because I'll have to refund if I cancel their stays, and I've already used that income to put toward the last of the renovation expenses.

My mind is a swirl of thoughts, coming so quickly that I can't pause to find a solution to any of them before the next problem surges to the forefront.

Holden's eyes slice toward me. "Wren, breathe."

It's only then that I realize how quick and shallow my breaths are, how my chest is rising and falling rapidly, how it feels like my heart is beating in my throat fast enough to cut off my oxygen. I'm panicking, and I can't stop.

Before I know what's happening, Holden has pulled the truck over onto the side of the road.

"What are you doing?" I ask, looking around at the familiar surroundings. We're about a mile from the turnoff that leads up the mountain to the cabin, and up ahead, breaking through the trees, I can see smoke gathering in the air. "We have to get to the cabin."

Holden puts the truck in park and turns to face me, his large, warm hands cupping my face. "Wren, I need you to breathe."

I've never seen him worried like this before, his eyes desperate in their concern. Every line of his body is taut, a string pulled tight enough to snap.

My breaths are coming so fast that I'm panting, clouding up the minuscule space between us. It's so hard to breathe, and that makes me panic more.

"I can't," I pant, fear clawing its way up my throat. Out of the corner of my eye, I can see the smoke billowing in the distance, my entire life savings going up in flames.

"Wren, look at me." Holden's voice is firm, so authoritative that it makes me listen without hesitation. He's scared, he must be, I saw it in his eyes just moments ago, but now that emotion is wiped from his face. Now he looks steady, like the rocks at the beach that are able to withstand the harsh elements without eroding or breaking. And *that's* what finally makes me breathe, what begins to steady my heart rate. For so long, I've been on my own, taking care of myself the best way I know how, but for the first time, I realize I don't have to anymore. That if I crumple, there's someone here to pick up the pieces. With Holden, I'm safe to fall apart.

And that's exactly what I do. As my breathing slows, the tears come. The adrenaline crashes, and the seriousness of the situation washes over me, rocking me to my core.

Holden gathers me to him, holding me against his chest. His lips are at my temple, and he rocks us back and forth. "It's going to be okay," he says over and over again, and although I know he can't possibly be right, I want to believe him. I think I do believe him. Because no matter what happens, I'm not alone.

When the tears slow and Holden pulls back, his thumbs swiping away the damp hairs sticking to my face. His eyes are hard again, the line of his mouth firm. "We will figure this out," he says, and it seeps right into my soul. "Together."

I nod, my head still in his hands, and he presses a soft, lingering kiss to my lips. We've shared so many kisses over the last two months, but this one feels like the night of the musical, like a promise.

Holden rests his forehead against mine. "Are you ready to go up there?"

This time, I don't let my eyes drift to the smoke up ahead. This time, I keep them focused on him, my steady rock in this storm. "I'm ready."

His hand latches on to mine, fingers threading together, and we turn back onto the road. I don't let myself look at the smoke. I just watch his profile in the gray light of the cab. I memorize how he looks right now, his jaw set, his shoulders tight, his tattoos peeking out of the rolled-up sleeves of his flannel, color stretching up the length of his forearms.

When we turn into the driveway of the cabin, I finally allow myself to look forward. Smoke pours out of the front windows, and the firefighters are trying valiantly to douse it.

Holden squeezes my hand. "Together, Red. We're going to figure this out."

All I can bring myself to do is nod.

Grey meets us at the truck as soon as we climb out, motioning for us to stay back. Rain pelts us, soaking us through in seconds. "We've almost got it out."

Beyond the windows, I can see the orange dance of flames, and if this is close to being out, I'm glad I wasn't here at its worst.

"What do you think caused it?" Holden asks, and if I'm not mistaken, I think nerves tinge his voice. Suddenly, I realize he's worried it's his fault.

Grey is still watching the fire, his suit covered in soot that's streaked with rainwater. "We won't know for sure until the fire chief can get in to assess it, but I think it was lightning."

Holden's shoulders heave, losing some of their tension immediately, and I squeeze his hand. When he squeezes mine back, I scoot closer to him, seeking his warmth under the chilly rain.

"It looks like the fire started on the porch and went into the living room, which is what leads me to believe a lightning strike. Unless you had something else on the porch that could have caused it, like a lithium battery."

"Nothing," Holden says, and once again, I'm so thankful to have him here, to have someone who knows this place as well as I do to answer the questions. I don't think I could give coherent answers right now.

Grey's warm blue eyes settle on me now, softening. "I'm so sorry, Wren. We're working hard to get it out."

I nod, not trusting myself to say anything.

Holden, bless him, asks the question I'm too afraid to ask. "How bad is it?"

Grey's jaw tightens, his gaze returning to the cabin, which thankfully just looks full of smoke now. No more flames in sight. "We won't know for sure until the fire chief can get inside, but honestly?" His statement is more of a question, his focus turning back to us. "I think there's fairly significant damage to the porch and maybe the living room, but the rest of the cabin looks untouched. We got here quickly, so I think those rooms will just have smoke damage."

I'm not sure what I was expecting to hear, or even if that's what I wanted to hear, but I know that it doesn't make me feel any better or worse. I guess it's a good thing it was localized, but regardless, I'm not going to have it fixed and ready for guests in two weeks.

My shoulders feel heavy again, my knees weak, and it's like Holden can sense it, because he drops my hand, his warm, strong arm coming around my waist instead, holding me upright. I lean into him shamelessly, needing to siphon his strength when I feel on the verge of collapsing.

"Is there anything we can do?" Holden asks, and I'm a little transfixed by the raindrop clinging to the tip of his nose. It's something to focus on besides the way my life is falling apart.

Grey shakes his head. "No, the fire chief will be in touch probably tomorrow. Once he does his walk-through, he should be able to tell you when you can get back inside."

Holden nods, his arm tightening around me. "I think I'm going to take Wren home, then." Hazel eyes focus on me. "Is that okay? Do you want to stay?"

I'm chilled to the core and numb, my voice frozen in my throat, so all I can manage is a shake of my head. I don't want to stay. I don't want to look at it any longer, not when that clawing sensation is climbing back up my chest.

He presses a kiss to my temple and murmurs, "Let's go home, Red."

I don't remember the walk back to the truck or Holden buckling me into the front seat or the drive back. It's all a blur, but before I know it, he's turned into the driveway of his house instead of my cottage. The house is dark, and I remember that we left June at Jodi's house for her weekly sleepover, so it's just us.

That's good, because I don't want June to see me fall apart, and I know I'm dangerously close to it, despite all of Holden's talk of everything being okay and us figuring things out together. I don't know *how* this can be figured out, at least not in time.

Everything is over. I focus on my cottage across the yard separating our homes, and I wonder if I'll lose it. I won't be able to sell the cabin in the state it's in, but I won't be able to afford the mortgage without the income it was going to generate. Maybe the bedroom there hasn't suffered too much smoke damage and I can stay there and work on the renovations.

That's a plan, a step.

"What's going on in that head of yours, Red?" Holden asks, reminding me that I'm not in this truck alone.

"I'm going to sell my cottage," I say, noticing how hollow my voice sounds.

Holden shakes his head, and I can hear the movement of his damp hair against his collar. "You're not going to sell your cottage."

"What am I going to do?"

"We'll figure something out," he says, but I'm shaking my head.

"You keep saying that, but *how*, Holden? There's no plan. I messed up." I sound ragged, wrung out, just like I feel.

His hand finds mine, massaging the palm, and it's only then that I realize how sore it is from how tightly I was holding them together in my lap. "It was an accident, Red. A freak accident of nature. There was nothing you could have done." His eyes lock on mine, and there's a firm set to his jaw, just like before. "But we *will* figure this out."

I want to believe everything's going to be okay. I want to reclaim my role in our relationship as the glass-half-full partner, but everything feels so bleak. So I just nod, even though I don't think what he's promising can come true.

"Let's go to bed," he says, and I finally notice that it's grown dark, too cloudy from the rain to see the moon and stars. I wish we could watch them together tonight, because staring up at the inky vastness has a way of making me feel minuscule. But tonight, the fog is heavy, both literally and figuratively, and my problems feel like a beam of light slicing through it, finding me even in the darkness.

Holden leads me inside, pulling me gently by the hand to his bedroom. He only lets go to pull out a pair of sweatpants and a T-shirt that looks like it will hang to my knees. He sends me into the bathroom to change, and I'm haunted by the purple half moons under my eyes, the emptiness inside them. I look as hollow and ragged as I feel.

When I come back out, Holden has changed and pulled back the blankets. He helps me into bed and then climbs in beside me. His arms wrap around me, and I breathe in his familiar scent, sawdust and pine-scented soap, the only thing tethering me to reality.

"Sleep, Wren. Everything will be okay in the morning."

I don't believe him, but I cling to that sentiment, chanting it over and over again until I finally drift off to sleep.

Twenty-Six
- HOLDEN -

When I wake up, I'm alone, Wren's side of the bed cold and empty. The first rays of light are bleeding through the curtains in shades of pinks and purples, and I wonder how early Wren must have been up. If she traversed my house in the darkness to leave. Not for the first time since we got the call, I wonder what she's thinking. She usually wears her every emotion on her face so clearly, but last night, there was only a blank emptiness that cut me straight to the core.

I slide out of bed, the hardwood cool against my feet as I search the house for Wren. She's nowhere to be found, and her car isn't in her driveway where Mom and Finley must have dropped it off last night while we were at the cabin. There's only one place I can imagine her going, so I get dressed quickly and hop into my truck, heading up into the mountains.

I'm not at all surprised to find Wren's little yellow VW Beetle parked in front of the charred, ashy remains of the cabin. She's sitting on the hood bundled in one of my jackets. Grey was right. It looks like the fire was localized to the front of the cabin, because the back looks relatively untouched, but the damage is still extensive.

When I climb up on the hood next to Wren, her eyes are red rimmed, her nose and cheeks pink from the early morning chill and from crying. She looks wrecked, and it makes my chest physically ache. I have to press my hand there just to dull it.

Her boots are soot stained. "Did you go inside?" I ask, already knowing the answer.

She nods, just a barely there dip of her chin. "Yeah."

"Wren," I sigh. "It's not safe. You should have waited on the fire chief, or at least for me, to go in with you."

She shrugs, and the movement looks so lifeless that the ache in my chest moves deeper, piercing my heart. "It's bad, Holden. The kitchen, bedroom, and bathroom look okay, just dusty and dirty, but the living room and the front porch are destroyed."

I want to tell her we'll figure something out, but I can tell it won't mean much when she's staring at the charred remains of her future. So I just wrap my arm around her, and when she melts into me, my chin settles on the top of her head. She feels so familiar to me now, and I can't believe that she was living next door to me for so long and we never fit together like this until now. I have a hard time not regretting the time we wasted, but I'm thankful for every second I have with her.

We sit there for so long, long enough for my muscles to grow stiff in the damp chill of the early morning. "C'mon, we should get out of here. Try to figure out a solution."

She nods against my chest. "Okay."

"Let me buy you a coffee."

"Coffee sounds good."

"We can leave your car here and get it later," I say, rubbing circles on her back.

"Okay."

My lips twitch. "Are you going to agree with everything I say?"

Wren nods again. "Yeah, I think so."

"How about we take your Christmas lights down?"

She pulls back, and relief whooshes through me at the hint of a smile on her face. "Not a chance."

I hold her tight one last time, my lips finding that spot on her temple that I can't stop kissing, and then I hop off the hood of her car, holding out my hand. Nothing has felt more right than when she slips her hand into mine, squeezing once. I think she'd let me lead her into fire right now, but what she doesn't know is that she's nestled so deeply into my life that she's become mine. Mine to protect, mine to cherish, mine to serve, mine to take care of. Mine to love.

We're quiet as we make our way into town. I miss the musical sound of her laughter, the way she sometimes hums under her breath without even realizing it. I've never noticed how much sound and color she's brought into my life until she's quiet and gray.

I'm the first one to notice the signs in town, taped to every shop window, written in bright colors. The ones saying they're taking donations or giving a portion of their proceeds to Wren.

"Wren," I breathe. "Do you see them?"

She hasn't, and I can tell the moment she does by the way her body goes ramrod straight in her seat, straining against the seat belt as she reads the signs. Her hand comes to her throat, and when I slash my eyes in her direction, I see the way her tears have returned, brimming on the edges of her lashes.

I slow the truck to a stop in front of Smokey the Beans, and we both see Myra and Melissa at the same time, seated at their regular table, a line of people waiting to reach them. Even from here, I can see people writing checks or handing over cash to put in the cash box Myra is clutching in her bony hands.

Wren is speechless as she watches the scene unfold, silent tears streaking down her face. Her voice is choked as she asks, "They did this all for *me*?" She sounds so disbelieving, and I can't fathom why. The only thing I'm unsure of is why we didn't consider this happening. *Of course* the town rallied around her. She's constantly giving of herself to this town, and they're finally giving back.

I reach for her hand, squeezing once. "Of course this is all for you, Red. C'mon, let's go inside."

I think she's still in shock as I open the passenger door and help her down, her hand clinging to mine like it's her lifeline. When we open the door to Smokey the Beans, the usual noise and clamor dies down, everyone turning to face us. I see a myriad of expressions reflected back at us—pity, sadness, pride, but most of all, love. Every single person in this town loves Wren Daniels, and none of them will let her dream die.

The cacophony of noise returns simultaneously, and everyone rushes forward, offering condolences and hugs to Wren, promising to help her get back on track in no time. My hand slips from hers in the chaos, and when she turns around to look for me, finding me immediately in the crowd of people, something snags in my chest. That smile is returning to her face, the one that looks like sunshine, even if it's still tearstained and hesitant.

It brings a smile to my own lips, and when she notices it, hers grows wider. It feels like the warmth of a summer day spent in the mountains, nothing but wide-open space and blue skies ahead.

I motion to the bar, and mouth, "Coffee." Wren nods, and within seconds, her focus is pulled back into the crowd of well-wishing townspeople. For the first time since we got the call last night, I actually feel a kernel of hope. Everything actually will be okay, Wren most of all.

"Did the cabin look cool on fire?" June asks later that night when she, Wren, and I have just sat down to dinner at my dining table. Wren chokes on the sip of water she's just taken, and I have to press my lips together to keep from smiling.

June looks between the two of us, confusion written on her features. "What?"

"Nothing, June Bug," Wren says. My heart constricts, just like it does every time I hear her call my daughter that. "It did look a little cool, but not cool enough to want to try seeing something else on fire."

I don't know how she does it, answers June so effortlessly, keeps her curiosity piqued while still reinforcing safety. It's like she's been around June's whole life, not just the last few months, and I'm starting to wonder how we made it before she showed up. That thought should freak me out, send me into a tailspin, wondering what will happen if things end badly between us and June gets hurt in the process, but I can't see that happening. When I look at Wren, I see forever.

It's not until we've finished dinner and the two of them have successfully heckled me into allowing June to have dessert that the subject of the fire comes back up.

June licks chocolate syrup and melting ice cream off her spoon before saying, "Grandma said everyone in town is going to fix Wren's cabin."

Wren smiles. "They're certainly helping. They're giving me a lot of money to fix it."

"Will it still be done in two weeks?"

"No," Wren says, a little sadness tingeing her voice. "I'll have to cancel all the reservations for this year. Maybe we can get it up and running again by next spring."

June's eyes widen. "A whole year?"

Wren shrugs. "Well, I won't be able to work on it until tourist season is over, and your dad always works more then too."

It's true. I'm already booked solid for the next few months, and as much as I would love to be able to work on the cabin in my spare time, there won't be much of it, especially once school is out for the summer. Wren is probably right that it will be a while before the cabin can be fixed. Despite the donations for repairs, that means another year of being strapped with a mortgage on little income. It makes my dinner sour in my stomach.

I'm quiet for the rest of dessert, lost in my own thoughts, and when June runs into the living room to pick a movie for the three of us to watch, Wren asks me about it. There's concern in her eyes as she says, "Are you okay? You've been quiet."

I don't want to tell her I'm worried for her, that I'm racking my brain for solutions, because she seems to actually be okay, and the last thing she needs is me setting off anxiety for her. So I shrug and say, "I'm fine."

She nods, following me into the kitchen with our dishes, but I can tell she doesn't believe me. We rinse the dishes in silence and load them into the dishwasher as June scrolls through the streaming services in the living room.

After loading the last of the dishes, Wren stops me with a hand on my arm. When I look at her, something inside me cracks. Her eyes are still a little puffy and red from crying last night, and her cheeks are dotted with freckles from the time she's spent out in the flower fields lately. All the sunshine is starting to bleach her hair, making it more blond than red. She looks so beautiful it hurts.

Her hand tightens on my arm, her finger absently tracing over the june bug tattoo inked into my skin. "Are you sure you're okay?"

Suddenly, not touching her feels like torture, and I break my self-imposed rule to keep the physical intimacy to a minimum in front of June. I wrap her up in a hug, and after a second's hesitation, she melts into me, her arms snaking around me until it feels like we're one person instead of two.

"Yeah, Red, I'm okay." I slide my hand beneath her curls, gently squeezing her nape. "Just thinking."

She pulls back, just far enough to look into my eyes. I want to kiss her, to remind myself that even when everything seems to be falling apart, she's here with me. That she's flesh and bone and heat and softness.

"What are you thinking about?"

There's a thought in the back of my mind, something that I'm not sure would work. It would take a miracle, really, but I'm starting to believe in those.

Shaking my head, I say, "Nothing." My hands slide back down her spine, coming to rest on those spots on her hips, and I tug them against mine, aware of June just feet away, her focus secured on the TV.

Wren makes a silent little gasp when we line up everywhere, just an intake of breath, and I lean in until my lips are on the shell of her ear. She shivers against me as I ask, "Could you stay here with June and put her to bed? I need to run out for a bit."

When she nods, her curls snag in my beard. "Yeah, of course. Where are you going?" Her voice is breathy, and it makes me warm all over.

"Wait up for me," I say, and let my lips find that smooth expanse of skin just below her ear, the one that always makes a trail of goose bumps prick up across her neck.

And then I back up, pleasure zinging through me at the dazed look in her eyes, at the way she grabs on to the kitchen counter for balance.

She watches me push my feet into my boots, not moving from where I left her propped against the counter. There's a heat in her eyes that feels like a promise. It almost makes me kick my boots back off and stay here. But then I see the ash coating the soles of my boots and I remember why I need to leave. There's something I need to do.

It's late when I get home, the full moon shining through the gaps in the curtains. I rinsed my boots off with the hose outside, no longer wanting to see the ashes on them or bring them into the house, and I slowly kick them off now, careful to be quiet. The whole house is that kind of still that only happens in the dead of night, and I tiptoe to my room, looking for Wren.

She's not curled up in my bed, though, and when I backtrack to the living room to make sure I didn't miss her on the couch, she's not there either. Confusion lances through me, but when I see the sliver of June's warm night light slipping through her cracked-open door, I have a feeling I know where I'll find Wren.

Sure enough, when I gently push open the door to June's room, I find them both in her bed. June's head is resting on Wren's outstretched arm, her little body curled into Wren's. The sight does something to me, makes everything inside me turn warm and sticky, just like the heavy lump clogging my throat.

My girls.

Silently, I pad into the room and climb into the twin-size bed behind Wren. It's too small for the two of them, and especially too small for all of us, but Wren stirs enough to scoot over, her body molding into mine. My arm settles around both of them, securing them against me so we're all tucked on the tiny mattress. Their breathing settles into something heavy and rhythmic, and I breathe in their matching shampoo scent. My heart rate settles, beating in time with theirs until I drift off to sleep, more content than I've ever felt.

Twenty-Seven
- WREN -

There's a crick in my neck when I wake up, but I'm warm and cozy. A heavy arm drapes over my middle, and June's braids are pressing into my chin, sure to leave an imprint. Early morning sunshine slices through the curtains, illuminating the room in a golden glow. Despite everything, how uncertain my life is right now, this moment feels like magic, like something I so desperately wanted without even knowing it. If you'd asked me what my ideal life would have looked like a year ago, I wouldn't have said snuggling with a single dad and his precious daughter in a too small bed, but right now feels as close to perfection as I can imagine. It's like those brief moments in time when you look around in awe of what you're seeing or experiencing—standing atop a mountain, a breathtaking view ahead of you, laughing in a car with the windows down, making a memory that you will never forget, picking berries as a kid, the juices staining your fingers. It's all the little moments that don't mean so much when they're happening but that leave a little imprint on your soul, ones you can look back on and know they were forming you into something new.

That's how it feels right now, Holden's arm holding me close, June snuggled into me in a way that makes my heart ache in a beautiful kind of way.

Behind me, Holden stirs, his nose moving up the line of my neck, his arm tightening around June and me. He sits up enough to look down at the both of us, and when he sees I'm awake, that devastating little smile quirks his lips. I don't know how I got so lucky to be one of the rare people who experience his smiles, but I'll never stop being thankful for it.

"Morning," he says, his early morning voice a deep rasp that never fails to send shivers up my spine.

"Morning," I echo, surprise rushing through me when he leans forward, his lips brushing against mine softly. When he pulls back, I ask, "What was that for?"

His smile lines deepen. "I'm not allowed to kiss you?"

I glance down at June, still sleeping soundly in my arms. "June could have seen."

He leans down until his mouth is at my ear. "I wouldn't want her seeing me kiss just anyone, but I plan on keeping you, Red."

A warm feeling spreads through me at his words, making everything inside me turn to liquid.

Holden lifts a single eyebrow. "That is, as long as you want to stick around." He says it in a playful tone, but I can see the vulnerability shining in his eyes, the hurt from Mia that's healing but not gone.

It makes me soften, turning slowly onto my back to see him better, careful not to disturb June. I let myself catalog the lines of his face, the dark shadow of his beard, the strong curve of his nose, the ever-shifting colors in his eyes. I want to memorize him just like this, so that one day when I'm old and gray and my memory is failing, I never forget how he looked leaning over me in this twin-size bed.

"Holden Blankenship," I say slowly. "There's nowhere else I'd rather be."

Some of the light returns to his eyes, the tension leaving his shoulders, and I sigh when his lips settle on mine again, just a brush of his mouth that makes me want more. When he pulls back, he regards me for a long moment, looking like he's debating something.

Finally, he says, "I love you, Wren."

That's it, nothing more, nothing less. It feels exactly right for him to tell me *just* like that, with his daughter in my arms and his hand tangling in my hair.

"I love you too." It's so easy to say it back. It feels like I've said it a thousand times before, like this is years and years in the future and we've woken up just like this more times than we've woken up alone.

That little smile hitches up one side of his lips again, and when he leans in close to my ear, this time he uses a whisper. "I really wish we weren't in bed with my daughter right now."

A quiet laugh escapes me, and I let my eyes trail down to June nestled in the crook of my arm, her body wrapped around me. As much as I'd like to be alone with Holden, I can't say I'd rather be anywhere but here.

I think he sees my thoughts reflected in my eyes, because his face softens as he regards us. "Here is good too."

I look up at him, a smile playing on my lips. "Yeah, it's perfect."

He watches me for a long moment, something unreadable in his eyes. "You didn't wait up for me last night."

"I tried my best," I tell him, but the truth is that when June asked me to stay in bed with her, I knew my exhausted body was going to be out in seconds.

"I had something to tell you."

My eyebrows lift. "What?"

That smile returns to his face, this time a little mischievous and playful. I have to say, it's a good look on him. "You'll have to wait and see." He sits up, making a face as he does. I guarantee he's in as much pain from sleeping in this tiny bed as I am. "Go back to your house and get ready. June and I will be over to get you in thirty minutes."

I stare at him, unmoving. "Where are we going?"

"You'll see."

Thirty minutes later, I'm showered and changed, my hair wet and curling around my head. I dressed in light layers since I'm unsure of where Holden is taking me, and I'm pulling on my jacket when he knocks on the door before letting himself in.

"We're waiting, Red," he calls out from my living room.

I roll my eyes, coming out of my bedroom. "It's been thirty-two minutes."

"Exactly," he says, leaning against my doorframe. I can't help but take in the way the hem of his shirt hikes up over his hipbone, exposing a sliver of tanned, toned skin. I know how that skin feels against my palms, and suddenly, I don't want to go on whatever adventure he's taking me on. I want to stay right here with him.

"I gave you two extra minutes." When I look back up at his eyes, I know he caught me ogling by the way he's smirking at me. Pink climbs up my cheeks. "Now let's get out of here. June's waiting in the truck."

We move across the yard that's finally turning green again and climb into the truck before backing out of his driveway. He heads through town, and my heart softens at the fundraiser signs still up in the windows. It only takes a moment for him to take the turn to head into the mountains, following the familiar drive to the cabin. I don't know if I want to go there today. Not with the happy bubble we've been in all morning. I know I'm going to have to face it soon, that I'm going to have to talk to my insurance company and call guests to cancel their reservations and refund the money that I've already spent on things for the cabin, but I was hoping for a little more time. Just a few hours.

"Holden, I don't know if—"

His eyes cut to mine, and he says, "Just trust me, Red."

I nod. I do trust him. But that knot of anxiety is still tied tightly in my stomach as we climb farther and farther up the mountain road. A few minutes later, we come to a stop behind a line of cars parked on the side of the road. Holden throws the truck in park and turns off the engine. I just stare at him, confused.

"What are you doing?"

"Getting out." With that, he climbs out of the truck and opens June's door to help her down. I guess we're back to the two-word answers with him, because as we start walking up the steep mountain road, he doesn't say anything more.

It's not until we get closer that I start to recognize some of the cars. I'm too busy wondering why they're here to notice the construction noises up ahead, so it's not until we round the last bend and the cabin comes into view that I see what's going on.

My eyes blur as I stare at what looks to be the entire town at work on my cabin. There's fresh lumber in the yard and cans of paint on the open bed of someone's pickup truck. Jimmy Chin is giving directions to a group of men and women in hard hats and worn jeans. People move around with saws and hammers and supplies, so busy with their tasks that they don't even notice us approaching, which is good, because my feet have frozen to the ground, shock holding me in place.

"What is this?" I breathe. Holden's hand finds mine. He gives it a squeeze, his eyes focused on me even though I haven't torn my gaze away from the cabin.

"We didn't want you to have to put off the renovations for another year. So everyone's chipping in to finish it by next week."

"Next week?" June asks, bouncing on the balls of her feet, excitement lacing her voice.

"Next week, June Bug," Holden tells her before returning his focus to me. The sight in front of me still feels too surreal, too unexpected for me to process. But it only takes me a moment to look at Holden, understanding dawning. My throat clogs with emotion, the tears behind my eyes growing heavier and more persistent.

"Did you do this?"

He shrugs, avoiding my gaze, red staining the tips of his ears. It's answer enough. I move in front of him, dropping his hand to put mine on either side of his face, drawing it down until his eyes connect with mine. So many things about him feel so familiar now, but he's proving that he will never stop surprising me.

"Is this where you went last night?"

Holden doesn't speak, and for a long time, he doesn't move, but he finally tips his head in a nod.

"You did all this? For me?"

One of his hands settles on that spot on my hip, the spot that feels like it was made just for him, and the other twists around a lock of my hair. He's so close that I can feel his breath on my lips as he says, "I'd do anything for you, Red."

"Do you think Mr. Chin would let me use a saw?" June asks, interrupting the moment between Holden and me, and a laugh chokes out of me. Holden's lips twitch, but when he turns around to face June, his expression is stern.

"Don't even think about it."

The town works nonstop in shifts for the next two weeks, Holden and I spending long hours there working until our backs are sore and our eyes are heavy, and somehow, by some miracle, we finish in time. The sun is setting as the last of the townspeople hop into their cars, headlights disappearing down the winding mountain road, and Holden and I watch from the front porch. We're exhausted, sore, and hungry, but there's a contented hum in my veins, the kind of tired satisfaction that comes from hard work.

Holden's arm comes around my shoulder, pulling me into him, and I melt, using his strength to keep me up. After the first renter arrives tomorrow, I'm sleeping for a week. I've half fallen asleep on his shoulder when I hear another car pull up, followed by an opening door and a girlish squeal.

"Daddy, is it done?" June yells. Holden groans against the top of my head. I think it's possible that the two of us both just fell asleep standing up.

Holden pulls himself taller, rubbing his eyes with the heels of his hands. "It's done, June Bug."

I look up to see Jodi getting out of the car, her hands full of paper bags. "I brought takeout. Thought you all could use dinner."

The truth is, I'm too tired to eat, but I don't say that. Instead, I paste a grateful smile on my face. "Thanks, Jodi."

She and June climb the stairs to the cabin, inspecting the finished work. It actually looks better than it did before the fire, and with the money the town raised, I was able to get nicer furniture for the living room and some cute vintage rockers for the porch. I'll never be able to thank everyone for their generosity.

"It looks amazing, Wren," Jodi says, a smile tilting her lips. She's one of the few people who haven't been here working on the cabin this week, instead keeping June so Holden and I could be here as often as possible.

I look around at the cabin, emotion making my throat thick. "Everyone really came through for me."

She fixes me with a stare, the kind I've seen her use on her own children dozens of times now. "You deserved it, and don't you dare go thinking you didn't. You've given back to this community for years now. It was our turn to do something for you."

Tears pool in my eyes, hot and heavy, and Holden's hand finds my back, drawing wide circles over my spine.

He says, "I couldn't agree more."

Jodi regards the two of us, something softening in her expression. I don't have to wonder if she's pleased with the way things have turned out between us. She looks at me like I'm something she's spent years praying for.

Extending the food in Holden's direction, she says, "Well, I'm going to get out of here. You both did a wonderful job. Go enjoy that view." She nods in the direction of the front door, and when I turn around, I realize you can see straight through to the back windows that open up to the mountains beyond. I'll never tire of that view. It's breathtaking.

Jodi leaves, her feet kicking up dust in the dirt driveway, and Holden hooks an arm around my shoulders, leading me through the front door. June is already on the back porch, sitting in one of the Adirondack chairs. From here, I can see her hunched over the friendship bracelet kit I didn't even notice her carrying when she arrived.

"Too tired to eat?" Holden asks, his lips brushing my ear.

I hum under my breath, my eyes falling closed.

"Me too," he murmurs. "Maybe we can just take a quick nap."

"Sounds good to me."

From the back porch, June yells, "I'm hungry!"

Holden sighs, his breath ruffling my hair, and I can't help but laugh. I'm exhausted, but I've never felt lighter.

I nudge his side, wrapping an arm around him and pulling him toward the back door. "C'mon. The sooner we eat, the sooner we can go to bed."

He nods, his chin resting against my head, his beard catching in my hair. "Okay."

We shuffle out the back door, clinging to each other, the paper bags crinkling between us. As Holden sets the bags on the end table between the two Adirondack chairs and begins to sift through them, I crouch down next to June, inspecting her handiwork.

"Whatcha working on, June Bug?"

She flashes me a smile, one that's sure to stop people in their tracks when she grows up, and turns the bracelet over so I can see it. The beads are in varying shades of green—pine, sage, and olive—and separated by plain white beads with black imprinted letters.

"Daddy said this is your little cabin off the beaten path," she tells me as I read the words she's spelled out. *OFF THE BEATEN PATH*.

A smile curves up the edges of my lips. "It's perfect."

Her eyes light up, bright as the summer sky. "Really?"

"Yeah," I say with a nod. "I've been thinking of what to name this place. All the rental cabins have names. I think The Cabin Off the Beaten Path is just right. What do you think?"

Her head bounces enthusiastically, and when I look up, I catch Holden staring at us, that little smile hidden beneath his beard. He looks happy in a way I haven't seen him before, like all his long-forgotten dreams are coming true in the most unexpected of ways.

I know the feeling.

June finishes tying off the bracelet, and when I extend my hand to her, she slips it around my wrist to nestle with the others she's made me. It fits perfectly, and I smile, tracing my fingers over the beads.

"Thank you, June Bug."

She grins at me, and I pick her up, settling her on my lap. Holden finishes pulling out the rest of the food.

He snorts a laugh, and when I look up, he's pulling out a very familiar bottle of cheap strawberry wine from the bag. My favorite brand. "Special present from Mom."

He cracks open the screw top and takes a long swig, his throat working, before he hands it to me, his face scrunched in disgust.

"That's nasty. Way too sweet."

I can't help but smile as I take it from him, my mind returning to just a few months ago when I stood in the demolished kitchen of the cabin with Stevie, drinking this exact wine, completely unaware of all the ways my life was about to change.

I take a sip and flash him a smile. "No, I think it's just right."

Epilogue

- WREN -
TEN MONTHS LATER

"This space heater is doing absolutely nothing," I complain, snuggling closer to Holden in the Adirondack chair, trying desperately to absorb some of his heat.

Holden snorts, his arms tightening around me. "I tried to tell you that."

I thought it'd be grand to sit under the stars with a space heater on the back porch at the cabin since it's empty this week. Most of the month, actually, since we're officially back in the post-Christmas lull in Fontana Ridge. I just underestimated how cold it was going to be. Outside. In the mountains. In January.

"In the books and movies, when the girl says she's cold, the guy will tell her not to worry because he'll keep her warm."

Holden nuzzles beneath my hair, the cold tip of his nose making me shiver. "I don't talk like that," he says into my ear.

Normally, this would make me feel warm all over, but I'm cold to the bone. And when a snowflake lands on the tip of my nose, my body racks with another shiver.

"Okay, that's enough of this nonsense," Holden says, hefting me up into his arms as he stands. My startled squeal echoes in the mountain night air.

Holden bends, yanking the space heater cord from the outdoor outlet and picking it up. Then he carries it and me inside, depositing the space heater by the door and me on the kitchen counter.

I shiver again, my skin pricking against the almost too-warm heat inside the cabin. Holden's eyes catch the movement, and he moves in closer, stepping between my thighs until we're touching everywhere. Slowly, his fingers wrap around the zipper of my coat, pulling it down. The sound of the zip and my breathing are the only noises. Once it's completely unzipped, his hands dive inside, coming around my waist, slipping under the hem of my sweater.

I gasp at the feeling of his chilled palms against my skin, and his lips twitch in that barely there smile I love so much. "Skin on skin is the best way to warm up."

I roll my eyes. "Yes, that's the only reason."

He leans in, pressing a quick kiss to my lips. "I need my hands warm so I can show you something."

I lift my eyebrows suggestively, and he lets out an aggrieved sigh that brings a smile to my face.

"You're ridiculous," he says, tugging me closer.

I slide my hands up his chest, fingers bumping over the buttons on his jacket. It's really unfair that he got to take mine off, but his is on. So I stop on one of the buttons, pushing it through the hole. Holden watches the movement before looking back at me, one brow raised.

"My hands are cold too," I say, but really, I just want to feel his skin beneath my palms. He knows it too.

The buttons come undone one by one, the ring on my left hand glinting under the warm cabin lights. It still surprises me sometimes when I see it. It's only been there for a few weeks, after all. I can remember the moment he proposed with vivid clarity, lit up under the sparkling colorful lights of the Christmas tree. There was a present for me from June beneath the tree, poorly wrapped in bright yellow paper that made my chest hurt just to look at. I could imagine her wrapping it herself, using too much tape, her bottom lip trapped between her teeth. I wasn't at all shocked to find a friendship bracelet inside the box, but my heart stopped when I read the beads. *WILL YOU MARRY MY DADDY?* When I turned around, Holden was on one knee, tears shimmering in his eyes. I'd never seen him look so sure of anything, like he knew without a doubt that this was exactly what he wanted. It made it easy to say yes, makes my throat go thick with the memory every time the ring catches the light.

When the buttons are finally undone, I slip my hands inside, lifting the hem of his shirt just like he did with mine. He's so warm, and I sigh at the feel of him. His eyes go hazy, and he looks like every daydream I've had over the last year. All the ones I never thought could have come true.

His lips find mine once more, slow and steady, unlike those first few kisses we shared. There are still times when we're frantic, grasping for each other like we can't move fast enough, but the majority of our kisses are just like this, like we have all the time in the world.

I like knowing I have all the time with him.

Holden pulls back, his forehead resting against mine. "I have something I want to show you." When I lift my eyebrows again, he sighs and pulls back, taking his warmth with him.

I watch as he moves across the small kitchen, opening the drawer beside the sink where all the odds and ends go. Confusion ripples through me when he pulls out a large rolled-up piece of paper.

He brings it back to where I'm still seated on the counter, unrolling it so it lies flat beside me. It's a blueprint, from what I can tell. Although I'm not sure of what.

"What is it?"

Holden's eyes fix on mine, more green today than brown, like the pine trees outside. They refract in the kitchen lights, all the shades of nature in one. "It's a blueprint. For a cabin."

I smooth my fingers over the paper, examining the straight lines on the page. "For a project you have coming up?"

He shakes his head. "No, it's for here."

My gaze snaps to his, confused. "What do you mean for *here*?"

Holden searches my face, and for the first time, I see a hint of hesitation, maybe nerves, reflected in his expression. "You can say no. I just had an idea."

I watch him for a long moment. "Okay."

"I know this cabin is important to you, but I know it's also not what you want it to be."

He's right. The cabin is too small for most of the families coming to Fontana Ridge, and despite the upgrades we made, it's still old, with a lot of quirks. Like the shower in the bathroom that goes ice cold when the kitchen sink is on. And the wood floors that creak with every step. And the spindle that a guest broke on the back porch that we've yet to fix. It's something on our long to-do list for the off-season.

"I was thinking..." he says and trails off. "What would you think of tearing it down?"

I blink at him, unsure if I heard him correctly. We worked ourselves to the bone to get this cabin in the condition it's in. I can't imagine why he'd want to tear it down, especially when it's just starting to make a profit.

"Hear me out," he says quickly, no doubt noticing the confused, hesitant look on my face. He sidles closer to me, fitting in the gap between my knees once more. His hands settle on my neck, lifting my chin up so I can look into his eyes. They're serious, but...hopeful too.

"We're getting married," he says, voice soft, tender.

A smile hitches up the sides of my mouth. "Is that what the ring's for?"

"I don't want to start our life together in my house. That house, as important as it's been to me, was the place I bought for me and June after Mia left. It was a place for us to start over. And," he pauses, sighing, "it's been that. It's been everything we needed. But we need something different now. We need a home with you."

His words fill me up, full to bursting, and I want to cry because of them. I want to cry for all the times over the last year that Holden has been everything I didn't know I needed or wanted. I don't know how I got so lucky to find him and June, how I ever lived without them.

"I thought we could build one here. Like the cabin we went to on our first date. You loved that cabin."

Tears brim behind my eyelashes as I look down at the blueprints, the shape of the building now familiar. It's similar to the cabin we visited, although not exactly the same. There's a large living room with what looks to be a fireplace, and a kitchen that looks out on the space. I can imagine the three of us there, making dinner together, June and I sneaking chocolate chips from the pantry when Holden isn't looking.

There are bedrooms and bathrooms too, more than the three of us need, and when I look back at Holden, his eyes have gone soft. He points to one of the bedrooms, a smaller one beside what looks to be the primary suite.

"I thought this one could be a nursery."

We've talked about kids, how we both want more, but this is the first time I'm seeing a way for that to happen. Holden's house has a third bedroom that mine does not, but really, it would be hard to have more kids there without all of us being on top of each other.

This cabin would be plenty large enough, though, and suddenly, I want it more than anything. The life in this cabin. The one I can picture perfectly. The three of us sitting on the Adirondack chairs, June holding her little hand to my belly to feel her little brother or sister kicking. I want it all. I want it all with them.

"Let's do it," I say around the lump in my throat.

"Really?" Holden asks, and I don't miss the hopeful tone of his voice.

I nod, just as sure about this decision as I was when he asked me to be his wife.

With Holden, I've never been more sure of anything.

Also By

NASHVILLE IS CALLING SERIES

Just Go With It
Wes + Lo

Just Between Us
Cam + Ellie

Just Friends
Alex + Hazel

Acknowledgements

Writing a book always has challenges. For this one, I was battling the worst flare up of my chronic illness that I've had since my diagnosis. The first day I woke up and told my husband that I wasn't in pain, my grandfather suffered several major strokes while visiting family out of state. We spent the next month traveling back and forth to be with him in his final days and to be with family after he passed. All of this happened while I was writing *Off the Beaten Path*. This book, in many ways, was. an escape for me. My life was hard, but this book and these characters were easy. I didn't always feel like writing about two people falling in love, and I didn't always have the time to, but when I did, it was probably my smoothest and easiest writing process.

I have so many people to thank for being my support system through these last few months. My husband, who is my very best friend, is a real champion when I have to disappear into my head or my office to write these stories. My best friends, Kelsey, Juliana, and Jamie, thank you for always being there for me. I can never feel lonely with you all by my side.

To my lovely team. I could never write books without my editors, cover designer, and beta reader. Mel, you made everything about this process so seamless and easy. I can't imagine writing without you now. Beth, my copy editor, is a saint for handling all my typos. I'm so sorry I still don't know when to use blond or blonde. Sam, my cover designer, makes all my dreams come true again and again. I gave her complete nonsense for this cover and she made it stunning. Melissa, thank you for being the first set of eyes to read my books. It's so good that you do. They're not fit for human consumption when you get them and you help make them what they are today.

To my readers, I love you all for being so supportive the last few months as I was dealing with all the things in my personal life. You told me over and over again that you'd be here for me when I came back, and you were. I will never stop being grateful for that.

Lastly, to my Savior, for being my rock when things are unsteady and my comfort when life is hard.

About the Author

MADISON WRIGHT IS A rom-com writer living her own happily ever after in Nashville, TN! After falling in love with reading at a young age, she always dreamed of being an author.

Madison spends most of her time with her head in a book—whether that be in the car, at the grocery store, or in her reading chair. When she's not reading, she's probably watching The Office, buying excessive amounts of chocolate, or spending time with her husband and dog.

Follow Madison for more!

Follow on Instagram @authormadisonwright

Follow on Tiktok @authormadisonwright

Join her reader group on Facebook

Sign up for her newsletter

Check out her website for signed books and merch

Printed in Great Britain
by Amazon